TITANIC

TITANIC

One Newspaper, Seven Days, and the
Truth That Shocked the World

Written and Edited by
STEPHEN W. HINES

CUMBERLAND HOUSE™

Published by Cumberland House, an imprint of Sourcebooks, Inc.
P.O. Box 4410, Naperville, Illinois 60567-4410
(630) 961-3900
Fax: (630) 961-2168
www.sourcebooks.com

Library of Congress Cataloging-in-Publication Data

Hines, Stephen W.
  Titanic : one newspaper, seven days, and the truth that shocked the world / Stephen W. Hines.
     p. cm.
  Includes bibliographical references and index.
  1. Titanic (Steamship)–History. 2. Titanic (Steamship)–Press coverage. 3. Titanic (Steamship)–In mass media. 4. Daily telegraph (London, England) I. Title.
  G530.T6H56 2011
  910.9163'4–dc23

                              2011022562

Printed and bound in the United States of America.
VP 10 9 8 7 6 5 4 3 2

For Gwen, life partner and ardent supporter

CONTENTS

———•———

INTRODUCTION

———◆———

APRIL 14, 1912, 11:40 P.M.

It is too late.

Frederick Fleet has just cried down from the crow's nest to the bridge of the Royal Mail Ship *Titanic*, "Iceberg, right ahead," but First Officer Murdoch cannot stop the ship. He can do no more than turn the liner slightly to port (left) before the berg gouges a path of destruction along the ship's starboard (right) side. The sea pours into six openings—flooding the forepeak, three cargo holds, and two boiler rooms (Eaton and Haas, *Titanic: Triumph* 137–38).

If only four cargo holds had flooded, the ship would have remained afloat. Six punctures in the hull mean it will not survive.

In just two hours and forty minutes, RMS *Titanic*, the largest passenger ship in the world, will sink with a loss of 1,517 lives out of 2,223 on board; its resting place over 12,000 feet beneath the waves. [Accurate figures are hard to come by. British historian John P. Eaton writes that there were "2,228 passengers and crew, of these 1,697 were men (12 years of age and older) and 528 were women and children" (Geller 8).]

During the early hours of Monday, April 15, the ship's architect Thomas Andrews will give the *Titanic* only about an hour to live. He himself will make no attempt to survive the sinking.

Captain E. J. Smith will see a nearby ship that fails to respond to his distress rockets. This mystery ship is so close that some lifeboats will try to row to her until she finally disappears, apparently sailing away from a rescue.

Second Officer C. H. Lightoller will break out handguns so that the crew can be armed against panic-stricken passengers.

Chief Telegrapher Jack Phillips had scolded the operator of the *Californian*'s wireless for interrupting his "traffic" with Cape Race, Newfoundland. The *Californian* stands at most only twenty miles away and operator Cyril Evans only wanted to tell Phillips about ice in the vicinity. Upon receiving Phillips's rebuke, he turned off his set and went to bed.

The crew will send away the first lifeboats half empty because the British Board of Trade has neglected to inform captain and staff that the boats are safe to be filled on the boat deck and can be safely lowered to the water at full capacity. (Lightoller will lower the first boat away with only twenty-eight passengers in it, fearing the boat may break apart in the air.)

Third-class passengers, only 25 percent of whom will survive, will learn there are not enough lifeboats left to save them.

Only two lifeboats out of the twenty launched will make a serious effort to rescue the freezing passengers in the water (Heyer 26). Although there is room in the rescue boats for an additional four hundred people, all lifeboats will be reluctant to return to the scene of the disaster, either for fear of being swamped or for fear of being sucked under by the fall of the *Titanic* to the bottom.

The sinking of the *Titanic* is human drama on such a scale that it is hard to take in. There were so many eyewitnesses who survived, all having different points of view, and so many experts who were willing to venture a guess as to what had happened, or what might have been done to save the ship, that a welter of confusing facts will always surround the sinking of the *Titanic* (Lord, *The Night* 241).

Launching the SS *Titanic*.

But it is less difficult to understand why there is everlasting fascination with the fate of the *Titanic* and those aboard her. All the elements of human tragedy are in her story.

First of all, Very Important People, many of the world's celebrity rich, lost their lives on the *Titanic*, the "almost unsinkable" ship (Tibballs 10). On April 16, 1912, the *Daily Telegraph* itself listed John Jacob Astor, Isidor Straus, Charles M. Hays, George D. Widener, Benjamin Guggenheim, and J. B. Thayer, all millionaires at that time, along with some twenty passengers who together could be valued at £100,000,000; all would be billionaires by today's standards (11). Among the famous were Archie Butt, an aide to President Taft; the writers Jacques Futrelle and W. T. Stead; American artist Francis Millet; and Broadway theater owner Henry B. Harris.

Second, British pride was shaken by the apparent fact that one of its most prized ships could sink less than three hours after hitting an iceberg. At the time, Britain ruled a fifth of the earth's people. It was a Very Important Country. Counsel Sir Rufus Isaac, representing the British Board of Trade, took care to point out that in the previous ten years, only seventy-three persons had lost their lives in British ships out of three and a half million passengers carried (Eaton and Haas, *Titanic: Triumph* 265). Somehow, he found it comforting that British shipping was generally safe—even if the *Titanic* hadn't been.

Third, moralists, both then and now, laid a large portion of the blame for the loss of the *Titanic* on the greed of the men who built the ship, who supposedly cut corners with regard to cost in a reckless disregard for safety. Brad Matsen, in his book *Titanic's Last Secrets*, claims Director J. Bruce Ismay of the White Star Line had asked the ship's architect to reduce the *Titanic*'s rivets from a full inch thickness down to seven-eighths of an inch to make the ship lighter and save on coal (103–04). Architect Thomas Andrews felt pressured to agree against his better judgment.

No one who reads about the *Titanic* can help but wonder what "might have been" if only there hadn't been such an assured complacency of competence on the part of the British Board of Trade; the ship's owners, both British and American; and the officers and crew of the ship itself.

Lastly, we remember the *Titanic* because its sinking signaled the end of a hubristic confidence in the Age of the Machine. As the writer J. B. Priestly observed many years ago: "A rapidly developing technology, because it has to make things work successfully to achieve anything at all, is always in danger...of seeing itself as being irresistible in its might...There are some places that might be healthier if they displayed large notices: Remember the *Titanic!*" (232).

★ ★ ★

Britannia rules the waves, but its greatest ship has just gone down. *Titanic: One Newspaper, Seven Days, and the Truth That Shocked the World*, then, is a "you-are-there" account of the ship's sinking and its aftermath, examined and experienced through the *Daily Telegraph* of London.

What was it like to pick up the world's largest daily circulating newspaper and read the unfolding drama? What was it like to feel the pride of the British people that women and children had been saved first? That Captain Smith had supposedly cried out "Be British!" to encourage his men to do their duty? That King and country were rallying to the cry to give generously to the widows' and orphans' funds?

Although the *Daily Telegraph*'s task is enormous, it will attempt to overcome all obstacles in getting at the truth of the disaster. In the week of the sinking, it will print over 200 articles on the *Titanic* and the dangers of ice at sea—striving to separate fact from fiction with varying degrees of success.

The paper will use its extensive staff of personal correspondents and hire others for special reports. As a national paper, it will want to set the tone of British reactions to the sinking and will take pride in the heroic behavior of British citizens and crew who all calmly did their duty and faced death without flinching.

Explanatory notes from a variety of printed and Internet sources will be found in starred boxes throughout *Titanic*. Citations are in parentheses and refer to the bibliography at the back of the book. News reports were lengthy in the days before television and Twitter, so points of ellipsis have been used to show where a report has been shortened to eliminate redundant or space-filling passages; some articles have been eliminated altogether out of necessity to make this book of manageable length.

All articles are taken from the *Daily Telegraph* just as they appeared. Therefore, only a few typographical errors have been corrected by notes in brackets. In general, typos are a part of journalistic life: always have been, always will be. So don't be shocked at the misspelling of names and of ships; there will be many. The *Telegraph*'s reporters were writing history in a hurry.

References to time throughout the *Telegraph* are from the points of origin of where the article was written except where otherwise indicated by the paper itself.

Here, then, is the unfolding drama of the *Titanic* as readers of 1912 experienced it, a commemoration of this great vessel one hundred years after her tragic loss.

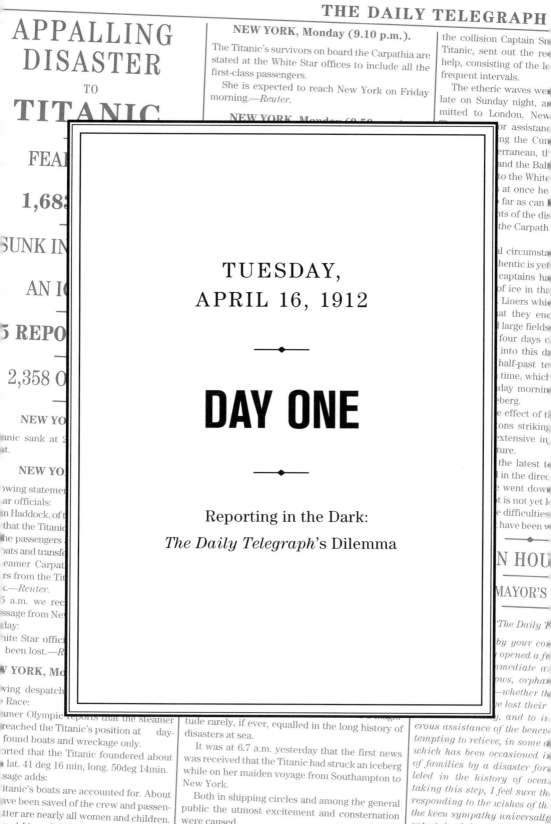

APPALLING DISASTER

TO

TITANIC

FEA...

1,68...

SUNK IN

AN I...

5 REPO...

2,358 O...

NEW YO...

...anic sank at 2...
st.

NEW YO...

...owing statemen...
...ar officials:
...n Haddock, of t...
...that the Titanic...
...he passengers...
...oats and transfe...
...eamer Carpat...
...rs from the Tit...
...k.—*Reuter.*

...5 a.m. we rec...
...ssage from Nev...
...day:
...hite Star offici...
...been lost.—*R...*

...Y YORK, Mo...

...ving despatch...
...Race:
...amer Olympic reports that the steamer
reached the Titanic's position at   day-
found boats and wreckage only.
...orted that the Titanic foundered about
...lat. 41 deg 16 min, long. 50deg 14min.
...sage adds:
...itanic's boats are accounted for. About
...ve been saved of the crew and passen-
...tter are nearly all women and children.
...and Liner California is remaining and
...e vicinity of the disaster

NEW YORK, Monday (9.10 p.m.).

The Titanic's survivors on board the Carpathia are stated at the White Star offices to include all the first-class passengers.

She is expected to reach New York on Friday morning.—*Reuter.*

NEW YORK, Monday (9.50...

TUESDAY,
APRIL 16, 1912

◆

DAY ONE

◆

Reporting in the Dark:
The Daily Telegraph's Dilemma

...tude rarely, if ever, equalled in the long history of disasters at sea.

It was at 6.7 a.m. yesterday that the first news was received that the Titanic had struck an iceberg while on her maiden voyage from Southampton to New York.

Both in shipping circles and among the general public the utmost excitement and consternation were caused.

As has happened on several previous occa-

---

the collision Captain Sm...
Titanic, sent out the re...
help, consisting of the le...
frequent intervals.

The etheric waves we...
late on Sunday night, a...
mitted to London, New...
...or assistance
...ng the Cu...
...erranean, th...
...and the Bal...
...to the White
...s at once he...
...far as can...
...ts of the dis...
...the Carpath...

...al circumsta...
...hentic is yet...
...captains ha...
...of ice in tha...
...Liners whi...
...at they en...
...l large fields...
...four days o...
...into this da...
...half-past te...
...time, which...
...day mornin...
...eberg.

...e effect of t...
...ons striking...
...xtensive in...
...ture.

...the latest t...
...in the direc...
...e went dow...
...t is not yet...
...e difficulties...
...have been w...

N HOU...

MAYOR'S...

The Daily T...
by your co...
opened a f...
mediate a...
ows, orpha...
—whether th...
e lost their...
, and to in...
erous assistance of the benev...
tempting to relieve, in some d...
which has been occasioned i...
of families by a disaster for...
leled in the history of ocea...
taking this step, I feel sure th...
responding to the wishes of th...
the keen sympathy universall...
entertained for those who ha...
been plunged into misery an...

INTRODUCTION

———◆———

IT IS THE MORNING OF APRIL 15, 1912: THE SEA IS SMOOTH, the sky is filled with stars, and the view from the lifeboats is clear.

All that is ever going to happen to make the Royal Mail Ship *Titanic* synonymous with the worst maritime disaster in history has already happened. She has gone down in two hours and forty minutes after striking an iceberg, and all who will ever be saved have already been saved by the dawn of that Monday morning.

Yet with no cell phones, no satellite photos, and no Internet, the rest of the world still knows nothing of the loss of more than 1,500 souls. The challenge of getting this story out will be the London *Daily Telegraph*'s dilemma. How to gather information and report on this story will consume this proud paper's editorial energies and staff. Not the least of the *Telegraph*'s problems will be attempting to sort through the messages of ship-borne wireless operators delivering fragmented, inconsistent reports.

Maybe a total of only ten to twenty maritime telegraphers on both sides of the Atlantic have any inkling that the world's largest passenger ship has gone down. A massive comedy of errors, unparalleled in the history of news reporting, is about to begin…

Breaking the quiet of early Monday, April 15, is a flurry of urgent distress signals: C.Q.D. M.G.Y., C.Q.D. M.G.Y. "Distress, *Titanic*; Distress, *Titanic*." *Titanic* telegrapher Jack Phillips is filling the airwaves, letting all who could hear him know that the "practically unsinkable" liner had struck an iceberg (Butler 82–3). It is only 12:15 a.m., and Phillips still hopes that a nearby ship will answer and come to the rescue.

But wireless telegraphy is in its infancy. Not all ships having wireless are even listening. Some telegraphers have turned in for the night. Many smaller ships still have no telegraph at all. And reception is spotty. A ship four hundred miles away may hear signals and one lying nearby may not, owing to inconsistencies in the reception and strength of telegraph receivers.

Fortunately, *Carpathia*'s response is swift and helpful. Only fifty-eight miles away, she receives a distress signal at 12:35 a.m. (Kuntz 24). Being the closest ship to hear *Titanic*'s message, *Carpathia*'s efforts take precedence over all others. Captain Rostron heads his ship at full speed toward *Titanic*, dodging icebergs, but can only arrive more than an hour and a half too late. *Carpathia* picks up all survivors and heads to New York, leaving other ships to search for the dead.

Yet on the morning of April 15, 1912, New York, London, Paris, and Berlin—the historic centers of commerce—know virtually nothing of this five-hour-long drama. The world's largest passenger liner has encountered catastrophe, and they remain in ignorance. True, David Sarnoff, one day to head Radio Corporation of America, has received telegraph relays on the wreck from ships at sea and from Cape Race, Newfoundland, but information has been sketchy and contradictory.

Little wonder, then, that the *Daily Telegraph*, as astonished as the rest of the United Kingdom, will struggle to comprehend the epic story that unfolds.

And so the world's largest circulating daily newspaper does the best that it can, creating a sort of moving picture of events as it searches for accurate news. This may well have been the first time it had ever had to report on what we now call "breaking news." In extenuation of the disjointed nature of the *Telegraph*'s efforts is the fact that for two days the *Carpathia* only telegraphed lists of survivors to Cape Race and then on to New York. Overworked operators Harold Bride, a survivor from the *Titanic* with badly frostbitten feet, and Harold Cottam, of the *Carpathia*, were also sending survivors' own messages to family and friends. These matters were priority. Nothing else mattered as much as helping the rescued (*Encyclopedia*, "Rostron's Lost Report").

But the built-up demand for real news created a frenzy of speculation nobody of that time could have foreseen.

A managing news editor for the *Wall Street Journal*, Maurice Farrell, tried to defend the mistakes of his own newspaper this way:

Reports published by Dow, Jones & Co. on Monday April 15, regard-
ing the *Titanic* disaster came chiefly from three sources—office of the
White Star Line, the Laffan News Bureau, and the Boston News Bureau.
At 8 A.M. on that day, upon interviewing representatives of the White
Star Line in their New York office, a reporter received information which
was summarized on the Dow, Jones & Co. news tickers as follows:

"Officers of the White Star Line stated at 8 o'clock this morning that
passengers on the *Titanic* were being taken off in boats and that there
was no danger of loss of life. The *Baltic* and the *Virginian*, they stated,
were standing by to assist in the rescue..." (Kuntz 481).

Apparently, the phrase "standing by" confused inexperienced reporters on both
sides of the Atlantic, because the *Baltic* and the *Virginian* were not "on the
scene" of the wreck but still steaming toward it.

Farrell goes on to explain:

No one was willing to believe, and, in fact, at the time could believe,
that the *Titanic* had sunk. Every scrap of what purported to be news
indicating safety of the passengers was seized with avidity and rushed by
telephone, telegraph, or cable to all parts of America and Europe. This
process doubtless entailed duplication of the same messages flying back
and forth, which was erroneously construed as confirmatory evidence...
(Kuntz 482).

It is a marvel, then, that the *Daily Telegraph* did as well as it did. After all, it
couldn't believe the *Titanic* had sunk either.

APPALLING DISASTER

TO THE

TITANIC.

—◆—

FEARED LOSS

OF

1,683 LIVES.

———

SUNK IN COLLISION

WITH

AN ICEBERG.

———

675 REPORTED SAVED

———

2,358 ON BOARD.

———

NEW YORK, Monday.

The Titanic sank at 2.20 this morning. No lives were lost.

NEW YORK, Monday.

The following statement has been given out by the White Star officials:

Captain Haddock, of the Olympic, sends a wireless message that the Titanic sank at 2.20 a.m. (Monday) after all the passengers and crew had been lowered into lifeboats and transferred to the Virginian.

The steamer Carpathia, with several hundred passengers from the Titanic, is now on her way to New York.—*Reuter.*

At 1.45 a.m. we received the following additional message from New York, despatched at 8.40 p.m. Monday:

The White Star officials now admit that many lives have been lost.—*Reuter*

NEW YORK, Monday (8.45 p.m.)

The following despatch has been received here from Cape Race:

The steamer Olympic reports that the steamer Carpathia reached the Titanic's position at daybreak, but found boats and wreckage only.

She reported that the Titanic foundered about 2.20 a.m., in lat. 41 deg 16 min, long. 50deg 14min.

The message adds:

All the Titanic's boats are accounted for. About 675 souls have been saved of the crew and passengers. The latter are nearly all women and children.

The Leyland Liner California [Californian] is remaining and searching the vicinity of the disaster.

The Carpathia is returning to New York with the survivors.—*Reuter.*

NEW YORK, Monday (9.10 p.m.).

The Titanic's survivors on board the Carpathia are stated at the White Star offices to include all the first-class passengers.

She is expected to reach New York on Friday morning.—*Reuter.*

NEW YORK, Monday (9.50 p.m.).

The White Star officials now admit that probably only 675 out of the 2,200 passengers on board the Titanic have been saved.—*Reuter.*

NEW YORK, Monday (9.35 p.m.).

Mr. Franklin now admits that there has been "horrible loss of life." He says he has no information to disprove the press despatch from Cape Race that only 675 passengers and crew had been rescued.

The monetary loss could not be estimated tonight, but he intimated that it would run into millions. "We can replace money," he added "but not lives."—*Reuter.*

All the above telegrams are given in the order in which they were received in London in the early hours of this morning.

It is as yet impossible to estimate the full magnitude of the disaster, the statements being in many respects contradictory, but it is gravely to be feared that great loss of life has been involved.

On board the Titanic when she sailed were 2,358 passengers and crew, the passengers alone numbering 1,455. Of these, so far, 675 souls have been accounted for. They are, says the message, "nearly all women and children."

For the time mystery surrounds the fate of the remainder. When the Carpathia, the vessel which is bringing these survivors to New York, arrived on the scene of the wreck, the Titanic had already foundered. The boats containing these passengers and the floating wreckage only were seen.

Absolutely nothing is known of the others. Indeed, the White Star Company, in a message which reached London at 2.40 a.m., admitted that probably these 675 passengers on board the Carpathia are the sole survivors of a company of 2,358.

The utmost significance attaches to the fact that when the Carpathia steamed on to the scene of the wreck she found mostly women and children in the boats.

It was at the outset hoped that other vessels had taken off the remaining 1,683 passengers and crew. But the grave improbability that any succouring vessel would have taken the men on board and left the women still afloat in the boat points, it is to be feared, to a disaster of a magnitude rarely, if ever, equalled in the long history of disasters at sea.

It was at 6.7 a.m. yesterday that the first news was received that the Titanic had struck an iceberg while on her maiden voyage from Southampton to New York.

Both in shipping circles and among the general public the utmost excitement and consternation were caused.

As has happened on several previous occasions, the first news of the accident came by wireless telegraphy, which once more establishes its value as a life-saving medium. Immediately after the collision Captain Smith, who commands the Titanic, sent out the recognised code signal for help, consisting of the letters C.Q.D., repeated at frequent intervals.

The etheric waves were received at Cape Race late on Sunday night, and were thence retransmitted to London, New York, and elsewhere. The appeal for assistance also reached several liners, including the Cunarder Carpathia, bound for the Mediterranean, the Allan liners Virginian and Parisian, and the Baltic and Olympic, both of which belong to the White Star Company.

These ships at once headed in the direction of the Titanic. So far as can be judged from the very meagre accounts of the disaster which have as yet come to hand, the Carpathia was the first to arrive on the scene.

Of the actual circumstances attending this accident little authentic is yet known. During the last few days ship captains have noted an unusually large quantity of ice in that portion of the North Atlantic Ocean. Liners which have arrived at New York report that they encountered many enormous bergs and large fields of drifting ice.

When about four days out from Southampton the Titanic ran into this dangerous icefield, and shortly before half-past ten o'clock on Sunday night, American time, which corresponds to three o'clock on Monday morning in London, she collided with an iceberg.

Obviously, the effect of the impact of this ship of over 46,000 tons striking the berg must have been to inflict extensive injuries to the forward part of her structure.

According to the latest telegrams, the Titanic was being towed in the direction of Halifax, Nova Scotia, when she went down, but whether in the deep water or not is not yet known.

In any case, the difficulties in the way of salving so big a ship must have been well-nigh insuperable. **2**

———◆———

"VESSEL SINKING."

———

NEW YORK, Monday.

An official message received here, via the cable ship Minia, off Cape Race, says that steamers are towing the Titanic, and endeavouring to get her into the shoal water near Cape Race, for the purpose of beaching her.

A message from Halifax states that the Government Marine Agency has received a wireless message to the effect that the Titanic is sinking.—*Reuter*.

1. These telegrams apparently originated with on-shore wireless operators who were just trying to be helpful and positive. Since the *Titanic couldn't sink*, some ship or ships had to be towing her to the nearest harbor, Halifax. One wireless message that somehow reached the newspapers had the *Virginian* towing the *Titanic* to Halifax, a spurious bit of information never successfully traced. The *Virginian* did hear the *Titanic*'s distress signals but was some 170 miles west of the sinking ship. She was completely unable to render assistance (Eaton and Haas, *Titanic: Triumph* 174, 202–04).

2. The *Titanic* was built with every possible safety feature in mind for surviving a collision with another ship. If struck amidships by another vessel, she was designed to float with as many as four compartments damaged. However, as far as protections from icebergs were concerned, little if any thought was given. The last major iceberg collision dated back to 1879 when the *Arizona*, a British ship, had rammed an iceberg head on—with no loss of life! There was simply no danger from icebergs (Cox 47).

RACE TO THE RESCUE.

EXCITEMENT IN NEW YORK.

From Our Own Correspondent.

NEW YORK, Monday Afternoon.

Despatches to the White Star Line's New York office report that the Titanic, at 4.30 this afternoon, was being towed to Halifax by the Allan liner Virginian. The sea was calm and the weather conditions fair.

Her passengers are on board the Cunarder Carpathia and the Allan liner Parisian, which are proceeding for Halifax. They will be brought to New York overland.

It is added that the transfer was made safely, in calm weather.

The White Star liner Baltic was reported at three p.m. as hurrying to overtake the other vessels with the purpose of taking the Titanic's passengers from them. This second transshipment is likely to be made early this evening, and the passengers may reach Halifax more quickly. The Baltic performed a like service for the Republic's passengers in January, 1909, taking them off the Florida, which had rammed the Republic.

The Titanic's watertight bulkheads forward are reported in the latest wireless despatches to be holding up well, and the prospect of getting her to port is regarded as good.

Most of the crew remain on board.

It was only when the Olympic, bound east, and 260 miles from the scene, got into wireless touch with the Virginian at noon that the first reassuring word was received. Captain Haddock, of the Olympic, ended many hours of suspense, in which even the White Star Line officials were without any authentic news.

From Our Own Correspondent.

NEW YORK, Monday Evening.

The first call for help from the Titanic was at 10.25 last night, and it was received at Cape Race at almost the same hour. The captain of the Virginian received a like message. He at once headed his ship to the Titanic's rescue.

About one o'clock this morning the Allan Line offices in Montreal received information of the Titanic's plight. The information was immediately made public, and this was the first intimation the world received of the mighty ship's peril. The fact that the greatest ship ever launched might possibly be sinking on her maiden voyage made the situation one of dramatic intensity.

About midnight the Virginian sent a marconigram saying that she was under forced draught, and some 170 miles on the American side of the endangered liner.

The Titanic's sister ship Olympic about this time reported to Cape Race by wireless that she was in latitude 40.32deg N. and longitude 61.18deg W., and was in communication with the Titanic, and using every ounce of steam on both her turbine and reciprocating engines. She was then about 200 miles away from the scene of the trouble.

At 12.27 a.m. communication between the Titanic and the Virginian suddenly stopped. The wireless operator on the latter ship said that the signals first became blurred and then ceased. The first message from the Titanic read, telling of her trouble:

"Have struck iceberg; badly damaged; rush aid."

WIRELESS INTERRUPTED.

About 4:30 a.m. a message reached Halifax announcing that most of the passengers were then in the lifeboats, and that the Titanic was sinking slowly by her head. After that[,] wireless communication direct from the vessel was interrupted. The White Star line officials at New York received nothing more definite than this up to seven a.m. They announced that the stoppage of the Titanic's wireless meant little or nothing. They likewise expressed the belief that the Titanic was unsinkable, and would remain afloat indefinitely. Even if she sank many feet forward, they said, she had fifteen watertight compartments, and that the smashing of several of those forward would not sink her.

Not long after this came a welcome and reassuring, though unsigned, Marconigram, which read: "All Titanic's passengers safe." Almost as welcome was the information from the Marconi operator at St. John's, Newfoundland, which indicated that the Titanic herself was to be saved. This wireless read: "Titanic, according to messages from Cape Race to St. John's, Newfoundland, and other near-by points, is nearing the vicinity of Cape Race."

In the meantime, and despite these words of cheer from the Titanic and the ships on the way to her rescue, the White Star line officials at New York were extremely worried. Vice-President Franklin was at his office long before daylight, and sent requests to both the Titanic and the Olympic, asking for the fullest information.

The suspense of the thousands of relatives of the passengers and crew was pathetic. They made every effort to get news, and there was little or no news to give them. By telephone and in person they pleaded with the officials to tell them the latest information.

It was eleven o'clock before Mr. Franklin got anything really worth while. This was a despatch stating that the Carpathia, of the Cunard, and the Parisian, of the Allan, line, were standing by. It was also announced that the Carpathia had taken off twenty boatloads of women and children.

This despatch came from Captain Haddock, of the Titanic's sister ship Olympic, and was all the more welcome as it was the first news since daybreak from him. His silence had been both inexplicable and exasperating to the officials here. He said to them that he was 260 miles from the Titanic, and that he had received the information he reported from the wireless operators on the Parisian and the Carpathia, both of which were standing by the Titanic. **3**

★ **3.** Haddock could have done nothing that would have pleased White Star officials. When he discovered he was too far away from the *Titanic* to rescue her, Haddock's radio fell silent after sending word to the *Parisian* of his situation. There was already too much "noise" on the airwaves, and there was nothing he could do for the sinking ship that would be of any help. Best to stay off the airwaves and let others provide "firsthand" information.

The next welcome bit of information was a wireless message to Mr. Franklin stating that the Baltic, bound west, was within sight of the Titanic and going to her rescue under full steam.

———◆———

MILLIONAIRES AFLOAT.

———

From Our Own Correspondent.

NEW YORK, Monday Evening (Later).

Such a sensation was created in New York by the news of the accident that the pavements outside the shipping offices were blocked by inquirers. The majority of the passengers are domiciled in New York or within easy distance, **5** and the relatives who called waited patiently at the office of the White Star Line, where bulletins were posted up frequently.

Mr. J. P. Morgan, jun., who is greatly interested in the International Mercantile Marine, **6** was amongst the callers about midday, and went home apparently much relieved. There are many wealthy people aboard the Titanic. I give a list of the millionaires, and the extent of their wealth:

Colonel John Jacob Astor, £30,000,000. **7**
Mr. Isidor Straus, £10,000,000.
Mr. Alfred Vanderbilt, £15,000,000.
Mr. George D. Widener, £10,000,000.

---

4. Most of what people "knew" about the *Titanic* and its collision was false. At this stage, unconfirmed wireless messages were coming in from ships at sea, some of whom were reporting secondhand what they had intercepted over the airwaves. There were no rules for sorting out garbage traffic, and two ships might report the same message in such different ways that no one could be sure if there was one source or two.

As for the *Parisian*—a ship purported by dispatches to be carrying passengers to Halifax—congressional testimony indicates she was 505 miles away from the stricken ship and in no position to help at all other than to relay messages picked up from the *Olympic*.

5. This was hardly the case for third-class passengers, most of whom were emigrating to America.

6. J. P. Morgan Sr. had formed this company in order to profit from the lucrative Atlantic trade. Oddly, the *Titanic* was wholly owned by an American company yet somehow considered a British ship (Tibballs viii).

7. Roughly $100,000,000 in terms of 1912 wealth but worth perhaps $3,430,750,000 in today's dollars (Officer).

Mr. Benjamin Guggenheim, $19,000,000. **8**

Colonel Washington Roebling, $5,000,000.

Mr. J. B. Thayer, $2,000,000.

Total, $91,000,000.

A prominent New York banker to whom I showed the Titanic's passenger list said he knew twenty persons aboard who between them were worth easily $100,000,000, to say nothing of the increases due to the rising stock market here, of which the above list takes no account.

Great sympathy is felt here for Captain Smith, of the Titanic. "He's a fine seaman," they say, "but unlucky." American shipping men are decidedly superstitious, and they talk of Captain Smith's "Hoodoo." **9** When he was transferred from the Olympic to the Titanic they shook their heads, and declared that the gods of the deep meant the Hawke collision to serve as a warning. **10**

Wireless details are contradictory regarding the exact time of transferring the passengers from the Titanic to the Carpathia and Parisian. It seems most probable that the transshipment was completed before noon, aided by a calm sea and bright sunshine, and a few hours later the giant Baltic received the passengers from the Carpathia and the Parisian. The Baltic should reach Halifax late to-morrow.

As soon as the safety of the passengers was assured, a wireless to the Olympic and to the other vessels hastening to the rescue, was sent, reassuring them, and enabling them to resume their voyages.

---◆---

CAPTAIN'S CAREER.

It almost seems as if the fates have suddenly turned against Captain E.

J. Smith, the master of the Titanic, at a time when he has reached the very height of his career as an officer of liners. The circumstances of the collision between the Olympic and his Majesty's ship Hawke, in the Solent, are still fresh in the public memory, and the litigation which followed it is not yet concluded. Captain Smith was acquitted from any blame for the collision, and, as commodore of the White Star Fleet, he was given the proud command of the last new boat, only to find that his ill-luck had followed him. He is a Staffordshire man, and was born in 1850. His apprenticeship to the sea was served in the ships of Messrs. A. Gibson and Company, and at 25 years of age he took his master's certificate. Eleven years later, in 1886, began his long connection with the White Star Line. He became chief officer of the Cufic, and two years later he received promotion to the post of captain of the Celtic.

★ At first, the general public was under the impression that the above wealthy persons were carrying vast hoards of money and jewelry with them. Insurance companies in particular were terrified about what the damages of claims against the Titanic might come to. Men in the stock market were also concerned about what would become of publicly traded companies linked to the likes of Benjamin Guggenheim (mining and smelting interests), Charles M. Hays (railroad interests), and George Widener (railroad and street car interests). However, the market did not suffer any collapse with the loss of these men.

The fortunes of Colonel John Jacob Astor and Isidor Straus were personal and made respectively in real estate speculation and in retail trade. Straus was a part owner of Macy's in New York.

The great majority of the wealthy people lost were American, since these people in particular were returning to the States after European holidays. Astor was returning from his honeymoon with his bride, Madeleine, age nineteen. Their marriage had created a scandal since Astor was a divorced man and old enough to be Madeleine's father. They were returning to America hoping to be readmitted to New York Society (Aldridge 40).

Colonel John Jacob Astor with his wife.

From that time onward his career was one of continuous advancement. Big ships were followed by others of greater dimensions, and each development in size and power saw Captain Smith taking a step forward in the importance and responsibility of his commands. Passengers liked him because of his breezy geniality, for he was the very personification of the typical liner "skiper." His employers trusted him because they knew him to be a good sailor and an able and careful navigator. He commanded seventeen White Star liners in succession, until the marvels of modern marine architecture brought him the Olympic and Titanic, which, in turn, drew down on him the temporary frown of fortune. **11**

Smith appears to be a favourite name for White Star Line captains, for in addition to Captain E. J. Smith there are also a Captain Will M. Smith and a Captain Harry Smith. To the veterans of the smoking-room Captain Smith of the Titanic is known by the nickname of "Two-Dollar Smith," for tradition has it that he loses every bill of that denomination which comes into his possession. If half the stories about him are true, it is not to be wondered at that Captain Smith is said to refuse bills of that currency whenever he can possibly get the money in some other form.

Captain Smith has served as a member of the Executive Committee of the Mercantile Marine Association, holds an extra master's certificate, and is an honorary commander of the Royal Naval Reserve.

11. *Titanic* experts John Eaton and Charles Haas say of Smith: "Captain Smith was regarded as a 'safe captain' and, for a period, he probably was. Yet...it seemed that Captain Smith—along with most contemporary liner captains—had much to learn about the displacement effects of so huge a hulk as the vessel he...commanded" (*Titanic: Destination* 77).

Captain E. J. Smith

—◆—

PRECAUTIONS
AGAINST
SINKING.

TITANIC'S SYSTEM.

It would be ridiculous to suppose that Lord Pirrie neglected to instal in the Titanic what he considered was the finest system of water-tight bulkhead doors. It should be stated, however, that it is associated only with the White Star steamers, and the doors are detailed in the company's own description of the vessels. Those giving communication between the various boiler-rooms and engine-rooms are arranged on the drop system. "They are," says the description, "of Harland and Wolff's special design, of massive construction, and provided with oil cataracts governing the closing speed. Each door is held in the open position by a suitable friction-clutch, which can be instantly released by means of a powerful electric magnet, controlled from the captain's bridge, so that in the event of accident, or at any time when it might be considered advisable, the captain can, by simply moving an electric switch, instantly close the doors throughout, practically making the vessel unsinkable. **12**

"In addition to the foregoing, each door can also be immediately closed from below by operating a releasing lever fitted in connection with the friction-clutch. Moreover, as a further precaution, floats are provided beneath the floor level, which, in the event of water accidentally entering any of the compartments, automatically lift and thereby close the doors opening into that compartment, if they have not already been dropped by those in charge of the vessel. A ladder or escape is provided in each boiler-room, engine-room, and similar watertight compartment in order that the closing of the doors at any time shall not imprison the men working therein, though the risk of this eventuality is lessened by electric bells placed in the vicinity of each door, which ring prior to their closing, and thus give warning to those below…"

Discussing the matter with a *Daily Telegraph* representative, a business man prominent in shipping said he would have assumed that a ship, properly provided with watertight bulkhead doors, would not have found any serious difficulty about keeping afloat. The impact with ice would crumple up the bows, but the rest of the ship, built as strongly as these liners are to-day, would in the ordinary way be safe. In these times, he added, it is the usual thing for the temperature of the water to be taken when the presence of icebergs is suspected, and, when evidence of their

---

12. Actually, this safety feature, as important as it was, never came into play. The doors were closed immediately by officer-in-charge Murdoch, but the ship was holed in six places and was going to sink anyway (Wade 180).

proximity is forthcoming, to close the doors at once as a precautionary measure. He also greatly doubted whether there was a dry dock large enough to accommodate the Titanic on the other side of the Atlantic. In that case, what would be done with her in respect of the necessary repairs?

———◆———

THE FIRST NEWS.

———

From Our Own Correspondent.

MONTREAL, Monday (6.0 a.m.)

"Titanic struck an iceberg. Sends marconigram asking for assistance. Virginian going to her rescue."

The above marconigram, which was received at Montreal from the Allan liner Virginian, via Cape Race, reached Montreal at midnight.

As the Virginian sailed from Halifax for Liverpool at eight o'clock on Sunday morning, she was fourteen hours out, and thus near Cape Race, when she received the Titanic's wireless call for help. It is impossible to guess the distance between the vessels at that time; probably it was between two and three hundred miles, so it was hoped that the Virginian would reach the mammoth White Star liner in time to prevent a disaster, no matter how severe might be her injuries.

It is stated here that the Virginian is capable of taking all the Titanic's passengers off if necessary.

This is the second mishap to the Titanic on her maiden voyage. **13**

———◆———

"C.Q.D." SIGNAL.

———

From Our Own Correspondent.

MONTREAL, Monday Afternoon.

The subjoined telegram was received here late last night:

It is difficult to know what could have been done to make the *Titanic* more iceberg-proof. Structurally, higher watertight bulkheads might have helped. Some of the ship's bulkheads were only fifteen feet above the waterline. Higher bulkheads would have given the *Titanic* more time to await rescue, but she would still have sunk.

If the *Titanic*'s sides had been more thickly plated, that might have saved her, but a heavier ship would have been a less glamorous and more expensive ship. The extra coal used to propel her would have been enormous.

★ ★

★ **13.** The *Titanic* nearly collided with the *New York* upon leaving Southampton, England, when the suction from her wake drew the smaller ship toward her side. A tugboat pushed the *New York* out of danger (Wels 61).

Cape Race, Sunday (10.25 p.m.).

At 10.25 to-night the steamship Titanic called "C.Q.D.," and reported having struck an iceberg. The steamer said that immediate assistance was required.

Half an hour afterwards another message came reporting that the Titanic was sinking by the head, and that the women were being put off in lifeboats. The weather was calm and clear. The Titanic's wireless operator reported, and gave the position of the vessel as 41.46 N. latitude, 50.14 W. longitude. **14**

The Marconi station at Cape Race notified the Allan liner Virginian, the captain of which immediately advised that he was proceeding to the scene of the disaster. At midnight the Virginian was about 150 miles distant from the Titanic, and expected to reach that vessel about ten a.m. on Monday. The White Star liner Olympic, at an early hour this (Monday) morning, was in latitude 40.32 N., and longitude 61.18 W. She was in direct communication with the Titanic, and is now making all haste towards her.

The White Star steamship Baltic also reported herself as about 200 hundred miles east of the Titanic, and was making all possible speed towards her.

The last signals from the Titanic were heard by the Virginian at 12.27 a.m.

The wireless operator on the Virginian says these signals were blurred, and ended abruptly.

Amongst the distinguished Canadians on the Titanic is Mr. Charles M. Hays (president and general manager of the Grand Trunk Railroad and Grand Trunk Pacific Railroad), who is returning from a business trip to England.

Shipping men here are inclined to the opinion that the mammoth liner was simply unable to make her way along to any extent, and had been heading for Halifax, when she got in communication with the Virginian. With her thirty-eight water-tight compartments **15** the danger had been reduced to a minimum, as far as marine and engineering science could make a ship.

New York received from Montreal its first news of the accident to the Titanic. The only information received on land from either vessel was the Marconigram from Captain Gamble, of the Virginian, which was in turn transmitted by land from Cape Breton to Mr. George Hannah, at the Allan Line offices here. From Montreal the message was communicated to New York, where the news caused a big sensation.

Early this morning a flood of messages came from New York, asking for additional details, but up to three o'clock this afternoon nothing more had come from Captain Gamble.

★ **14.** The *Titanic* was approximately 2,300 miles west of London and 1,000 miles east of Boston and just above New York's latitude.

15. Really, it was only sixteen watertight compartments (Tibballs viii–ix).

—◆—

ICE PERILS
OF THE NORTH
ATLANTIC.

ENORMOUS BERGS.

AN ABNORMAL SEASON.

RISKS OF NAVIGATION.

**By OUR SHIPPING
CORRESPONDENT.**

The catastrophe to the Titanic is a sharp reminder of one of the gravest perils of the North Atlantic. Gale and sea can do their worst against the liner of to-day. She rides triumphant through the fiercest storm. But there is an ever-lurking danger at certain seasons of the year—the danger of contact with icebergs. How many North Atlantic mysteries have been due to the cause we shall never know. We can only conjecture. Here is a typical case. The steamship Erna left the Clyde **16** on Feb. 28 last for Newfoundland. She was commanded by Captain Findlater, who had his family on board with him. This fairly big tramp steamer is missing, and she is assumed to have met her fate at the hands of an iceberg. We shall never know, of course, but that is the inference.

Wireless telegraphy is putting the mariner in a better position, if, that is to say, his vessel is fitted with wireless. He can get from other vessels warnings of icebergs which will induce him to keep a specially good look-out for these ocean pests. Or he can, as the Titanic did, appeal for help on meeting with misfortune through ice. We are in a better position as regards knowledge of risk and knowledge of disaster, but the root mischief remains. We can never get rid of icebergs. A facetious American once proposed to send out ships with guns, with a view of blowing icebergs to pieces. He had a limited sense of proportion. He might as well have talked of blowing up the Isle of Wight.

THE APRIL DANGER.

Roughly speaking, the ice season in the North Atlantic extends from April to August, both months inclusive, although bergs have been met with at all seasons of the year northward of 43 N., and occasionally as far south as 39 N. It will be seen, therefore, that the disaster to the Titanic has occurred at what may be called the opening of the ice season. There is evidence that at the present time the ice conditions in the Atlantic are quite abnormal. The Canadian Pacific liner Empress of Britain, arriving at Liverpool from Halifax (N.S.), yesterday, reports immense quantities as afloat. Last Tuesday, when three days out from Halifax, she encountered an icefield one hundred miles in extent, with enormous bergs. She states that the extent of the ice was phenomenal, the bergs appearing to be joined to the icefield, which is described as an enormous white line on the horizon. It seems that the Allan liner Virginian warned the Empress of Britain of this icefield. It is also learned from New York, by a telegram dated yesterday, that the Carmania and the Nicaragua, which have arrived at that port, both had a perilous time in the ice, the Nicaragua sustaining considerable damage.

We may picture the North Atlantic at the present time as the scene of innumerable wireless messages, passing from ship to ship, and between ship and shore, which are designed as warnings against the special seasonal danger. It may therefore be taken that the Titanic was fully informed of the risks which lay ahead of her, and to which she has succumbed, doubtless after the exercise of the utmost vigilance, when something over a thousand miles from New York, her port of destination…

SOME RECENT COLLISIONS.

The casualty to the Titanic follows upon at least two similar accidents to Atlantic liners within the last nine months. The Anchor Line steamer Columbia arrived at New York on Aug. 6 with her bow-plates crushed in for a distance of 15ft. She lost her port anchor, and the presumption is that she left it on the iceberg with which she collided. Her experience

was undoubtedly a very unpleasant one. Again, on Aug. 15 last, the Donaldson liner Saturnia struck on a ledge of an iceberg, when 110 miles from East Belle Isle. She completed her voyage from the St. Lawrence to the Clyde, but on arrival was found to be taking in water. A third steamer at the time was subject to a somewhat similar experience. It may reasonably be inferred that in August last, just at the very tail end of what may be called the ice season, the Atlantic, so far as its more northerly waters are concerned, was in a condition not wholly dissimilar from that which now obtains.

The Columbia is a steamer of between 8,000 and 9,000 tons. The Titanic is of 46,000 tons. These figures are worth noting, because they help to explain the more serious damage to the White Star liner. If the Anchor liner, with less than one-fifth of the weight, got her bows so badly damaged, it is pretty clear that the Titanic was bound to suffer to some extent in proportion. To that extent, and to that extent only, is it conceivable that the huge size of the new liner could have influenced this latest disaster. All idea that it could have been brought about, or be in any way explained, by the theory of suction, is ridiculous, in view of the fact that the liner was in deep water, and meeting the iceberg, it may be assumed, end on.

POSSIBLE PRECAUTIONS.

In dealing with ice the mariner has to allow for something that is wholly uncertain. One season will differ from another, and it is often impossible, even with the best system of intelligence that can be set up, to give warning where serious obstruction is likely. The main precaution must necessarily be the keenest possible lookout…

It is pretty generally known that, in part with a view of avoiding ice, Atlantic liners vary their route according to the season, selecting the more southerly when the risk is at its height. **17** It is well, however, to get away from the idea that the danger always lies to the northward. It would appear that ice has been prevalent in the western part of the North Atlantic much farther south than usual during the last few years. Instances of an exceptional nature are recorded of bergs being met with about sixty miles W.N.W. of Corvo Island, in the Azores. In May, 1907, small pieces of ice were reported to have been passed in, approximately, 31 N., 33 W., southwestward of the Azores. In the same month two years afterwards, a piece of ice 60 ft long and 10ft high was seen in 33 N., 44 W.

WHAT CAN GOVERNMENTS DO?

Much has been written of late years about the danger of derelict ships in the North Atlantic. The United States Government has been at special pains to send out ships with a view to their destruction. But what can Governments do with regard to the destruction of the even more dangerous peril represented by icebergs? Plainly, they can do little

or nothing. They can help, as they do, in the circulation of information with regard to the break-up of the immense masses of ice which the currents at particular seasons bring down from the northward. They can, as they do, circulate charts which embody all the teaching of recent years with respect to ice risks and ice probabilities. Clearly, however, they can do but little more. The rest must remain with the shipowner and with his servants.

It is a question of navigation, and, unfortunately, navigation must to some extent be a question of luck. It is the worst possible luck that the Titanic should have made her début during a month in which ice dangers have been far in excess, so far as the Atlantic is concerned, of the Aprils of some former years. It is worse still that this magnificent ship should have been the first to come to grief this ice season.

SCENES AT LLOYD'S.

INSURANCES OF £730,000.

Our Marine Insurance Correspondent writes:

During the last six months the casualties to liners of the highest class have been unparalleled in the history of

---

★ **17.** The *Titanic* took the southerly route, but, even so, was not far enough south, as events proved.

Lloyd's; the oldest members own they have never seen their equal. They began with the collision of the Olympic, followed by the sinking of the Delhi and the Oceana. The burden of the two latter vessels did not touch the market, the P. and O. Company having an insurance fund of their own. The loss of the cargo and the claims on the specie **18** of both vessels fell on underwriters both inside and outside Lloyd's. **19**

A long spell of freedom from accidents to such big vessels of the liner class was certainly deserved, and with finer weather was looked for. The casualty to the Titanic which met those underwriters who were present at the opening of Lloyd's yesterday morning makes the fourth that has fallen on the marine insurance market since the Olympic's collision on Sept. 20 last. The casualty board on which the telegrams from the other side of the Atlantic were posted the moment they reached Lloyd's was surrounded by a big crowd of members and their clerks, and as fast as the first row, after having read them, passed away, their place was taken by another set, and this continued without interruption till after the closing of the "Room." Such a scene has not been witnessed before. This has arisen from the well-known character of the liner, the huge dimensions of the boat, and the enormous value of such a great floating hotel.

The insured value of the vessel in the policy is £1,000,000, of which £730,000 is covered by insurance; but as the cost of the vessel must have been at least £1,500,000, it follows that the owners are running at their own risk about £750,000, or an amount equivalent to that they have covered against all risks. So satisfied were the underwriters of the safety of the vessel and the almost impossibility of her total loss that the premium charged for the insurance of this £730,000 is ridiculously small. Apart from the insurance of the hull, a very considerable amount has been effected on diamonds and bonds by registered post. These, it is hoped, would, after the landing of the passengers, receive first attention. After looking to the safety of the valuables, if the steamer holds up sufficiently long the passengers' baggage might be dealt with.

Unlike the case of the sinking of the Delhi and the Oceana, the Titanic does not appear to have any specie on board, the flow of the market at the moment not being in a Western direction. The cargo in the hold of the vessel is insured in different quarters, and as she is no doubt full it runs into a very considerable sum.

---

18. Money in coins.

19. Lloyd's of London is a famous insurance company that got its start in a coffeehouse where ship owners and merchants met to negotiate coverage for losses of cargo at sea. The year was 1688. The company is famous for insuring just about anything, including dancers' legs. The company publishes *Lloyd's List and Shipping Gazette*, proclaimed to be the oldest newspaper in London.

RUSH TO RE-INSURE.

When the "Room" opened there was a rush among some underwriters, who had heavy lines, to get rid of their liability, and for this they had to pay 50 guineas [20] per cent. at which a considerable amount was done. Before lunch the rate rose to 55 guineas, and after two o'clock it reached 60 guineas. The ideas of experts were many and varied, but the fact that influenced most in taking the rate to 60 guineas for a steamer so splendidly equipped with watertight compartments as the Titanic was the sudden cutting off of the wireless messages, which some thought might mean that the vessel was sinking, while others imagined that the shock of the collision might have brought down the pole of the wireless apparatus.

Just before four o'clock a telegram was received at Lloyd's, giving the copy of a statement in the Montreal Star, to the effect that the Titanic was being towed towards Halifax. On this the rate dropped to 25 guineas, giving those who had written earlier in the afternoon a profit of 35 guineas.

When the collision occurred the Titanic was about 400 to 450 miles off Halifax and if possible she will no doubt be towed to that port. The question of repair will be a serious one, as there is no dock large enough on that side of the Atlantic to take her—the one at Belfast is the only one on this side—she cannot be beached or tipped; so that the building of a coffer dam, temporary repair, and towage to Belfast, is the only course.

This accident to the Titanic recalls a collision with an iceberg which befell the Guion steamer Arizona, a greyhound of the Atlantic, thirty years ago, when several tons of ice fell on her deck and her bows were crumpled up like matchwood.

OPERATOR'S MESSAGE.

A Godalming correspondent says:

"Mr. and Mrs. G. A. Phillips, of Farncombe, Godalming, parents of the wireless operator on board the Titanic, to-night received the following message from their son: 'Making slowly for Halifax. Practically unsinkable. Don't worry.'

"Mr. J. G. Phillips, the operator, was appointed to the Titanic for this voyage, after having served on the Teutonic, Lusitania, Mauretania, and Oceanic." [21]

20. A guinea was a sum worth a little more than a pound in value.

21. Phillips's parents denied ever receiving such a telegram in a later edition of the paper.

———◆———

WELL-KNOWN VOYAGERS.

———

We publish below some details concerning a few of the passengers who were well known on each side of the Atlantic:

Colonel John Jacob Astor is cousin to Mr. William Waldorf Astor. He built the Astoria Hotel, New York, in 1897; served in the Spanish-American War in 1898; presented to the Government of the United States a mountain battery for use in war against Spain; and has invented a bicycle brake, and a pneumatic road improver.

Major Archibald W. Butt is aide-de-camp to President Taft. He had recently been in Italy, and had paid a visit to the Pope.

Mr. Washington Dodge is a member of the American banking firm of Phelps, Dodge, and Company.

Mr. Jacques Futrelle, a well-known author and short-story writer, has also had experience in American journalism and theatrical management.

Mr. Benjamin Guggenheim is a member of the famous Guggenheim family of capitalists, associates of Mr. Pierpont Morgan, and world-famous in connection with Alaskan development and copper production.

Mr. Henry B. Harris, a theatrical producer and manager, is a son of the gentleman of the same name who owns many of New York's theatres.

Mr. Charles Melville Hays president of the Grand Trunk Railway, commenced his career as a clerk in the passenger department of the Atlantic and Pacific Railroad, St. Louis. He has had a wide and varied experience in railway work, and is at the head of several railway systems in America.

Mr. Christopher Head is well known to the inhabitants of Chelsea. He takes a great interest in art, and in the discussions at the Mansion House **22** respecting the King Edward Memorial he also took a leading part.

Mr. Joseph Bruce Ismay is chairman and managing director of the White Star Line, and president of the International Mercantile Marine Company.

Mr. C. Clarence Jones, a New York stockbroker, had been visiting European capitals in connection with the purchase of American Embassy sites.

Mr. Frank D. Millet is an American painter, who resided a long time in London.

Mr. Clarence Moore is well known in New York society. **23**

Mr. Washington Augustus Roebling is the head of the great wire cable firm of John A. Roebling's, Sons, and Co., Trenton (N.J.). The entire construction

22. The mayor of London's residence.

23. According to an article in the *New York Times* of April 16, 1912, Clarence Moore was a Washington, DC, banker and sportsman. He rode to the hounds and was Master of Hounds at the Chevy Chase Hunt. His business interests lay in mineral development.

of Brooklyn Bridge was left to him owing to the death of his father. **24**

The Countess of Rother [Rothes] was on her way to meet the Earl of Rother, whom she married in 1900. She was Lucy Noël Martha, only child of Mr. Thomas Dyer-Edwardes, of Prinknash Park, Gloucester.

Mr. W. T. Stead is the well-known journalist and editor of the "Review of Reviews."

Mr. Isidor Straus was a member of the United States Congress from 1893–5. He is a partner in the firm of L. Straus and Sons, importers of pottery and glassware, New York.

Mr. John Borland Thayer, born in Philadelphia, in 1862, passed through all the grades of railway administration, and is now president of the Pennsylvania Railroad.

Mr. George D. Widener is the son of Mr. Peter A. Widener, a Philadelphia millionaire, who recently bought the famous picture "The Mill," from the Marquis of Lansdowne.

PASSENGERS AND RAILROAD.

NEWHAVEN (Connecticut), Monday.

The traffic officials of the New York, Newhaven, and Hartford Railroad have been notified that the passengers of the Titanic will be landed at Halifax, Nova Scotia. About 600 will require transportation to New York by sleeping-cars and 800 by ordinary coaches.—*Reuter.*

LIFE SAVING
BY
WIRELESS.

A SPLENDID RECORD.

GIFT TO HUMANITY.

Once again a disaster which might easily have involved the loss of hundreds, if not thousands, of lives has been rendered bloodless by means of wireless telegraphy. **25** The instances of vessels which have stranded, or been in collision, or met with other accidents and have received prompt assistance in response to messages by radio-telegraphy have become so frequent that unless some great liner is involved they have almost ceased to attract attention, and no record of them is kept even at the head offices of Marconi's Wireless Telegraphy Company.

---

24. Not so. Washington Augustus Roebling II was the *nephew* of the man who built the Brooklyn Bridge. This mistake is repeated in many books and articles about the *Titanic* (*Encyclopedia*, "Mr Washington Augustus II Roebling").

25. What great hope they have in the magnificent *Titanic*, the unsinkable ship!

THE REPUBLIC AND **THE DELHI.**

It is something of a coincidence that the first instance in which the passengers of a great liner escaped destruction by this means was that of the White Star liner Republic, and that the vessel which took off her passengers and crew was the Baltic, which has played so prominent a part in saving the victims of yesterday's disaster. The Republic left New York on Jan. 25, 1909, with 710 souls on board, of whom 400 were passengers. She was a magnificently equipped vessel of 16,000 tons, and was known as the "millionaires' ship," on account of the number of well-known and immensely rich Americans who travelled by her. She was slowly making her way through a fog about a hundred miles from the American shore when she collided with the in-bound steamer Florida, and was badly damaged just aft of the midship section. The Florida also sustained great damage, and although she rendered all the assistance in her power it would have gone hard with many of the Republic's passengers if that vessel had not been equipped with one of the earliest installations of wireless telegraphy. The heroism of Jack Binns, the telegraphist, who remained at his post until he was literally washed out, will be still well remembered. In response to his messages the French steamer La Lorraine

and the White Star liner Baltic steamed full-speed to the Republic's assistance, and with the exception of six unfortunate victims, who were killed at the time of the collision, all on board were saved. The Republic sank while being towed back, and her captain and chief officer, who had remained on board, narrowly escaped with their lives. **26**

A more recent case in which prompt assistance was brought by wireless telegraphy is that of the wreck of the Peninsular and Oriental steamer Delhi, on Dec. 13 last, three miles south of Cape Spartel, when the Princess Royal and the late Duke of Fife and their daughters underwent terrible experiences. It was the receipt of wireless messages at Gibraltar from the stranded liner which brought his Majesty's cruiser, Edinburgh, the Admiralty tug Energetic, and torpedoboat, and salvage steamers to the scene of the disaster.

---◆---

A DISTURBING INCIDENT.

Sailors are a proverbially superstitious race, and an incident which happened when the Titanic started off on her first voyage will doubtless be pointed to now by them as a sign of ill omen. As she swung away from her berth she passed the New

---

★ ▶ **26.** A legend persists that the *Republic* was carrying gold, but if that were so, more of an effort would have been made to transfer the precious cargo along with the passengers ("Treasure"). Nonetheless, salvors still dream of finding treasure on her.

York, lying at anchor at Test Quay. The disturbance caused by such an immense displacement of water caused the stern ropes of the American vessel to part, and she began to swing out in the fairway. Tugs at once took hold, and hauled her out of danger, and the Titanic, which had stopped, proceeded on her course. **27**▸

---◆---

TITANIC IN COLLISION WITH AN ICEBERG.

THE WORLD'S GREATEST LINER.

DESCRIPTION OF THE SHIP.

A PALACE
OF
LUXURY.

When, at noon on Wednesday, the Titanic slipped her moorings at Southampton and steamed proudly down the Solent, **28**▸ the sailormen and others who watched her departure were filled with admiration and wonder at her gigantic proportions. There had never been a ship quite like her, even in those waters, where mighty triumphs of the shipbuilder's skill are a familiar sight. In point of size her sister ship, the Olympic, was her equal, but the fittings and appointments of this newest vessel were even more splendid and luxurious, and everything on her was the embodiment of, for the moment, the last word in the thousand and one things which go to make an ocean voyage swift, smooth, safe, and comfortable. The Titanic was designed, built, and engined by Messrs. Harland and Wolff (Ltd.), the world-famous Belfast firm, and her keel-plate was laid on March 31, 1909. Almost exactly a year after she was fully framed, and on May 31, 1911, she was launched. Part of her construction, at any rate, was carried out while the Olympic was building, and the spectacle of the two great hulls, gradually growing into shape on slips which stood side by side, was an unique one—a triumph of naval architecture and marine engineering.

STUPENDOUS FIGURES.

Some idea of the tremendous size of this creation of man, which is reported to have come off second best in an encounter with the creation of Nature in the

---

★▸ **27.** According to one source, "Another example of the force of the *Titanic*'s suction would be revealed later when Southampton authorities discovered that a sunken barge had been dragged in the *Titanic*'s wake 800 yards across the harbor bottom" (Wade 28).

28. The channel between the English mainland and the Isle of Wight.

shape of an iceberg, may be conveyed by the following figures:

Length, over all:	882ft 9in
Breadth, extreme:	92ft 6in
Total height, from keel to navigating bridge:	104ft
Gross tonnage:	46,328
Displacement (tons):	60,000
Horse-power of reciprocating engines:	30,000
Shaft horse-power of turbine-engine:	16,000
Speed (knots):	21

She has accommodation for 750 first-class passengers, 650 second-class, and 1,200 third-class, and her crew is reckoned at 860, of whom 65 are attached to the navigating department, 320 to the engineers' department, and 475 to the stewards', &c.

The details as to the construction of the ship are interesting. In the building up of every single part of her, stability and strength were the one consideration. A double bottom, riveted by hydraulic power, made for increased safety in the event of striking something under water, and was, at the same time, utilised for carrying water ballast. Stout steel girders, heavy beams, and stanchions which are really steel columns, are fitted right through the hull to give the maximum stiffness in a heavy seaway; and the deck plating, steel throughout, is thickened and strengthened on the shelter and bridge decks. The strength of the shell needed may be easily guessed at. The Titanic's exterior is composed of exceptionally heavy plating, the plates being 6ft wide and 30ft long, with the laps trebly riveted.

————

A MONSTER RUDDER.

————

Even the weights of the stern frame and rudder of such a monster are interesting. The former weighs 70 tons, and the latter 101 ¼ tons, with a length of 78ft 8in—the dimension of a good-sized craft in itself. What strength of steering oar is needed for the purpose of manipulating this rudder may be gathered from the fact that the rudder-stock is just half an inch under 2ft in diameter, and a triple cylinder engine is needed to work it. The gear is controlled from both the navigating bridge and the docking bridge, and the whole is so designed as to minimise shocks received in a heavy sea, and the chance of that once great danger with steamships— "steering gear out of order." A 15-ton anchor is necessary to hold her at her moorings, and for the accommodation of the 30ft lifeboats there are sixteen sets of davits, specially designed for handling two or three boats without waste of time, and with electric winches for launching. The water-tight compartments, the provision of which would prevent the ship immediately sinking in the event of such an accident as that of Sunday night, are fully described elsewhere, as is also the wireless telegraphic apparatus, which proved of such incalculable service. In addition to this there is a complete installation for receiving submarine signals, **29** and two

————

29. Why the *Titanic* would want to receive submarine signals is not clear, unless the signals could somehow detect jagged rocks beneath the sea.

electrically-driven sounding machines, by which soundings may be taken under the direct control of the officer in charge when the ship is going at full speed.

POWERFUL MACHINERY.

Equally as remarkable as the strength of construction is the tremendous power of the machinery. The Titanic is a triplescrew steamer, with a combination of reciprocating engines with a low-pressure turbine. Both from an engineering and a passengers' point of view, this is an advantage, for it makes for the smooth working of the ship. There are twenty-nine boilers in all, with 159 furnaces. All the boilers are 15ft 9in in diameter, and twenty-four of them are 20ft long, and they are accommodated in six water-tight compartments. Any of these six compartments can be isolated, the pumps being independent so far as the inrush of sea water is concerned, and air is supplied to the stokeholds by electric fans.

Cool drinks and fresh food are assured by the refrigerating installation, and the electric lighting plant is of a very complete character. Four engines and dynamos, in a separate water-tight compartment, are capable of generating 16,000 amperes, and, in addition to these, there are two other engines in another part of the ship, available for emergency purposes. There are electric lights from stem to stern, and the dynamos supply power for heating and for running seventy-five fans for ventilating passenger and crew spaces. **30**

PASSENGER ACCOMMODATION.

A recital of the details of the accommodation for passengers would, to ocean travellers of a century ago, sound like boastful exaggeration. The Titanic might be called a "floating palace" but for the fact that the term is so terribly hackneyed, and, further, that there are probably very few palaces even which offer the attractions to be found on board her. The vessel has ten decks—again figures convey an idea of her vastness. For first-class passengers there are thirty suite-rooms on the bridge deck and thirty-nine on the shelter deck, and they are so arranged that they can be let in groups to form suites, including bedrooms with baths, &c. For the payment of £870 **31** per voyage, indeed, one may get all the advantages of a well-appointed flat in the West-end of London. In all, there are nearly 350 first-class rooms; in the second-class the rooms are arranged for two and four berths; and in the third-class also there are a large number of enclosed berths, promenades, reading, writing, and smoking rooms, dining saloons, all are of a spaciousness

30. The *Titanic* was designed to have the best luxury accommodations in every way, and, at the time, it did.

31. Roughly $100,000 in today's money, though online estimates vary widely (Officer).

in keeping with the general size of this wonderful ship, the third-class dining saloon, for instance, seating nearly 500 passengers. In fact, everything about the arrangements conspires to combat that feeling of boredom which many days away from sight of land induces in some people. A splendidly-equipped gymnasium, a squash racquet court, swimming, Turkish, and electric baths, a well-stocked library, in addition to the many other well-known forms of shipboard entertainment, are provided to beguile the traveller and make the already short journey seem shorter; and the decorations of the apartments are truly charming. **32** A careful study of style at Hatfield and Haddon Hall have resulted in a faultless reproduction of the Jacobean style in the dining-room, and other styles and periods have been faithfully copied in other of the common apartments and state-rooms. And on the promenade deck is the Café Parisien, with walls covered with trellis, up which climbing plants appear to grow. Here the voyager may sip his after-dinner cup of coffee and ruminate on the great skill and ingenuity of the shipbuilders and engineers, upholsterers and decorators, whose combined efforts produced the most marvellous ship which ever sailed the seas, to come to grief, on her very first venture, through a cause which all their skill and ingenuity could not altogether foresee and guard against.

32. There was a lot of publicity attached to the *Titanic* that may have made it seem that she was a grander ship than she was. *Titanic* was the largest passenger liner afloat, but the *Olympic* was only a few feet shorter than the *Titanic* and had virtually the same amenities—except for *Titanic*'s exclusive enclosed promenade deck and luxurious Café Parisien.

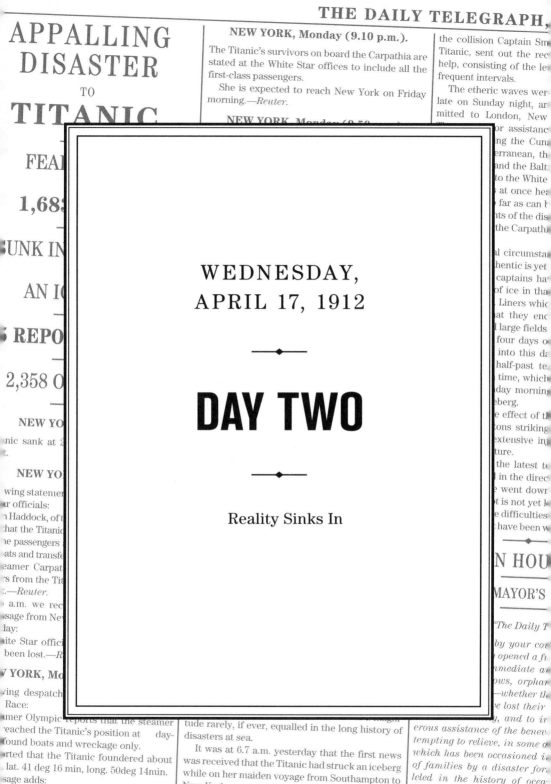

WEDNESDAY,
APRIL 17, 1912

DAY TWO

Reality Sinks In

INTRODUCTION

———◆———

A S   O F   T O D A Y,   I T   I S   N O W   C L E A R   T H E R E   H A S   B E E N   A   G R E A T
loss of life. Perhaps only 868 souls have been saved, though some news outlets
report even fewer survivors.

There is great concern in the financial sector that some Very Important
People have been lost. Without these great captains of industry, how will businesses such as the Grand Trunk Railway of Canada go on? Can Macy's retain
its preeminence in retailing without Isidor Straus? And what of the widows
and children? Who will take care of them? In an effort to answer that last
question, the *Daily Telegraph* will launch a fund for survivors.

Of course, it is still hard to get accurate information. The rescue ship
Carpathia is still too far away at sea to make direct contact with Cape Race,
Newfoundland, or New York, and any news about VIPs such as John Jacob
Astor, Isidor Straus, and Benjamin Guggenheim is hard to get.

Not all answers can come today—or ever, perhaps.

How can so many well-to-do passengers, major representatives of the upper
class from the United States, Canada, and Great Britain, surrounded by riches
and all the security only money can buy, go down to such an ignoble death?

Is no one safe from risk and danger?

From an
Unsigned Editorial

◆

With profound sympathy for those who have been so suddenly cast into mourning, we have to record the most appalling disaster in the annals of navigation. The King and Queen, in that gracious spirit which their Majesties always exhibit in a national emergency, have been the first to send words of heart-felt sympathy to those who are bowed in overwhelming grief. The great White Star liner Titanic, which collided with an iceberg in the darkness of Sunday night when off the dread Newfoundland Banks, sank less than four hours later, carrying with her, "to sleep in the noiseless bed of rest," nearly 1,500 of her passengers and crew. When the first news was received of the disaster to this wonderful vessel— the last word in ocean comfort—good ground existed for hoping that all her passengers would be rescued, and that the maimed leviathan would be able to reach the coast near Halifax, there to be beached—for the American continent has no dock which could have accommodated her. In shipping circles, familiar with the staunchness of her hull and the minute precautions taken against the perils of sea traffic, it was confidently asserted that, however serious the damage, the Titanic would keep afloat. All these optimistic statements have proved baseless; the truth has undermined these too willing assurances. The ship which was unsinkable has sunk in two miles of water. Over one half of the passengers and most of the crew, who were safe, are lost. Probably not for some days—days of terrible suspense for many sad hearts—shall we see a full and authenticated list of those who have been rescued, but it seems apparent that at the highest estimate only some 800 of the persons on board, numbering upwards of 2,300 souls, are alive. The welcome stories of the arrival of the liners Virginian, Parisian, Baltic, Carpathia, Californian, and others, and of the transfer to them of the Titanic's human freight, were, it seems, merely figments of imaginations which outran the ascertained facts. [1] We now know, from a message received at Cape Race, that "the Carpathia reached the Titanic's position at daybreak, but found boats and wreckage only," the stricken liner having foundered about twenty minutes past two o'clock, in the hour just before the dawn. Fortunately, the sea was calm; the ship's boats had been able to keep afloat, and their occupants were taken on board the steamer without delay. The ocean waste, with its frail craft and its wreckage—all that remained of the proudest ship that ever rode the waves—told in a glance all that really matters of the grim tragedy. Within the measurable distance of the spot where that stout-hearted Devonian, Sir Humphrey Gilbert, the pioneer colonist of the American continent, sank in the Golden Hind of forty tons, the ice-cold

---

1. For an example of how this could happen, read the article in the *Daily Telegraph* for April 22, titled "Clearing a Mystery."

waters have closed over the twentieth century's greatest caravanserai of 46,000 tons. "We are as near to heaven on sea as on land" the famous navigator cheerily shouted to his companions when the end was near; though the Elizabethan age, with its small, trim ships, has given place to the age of steel and steam, though we have mastered many of the problems that puzzled Sir Walter Raleigh and his stepbrother in their voyagings, there are mysteries which remain unplumbed, and the consolation of Sir Humphrey and his brave companions is still the consolation of all who go down to the sea in ships. Over the storm-swept grave of these hapless passengers the English and American peoples will gather in spirit united by a common grief. We shall never know from anyone who was on board the Titanic when she sank what happened in the last hours and minutes, but the report that those in the boats were "nearly all women and children" bears eloquent testimony to the innate instinctive humanity of the men of Anglo-Saxon blood, which calls upon them to sacrifice their strength to the appealing weakness of those whom it is their duty and privilege to protect. At such moments what man gives a thought to the "war of the sexes"? In face of a calamity men are still men, and women are still women, and the cry of the children falls on no deaf ears; thus it happens that of those rescued "nearly all are women and children." **2** In the hour of mourning into which England and America have been suddenly plunged it is a healing thought that the old chivalrous cry of English seamen, "Women and children first!" ran from deck to deck, from end to end, of the leviathan before she sank beneath the waves. In the House of Commons the Prime Minister echoed the admiration which will be universally felt that "the best traditions of the sea" should have been observed under these heartrending conditions, and we, on our part, have felt it no more than our duty to appeal to the generosity of the nation to come to the aid of the dependents of the members of the crew who so bravely rendered up their lives in the hour of peril. Great sorrows make communities nations and make nations one, and throughout the English-speaking world the prompt message of the German Emperor and the sympathy of the Reichstag will be received with feelings of responsive gratitude. **3**

This disaster is another reminder that

---

2. Actually, of the 705 survivors, 52.5 percent were women and children, which gives a somewhat different picture. However, there were not that many women and children on board out of the 2,223 passengers. "Women and children first" is shown by the fact that 70 percent of all women and children on board survived; whereas, only about 20 percent of the men on board survived (Geller 8–9).

3. The *Daily Telegraph* ran messages of condolence that came in from various dignitaries worldwide, but Kaiser Wilhelm II was already intensely distrusted. He had given the *Telegraph* an exclusive interview in 1908 in which he had said: "You English are mad...mad as March hares" (October 28, 1908).

the horrors of war are equalled only by the horrors of peace. The strife of man with men in the past rendered villages and towns desolate; the present strife of man with the primeval forces of Nature casts over thousands of homes the shadow of death. These are still the days of bloody conquest, of devastating wars; but the struggle is against those inanimate, and yet seemingly animate, elements—immeasurable in their strength and unknowable in their mysteries—which have existed since time began, and which our distant forefathers regarded with awe as untameable. With each age man has made fresh efforts to conquer the sea and the air and the earth. He has attempted to put a girdle round the world, each link either a huge ship of steel ribs, with pulsating engines of colossal power, or an express train, with luxurious accommodation, designed to rival the wind in speed. In wringing from Nature her secrets the inventor has had many triumphs. He has annihilated distance by wireless telegraphy; he has bridged wide seas, and brought coast near to coast; he has enabled the pleasure-seeker and the trader to be in two Continent almost simultaneously; he has shown how man may fly over the earth with artificial wings, or swim under the water in a moving casket. Yet time and again we have rude awakenings from the natural satisfaction which these achievements occasion. The conquests are made, but the price has to be paid. Over 1,000 lives were lost on the railways of the United

Kingdom last year, though they are the best and most cautiously worked in the world. Not in dramatic fashion, but in dozens and scores, thousands of lives were sacrificed on the seas. In tens and twenties, hundreds of brave men have given their all in the development of submarine navigation, and the toll exacted by aeroplane and the airship is daily mounting higher. To-day, by the loss of a single ship engaged in peaceful navigation, we have to mourn the death of nearly 1,500 persons, of our own kith and kin, a battle's death-roll, and yet who will believe that even such a calamity will cause the hands of the clock to be turned back? There may be a momentary arrest in the tendency of the age, but assuredly the movement will continue, and as the memory of the fate of the Titanic becomes dim with the passage of time, the inventor, the shipbuilder, the worker in steel, and all who are engaged in the allied industries, will turn to the fight against the obstacles and embarrassments of the dumb forces of Nature with renewed zest for victory. **4**

The sinking of this great liner, representing probably a loss of about three millions sterling, including her valuable cargo, will assuredly occasion many temporary misgivings as to the wisdom of constructing ships of such unparalleled size. It is impossible for the ordinary Englishman to form any accurate conception of the dimensions and the complications of detail of such a maritime hotel, with its verandah restaurant

★ **4.** Why humankind is not included as a part of Nature is not clear here, except if one excludes man from being a part of the "dumb forces of Nature."

which displays the growing vine on its lattice-work, with its riding school, its swimming bath, its skating rink, its delightful garden, its fishpond, yielding trout for the dinner table, its gymnasium, its ball-room, and all the other refinements of ocean travel. It is the fashion to refer with awe to the immense size of Dreadnoughts, the latest development in warships. But the Titanic represented more than twice the deadweight of the largest vessel of any navy in the world, with a length of about one-sixth of a mile, and decks towering up above the level of the sea to a height of over one hundred feet. **5** She has gone—buried for ever beneath the waters off Cape Race, but already her greater sister, the Gigantic, is on the stocks in this country, and yet another of her class is building in Germany. **6** The world bows its head in mourning over the fate of the Titanic and the awful sacrifice of life it has involved, but there will assuredly be no lengthened pause. Great size means comfort, economy, and safety. The Titanic's hull was a honeycomb of well-wrought and well-riveted steel; she was protected from disaster as no smaller vessel could be protected; and her loss must have been due to a blow which rent open almost her whole side to the inrushing water. Because she has come to such an untimely end, and on her maiden voyage, her race will not cease to be seen on the seas. This overwhelming disaster will have its effects on the development of marine navigation, yet it will not tend to more moderate dimensions. While the world has become a small place owing to triumphs of mechanical science, men's ideas are ever growing. The field of achievement will, no doubt, be surveyed with care, with a view to devising additional precautions to guard navigation against the unforeseen blows of the elemental forces of Nature. Possibly some further measures may be taken for watching the movements of winds, fogs, ice-floes, and icebergs, and communicating the intelligence to the liners which are always on the great ocean tracks, proceeding outward or homeward with such marvellous certainty of movement. There is a need for further inquiry—inquiry on the broadest lines—and it is conceivable that by the tragedy of to-day generations yet unborn will benefit. Already the White Star Company announce that their ships will in future keep well southward of the ice-floes, and the travelling public will welcome the decision. The dominant thought at the moment is one of defeat—of the staggering blow which has been struck at all the confident beliefs of the ship designer and the shipbuilder. But oftentimes in the hour of defeat the seed of victory is sown. We can only trust that during the last hours, when the Titanic laboured under the iceberg's deadly thrust, the passengers and crew did not

---

5. Actually, about seventy-five feet from the boat deck to the waterline (Davie 68).

6. The *Gigantic*, another superliner, was built by the White Star Line, but the company changed her name to *Britannic* in an effort to use a less ostentatious name (Marriott 19–20).

realise what we unhappily know now, and that they were supported by the assurance that the ship would float under almost all conditions. We must cherish the hope that after the last great service had been rendered to humanity, and the women and children had been placed in the boats, this buoyant thought relieved the terrible tension on board of those who so soon were to land "on the silent shore, where billows never break, nor tempests roar." **7**

HEROES
OF THE
TITANIC.

PUBLIC APPEAL.

THE DAILY TELEGRAPH FUND
FOR THE WIDOWS & ORPHANS.

The Daily Telegraph appeals to-day to the generosity of the nation on behalf of those dependent upon the men who lost their lives in the performance of duty on board the Titanic.

Following upon the shock of horror with which the nation learned yesterday the full gravity of the disaster, came the realisation of the devoted heroism of the crew of the vessel, shown in the fact that so many women and children were got away in the lifeboats and subsequently rescued.

That eloquent detail, standing out among the few meagre facts which we have been able to learn as yet of this appalling catastrophe, means that officers and men unflinchingly maintained the noblest tradition of the British mercantile service. **8**

As a seafaring nation, British commentators grappled with what to make of the *Titanic*'s loss. Her sinking was almost a personal thing, a slap at national pride. England was in intense competition with Germany to build ever bigger, ever faster liners and win the bulk of the enormous trade in Atlantic passengers. If England couldn't rule the waves, it couldn't rule its Empire; it was as simple as that.

★ ★

7. Lines by Sir Samuel Garth from the poem "Dispensary."

8. Not according to George Bernard Shaw. The notable contrarian lamented the "outrageous romantic lying" of the press. From the vantage point of May 14, 1912, he wrote the *Daily News* that at least four romantic lies had been perpetrated by the press: All women and children had been treated with deference; nearly all the men had proved to be heroes; all the officers had been calm and professional; and everyone had faced death "without a tremor" (Foster 214–16).

The rule that directs the saving of "the women and children first" has cost the lives of innumerable gallant seamen in the past. It has been reserved for our time to provide the most splendid proof yet shown of this dauntless spirit of self-sacrifice in the cause of the weak.

It is believed that from 500 to 600 of the crew have perished with the ship from which they aided nearly 700 passengers, mostly women and children, to escape.

In case of shipwreck every man in the great liners has his allotted station, only to be left at the word of command, and upon the observance of discipline among them depends the life of every passenger on board. The men of the Titanic, as the facts entitle us to assume, stood by their stations until the end came. **9**

"The best traditions of the sea," said the Prime Minster **10** last night in the House of Commons, "seems to have been observed in the willing sacrifices which were offered to give the first chance of safety to those who were least able to help themselves.["]

All the White Star liners are manned by British seamen. Nearly all the crew of the Titanic had their homes in Southampton. Lamentation and misery are in those homes to-day, with the prospect of poverty to come. The appeal is to the nation to-day—"women and children first."

The Daily Telegraph has decided to open a fund for the relief of those whose breadwinners have died at the post of duty.

We have already received the following letter from Mr. H. J. Duveen:

Sir—As one who has crossed the Atlantic more than a hundred times, I can well imagine the heroism and self-sacrifice which must have been displayed by the crew of the Titanic in helping to save the women and children.

I feel that we must now think of the widows and orphans of the brave men who have willingly surrendered their lives.

No doubt some such idea will occur to many others, and I therefore beg to

9. Later British Wreck Commission proceedings would show that the crew was not trained enough in safety procedures for this assumption to be true (*Titanic Reports* 105).

10. H. H. Asquith

★ ★

Before the British government took over much of social welfare activity, it was up to the initiative of papers like the *Telegraph* to show what private compassion could do to help widows and orphans. Poor survivors also received charity. If anyone was overlooked in the public outpouring of concern, it was the unemployed men and women who survived the *Titanic*. Their salaries ceased with the sinking of their ship, and the White Star Line never paid them a cent more than their wages earned up to the night of April 14!

Eventually, a great amount of money was raised by a variety of charitable organizations set up specifically to take care of survivors. Some of these funds continued to pay out money into the late 1950s.

enclose my cheque towards any fund which you might have in your mind to initiate for this purpose.

I am, Sir, yours faithfully,

H. J. Duveen

38 Park-lane. W., April 16…

FINANCIAL EFFECTS.

Our City Editor writes: The accounts of the Oceanic Steam Navigation Company, the owners of the White Star Line, to whose fleet the Titanic was the latest addition, are made up to Dec. 31, and are submitted in April or May. For the past year the actual dividend declared is not yet known, though, including two interim distributions of 10 per cent. each, it is believed to be at least 30 per cent., which was the amount paid for 1910.

The entire share capital of £750,000, it will be remembered, was acquired by the International Mercantile Marine Company of New Jersey, in 1902, and the dividends of the Oceanic Company form one of the chief contributions to the earnings of the Morgan Shipping Combine. Hence, whatever loss results from the present disaster will fall on the shareholders of the Mercantile Marine Company, though, as the latter have never yet received the smallest return, their position will not be appreciably altered.

It is generally assumed that the cost of the Titanic was fully £1,500,000, apart from the stores, furniture, &c., on board. Since only £730,000 was insured, the Oceanic Company will lose £770,000 on the ship, in addition to whatever compensation may be payable to the families of the crew. It is possible that the latter item may be covered in a Protection and Indemnity Club which ensures steamships against risks not covered by Lloyds. In any event, the loss of steamship owners is limited to £15 per ton of the registered tonnage, which in the case of the Titanic's 46,000 tons, represents £690,000.

Consequently, so far as the Oceanic Company is concerned, the heaviest immediate pecuniary loss possible appears to be about £1,500,000. To meet it the company at the end of 1910 had capital reserves of £3,000,000, general reserves of £500,000, and other funds amounting to £200,000, making in all £3,700,000. With such a strong position, and only £2,450,000 outstanding in the form of Debentures and loans, the directors may decide to draw on the reserves for the whole of the loss, and not to interfere with the final dividend for 1911.

In view, however, of the decreased earning power which the loss of such a huge vessel implies until another ship can be built, and in view of the advisability of replenishing the reserves, future dividends are scarcely likely to be on so handsome a scale as for the past two years. The White Star Line has always been admirably managed, and its efficiency has never been impaired in order to assist the finances of the Mercantile Marine Combine. No dividend has ever yet been paid on the $52,000,000 Six per Cent. Cumulative Preferred stock of the latter, on which the arrears now amount to 60 per cent., and in spite of the great improvement which has taken place in the shipping trade, noticeably in the Leyland Line, which is one of the controlled companies in the Combine, the prospect of such an event is still very remote. It is therefore no surprise that the Preferred stock, which had gradually been manipulated up to 26 ½, fell yesterday to 21 ½, as a result of the terrible disaster to the White Star Line.

AT THE LONDON OFFICES.

INTERVIEW WITH THE MANAGER.

Early in the afternoon the official list of survivors on board the Carparthia [Carpathia] began to reach the London offices in Cockspur-street and Leadenhall-street, and soon after three o'clock some fifty names were posted at each office for the benefit of anxious inquirers. Long before this, however, much fuller lists had been telegraphed through Reuter's Agency, and these also were available for all seeking information.

Mr. Parton, the London manager, interviewed by a representative of *The Daily Telegraph* at about six o'clock, said apart from names of survivors no official news had reached the London offices since the early morning, when the despatch arrived announcing that the Carpathia had reached the scene after the foundering of the Titanic, and that 675 souls had been saved of crew and passengers, the latter nearly all women

Naturally, accounts vary as to how much the Mercantile Marine Company—owner of the White Star Line which owned the *Titanic*—paid out in claims. One positive note for the company, or companies, was that the British Wreck Commission did not find the Line guilty of negligence; neither could the U.S. Senate Inquiry prove negligence. Both investigations questioned aspects of the ship's navigation but concluded it was within acceptable standards of the day. The *Titanic*'s construction was judged to be superb, except that it would have been better if the bulkheads had gone all the way to the boat deck instead of stopping at deck E, as many of the bulkheads did. However, these generous conclusions did not withstand the scrutiny of court proceedings that finally led to the settlement of all claims. In 1915, at a U.S. District Court in New York, claimants brought a suit totaling $16,804,112. The White Star Line countered that its liability, by law, was only $97,972.12, a figure arrived at by its lawyers (about forty) and accountants. According to the *New York Times* of December 18, 1915, the claimants agreed to an out-of-court settlement of just $664,000 ("Titanic Claimants"). It was a triumph for White Star. Mrs. Henry B. Harris had claimed a million-dollar loss on the life of her husband. She got $50,000. Immigrants who had lost providers wanted $1,500 each. They received $1,000. British journalist Michael Davie points out these were not "inconsiderable" amounts of money: Meals on Fifth Avenue could be had for thirty-five cents; a five-day cruise of Bermuda could be had for $28 (Davie 136 and Marriott 140). The White Star Line did exceedingly well, paying out only about 5 percent of what it might have had to pay if the claimants had held on and won (Eaton and Haas, *Titanic: Destination* 120–22).

and children, and that the Carpathia was returning to New York with the survivors. "We hardly expect any other news to-night," Mr. Parton added. "The matter of first importance is to obtain a complete list of those who have been saved, and that will occupy some hours."

In response to inquiries to the boats carried by the Titanic, Mr. Parton said the vessel fulfilled all requirements in that respect to the full satisfaction of the Board of Trade; and since the first and second classes were only half full it was obvious that there must have been far more than ample boat accommodation for all on board.

In conversation with another Press representative, Mr. Parton observed: "What discipline must have been maintained! The fact that nearly all those who are saved are women and children is, I think, evidence of that."

Mr. Parton remained at the office until close upon midnight on Monday, had the telephone at his bedside all night to answer inquiries, and was in attendance almost without intermission yesterday from five o'clock in the morning.

WALL STREET.

A FIRM CLOSE.

From Our Financial Correspondent.

NEW YORK, Tuesday.

Leading issues opened strong to-day, despite the depressing influence in the Street occasioned by the loss of the Titanic, and closed firm. Business men were largely absorbed in watching for the latest news of the disaster, and the bulletins confirming the report that no passengers had been rescued by the Virginian and the Parisian, as had at first been hoped, dismayed even the most optimistic speculator…

The British Board of Trade rules did not require boats for every passenger. Having a full complement of lifeboats might cause passengers to worry about their safety. And, in any case, they were not needed on modern "unsinkable" ships. The Titanic had a lifeboat capacity of 1,178, more than regulation required (Wade 40–1). Her twenty lifeboats were four over the minimum thought necessary. Although the Titanic could carry well over 3,000 people, it was thought that if she were damaged in a collision with another ship, she would sink slowly, and passengers and crew could be transferred to a rescue ship called to the scene by Marconi telegraph. Such an example of this use of lifeboats and telegraphy had already occurred in the case of the R.M.S. Republic when she collided with the Florida in 1909. The Republic stayed afloat for several days, and all passengers and crew were saved except for those killed in the initial collision. Later the Republic sank as it was being towed to American shores, but no investigation was ever held, so the public was unaware that the ship did not have enough lifeboats for all on board. Salvors still search for her "lost" gold ("Treasure").

SUMMARY.

The King **11** has sent a message to the White Star Company:

"The Queen and I are horrified at the appalling disaster which has happened to the Titanic, and at the terrible loss of life.

"We deeply sympathise with the bereaved relations, and feel for them in their great sorrow with all our hearts."

According to an official statement issued by the White Star Line, 868 people have been rescued from the Titanic.

This represents a little more than one-third of the total passengers and crew.

Passengers numbered over 1,300, and the crew about 900.

The Carpathia, with the rescued passengers on board, is expected at New York on Thursday afternoon or Friday. **12**

A message from Captain Haddock, master of the Olympic, states that "all the Titanic's lifeboats have been accounted for."

Captain Smith, who commanded the ill-fated vessel, is reported amongst the drowned.

This morning *The Daily Telegraph* opens a fund for the relief of the dependents of the crew…

DISASTER
TO THE
TITANIC.

---

868 SURVIVORS
ON THE CARPATHIA.

PROCEEDING TO NEW YORK.

1,400 LIVES LOST.

★ **11.** George V was king at the time. He had no prominent friends aboard the *Titanic*.

12. The *Carpathia* ran into fog and was delayed until Thursday evening, April 18 (Eaton and Haas, *Titanic: Triumph* 180).

★ ★

The *Daily Telegraph* fund will eventually grow to more than $10,000 in only a week. Other British and American papers will also raise money to aid orphans and widows. The needy of Southampton, particularly hard hit by the loss of breadwinners, would begin receiving help almost immediately, according to the *Daily Telegraph* of July 23. The Mansion House Fund, sponsored by the Lord Mayor of London, eventually reached more than $130,000 by April 25, according to the *Times* of London, but this money had not yet begun to be distributed.

RECORD CATASTROPHE.

MESSAGES OF SYMPATHY
FROM THE
KING AND QUEEN. [13]

...There is now, unfortunately, no possible doubt that the maiden voyage of the White Star liner Titanic, the largest vessel in the world, has resulted in a catastrophe of unprecedented dimensions, even in the annals of ocean tragedy.

Down to an early hour yesterday morning it was confidently believed that the great vessel's collision with the iceberg had not given rise to loss of life, and that there was a fair chance of her being able to make the port of Halifax in safety. The earlier telegrams all led to the belief that the whole of the passengers had been removed from her in safety to other liners.

Unhappily, these optimistic views have been completely belied by events. As was stated in yesterday's *Daily Telegraph*, the Titanic sank at 2.20 on Monday morning, that is to say, about four hours after the collision. Of those on board, numbering about 2,200, by far the larger portion perished.

The latest official news received by the White Star Company indicates that only 868 of the passengers and crew were saved. This is the number which the Cunard liner Carpathia has on board, and is bringing to New York where she is expected to arrive either to-morrow (Thursday) night, or on Friday morning. It is not yet know exactly how many are members of the crew, but there seems reason to suppose that the staff saved number about 200, the remainder being passengers.

In all the death-roll will certainly exceed 1,200, and may approach 1,400.

Partial lists of the survivors have already been received, either direct by the White Star Line or through Reuter's Agency. These lists total about 350, leaving upwards of another 300 survivors yet to be recorded. It is explained that interferences by amateur wireless telegraphists have impeded the work of despatching these names, with the result that many of them have been mutilated or put into forms in which they do not appear in the liner's passenger lists.

The earliest intelligence of the sinking of the Titanic and of the terrible loss of life thereby caused came in shortly before one o'clock this morning simultaneously from Reuter's Agency and the Central News. The news of the foundering of the great liner appeared in the first edition of *The Daily Telegraph* yesterday, and that of the death-roll in all the subsequent editions.

13. This article begins by quoting messages of condolence to the White Star Line from the King and Queen. Then the White Star Line is quoted as replying with thanks to their majesties, and the newspaper continues with its story.

Among those definitely known to have been saved are Mr. Bruce Ismay, chairman and managing director of the White Star Line; the Countess of Rothes, Mrs. John Jacob Astor, Sir Cosmo and Lady Duff-Gordon, who were travelling under the names of Mr. and Mrs. Morgan, and Mrs. C. M. Hays, wife of the president of the Canadian Grand Trunk Railway. The fate of Mr. Hays is at present uncertain, but it is now stated that he was among those rescued. Colonel J. J. Astor, the millionaire, is believed to have been drowned, but this is by no means certain. The same remark also applies to Mr. W. T. Stead, whose name, however, does not appear among the list of the survivors, and who is probably drowned.

The fact that a whole day has passed without news of the safety of Mr. W. T. Stead leaves little hope that he escaped from the ill-fated ship…

The terrible calamity has created consternation, not only in this country and in the United States, but also on the Continent, and on all hands great sympathy is expressed for the bereaved.

The dead also seem to include Mr. B. Guggenheim, a member of the millionaire copper firm, and Mr. E. Widener, son of the art collector, Mr. P. A. B. Widener. Mrs. Widener is safe.

In the early morning a message from St. John's (Newfoundland) gave rise to the hope that the Allan liner Virginian had some of the survivors on board, and another straw eagerly clutched at was a statement made by the operator at Sable Island on Monday night, who, when asked as to the possibility of delivering messages to the Titanic's passengers, replied that it would be difficult to do so, as the passengers were believed to be dispersed among several vessels.

Later, however, the sad intelligence arrived from Montreal that the Allan Line had received a communication to the effect that they were in receipt of a Marconigram, via Cape Race, from Captain Gambell, of the Virginian, stating he had arrived on the scene of the disaster too late to be of service, and was proceeding on his voyage to Liverpool.

No mention was made of the rescue of any of the Titanic's passengers.

Another message also indicated that the Allan liner Parisian had no passengers belonging to the Titanic.

According to an official statement which arrived from New York early last evening, the White Star Line announced that they had received positive news that the number of survivors from the Titanic was 868. The despatch was transmitted by the Olympic.

At the West-end branch of the White Star Line in London there were numerous callers throughout the day to make inquiries as to relatives and friends on the ill-fated vessel.

The Allan Steamship Company has received a cablegram from their agents at Montreal stating that they have received a wireless message from the Virginian saying that she has no passengers on board from the Titanic, and is proceeding on her voyage to the British side.

Lord Ashburton, who was reported to have been on board the Titanic, is, as a matter of fact, a passenger on the Olympic.

As some doubt exists as to the exact number of persons on board the ill-fated Titanic, the Exchange Telegraph

Company is officially informed that the following is as near the correct compilation of those on board as for the moment it is possible to make:

Passengers (first class):	316
Second-class:	279
Steerage:	698
Total passengers:	1,293

In addition, the crew numbered between 800 and 900.

It now appears that the message stated to have been received on Monday night by Mr. and Mrs. Phillips, of Godalming, from their son, the wireless operator aboard the Titanic, did not come from him at all, but from a brother in London. On receiving the message, the father came to the conclusion that it was from his son on the Titanic, but yesterday morning he stated that he felt he was mistaken.

———◆———

THE SS. PARISIAN.

————

From Our Own Correspondent.

HALIFAX (Nova Scotia), Tuesday.

The Allan Line steamer Parisian was in communication with Sable Island this morning. She says she has none of the Titanic's passengers on board.  **14**

HALIFAX (Nova Scotia), Tuesday (Later).

It looks now as if the steamer Parisian might have some survivors of the Titanic aboard. The Canadian Pacific Railroad people have orders to have a special train ready for Colonel John Jacob Astor, who is said to be on his way to Halifax. **15**

———◆———

868 SURVIVORS.

————

OFFICIAL STATEMENT.

————

NEW YORK, Tuesday (11.40 a.m.).

The White Star Line announce officially that they have received positive news that the number of survivors from the Titanic is 868. The despatch was transmitted by the Olympic.—*Reuter.*

★

14. The *Parisian* is mentioned many times in the *Daily Telegraph* but was some 500 miles away when the *Titanic* was sinking and played no part in the rescue (Wade 34–7).

15. Col. J. J. Astor's body was found by the ship *MacKay-Bennett* on April 22 along with some three hundred other victims, most frozen, not drowned (Eaton and Haas, *Titanic: Triumph* 229).

FATE OF MR. C. M. HAYS. [16]

NEW YORK, Tuesday (11.0 a.m.).

A Montreal telegram states that a wireless message has been received there announcing that Mr. Charles M. Hays, president of the Grand Trunk Railway, is among the Titanic survivors on board the Carpathia. His wife and daughter have already been reported as saved.—*Reuter.*

NEW YORK, Tuesday (11.25 a.m.).

According to a wireless message received by the Customs, the Carpathia will arrive on Thursday afternoon.

The Treasury officials at Washington have directed that the Customs regulations shall be waived in order to facilitate the landing of everybody.—*Reuter.*

NEW YORK, Tuesday (11.30 a.m.).

Captain Rostron, of the Carpathia, in a wireless message to the Cunard Company here sent from lat. 41.45, long. 52.20, says:

I am proceeding to New York, unless otherwise ordered, with about 800. After having consulted Mr. Bruce Ismay, considering the circumstances, and with so much ice about, I considered New York best. There is a large number of icebergs and twenty miles of field ice with bergs amongst it.

Two messages received by the Marconi Company from Cape Race and Sable Island make it appear that none of the Titanic's passengers have been rescued either by the Parisian or the Virginian.

One reads:

Marconi Station, Sable Island: Been communication Parisian. Ship had no passengers from Titanic.

The other is:

Marconi Station, Cape Race, reports: Had no communication Virginian. Do not believe any Titanic passengers on that vessel.

A telegram from Montreal states that the Allan Line has issued the following communication:

We are in receipt of a Marconigram via Cape Race from Captain Gamble [Gambell], of the Virginian, stating that he arrived on the scene of the disaster too late to be of service, and is proceeding on his voyage to Liverpool. No

16. Charles M. Hays, a Canadian railroad magnate, comes in for a good deal of coverage in the pages of the *Daily Telegraph*. There is good reason for this. Hays had managed to convince the Canadian government to back a scheme to support a second transcontinental railroad across Canada. Hays's proposal promoted the idea that a series of destination luxury hotels, built as the Grand Trunk extended west, would draw traffic to the line and aid in the further development of Canada. British investors in Hays's vision felt, not unnaturally, that Hays himself was essential to its success. As it turned out, the Grand Trunk Railway failed in 1919 (*Encyclopedia*, "Mr Charles Melville Hays").

mention is made of the rescue of any of the Titanic's passengers.

MONTREAL, Tuesday.

Intelligence was received by the Allan Line officials this morning from Captain Gamble of the Virginian, that that vessel had continued her voyage to Liverpool. She has no survivors of the Titanic on board.

It is rumoured that Mr. Hays, president of the Grand Trunk Railway, and his son-in-law are among those rescued.—*Reuter.*

ordered the fast scout cruiser Salem to proceed to sea immediately from Hampton roads to meet the Carpathia. The cruiser is fitted with the best wireless apparatus, with a range of 1,000 miles, and, by instruction of the President, she will obtain a complete list of survivors, and send the names by wireless telegraphy to the Government here.

In the event of the Salem not having a sufficient quantity of coal in her bunkers, the Secretary has given provisional orders to the cruiser North Carolina, which is also at Hampton roads, to perform the mission.—*Reuter.*

CARPATHIA IN THE ICE.

NEW YORK, Tuesday.

Captain Roscon [Rostron] has sent a wireless telegram to the Cunard Company stating that the Carpathia has 800 survivors aboard and is slowly proceeding to New York through the field of ice.

The Leyland Company have instructed the captain of the Californian by wireless telegraphy to remain near the scene of the wreck and to render whatever aid is possible until he is relieved or until his coal supply runs low. **17** —*Reuter.*

WASHINGTON, Tuesday.

At the direction of President Taft, Mr. Meyer, Secretary for the Navy, has

PAINFUL SCENES IN NEW YORK.

ANXIOUS CROWDS.

WEEPING RELATIVES.

From Our Own Correspondent.

NEW YORK, Tuesday.

Unprecedented scenes marked the early morning hours in and around the White Star offices, and at dawn to-day the endless crowd of weeping, sobbing,

17. The *Californian* could do nothing by standing by the scene. Perhaps company officials in New York were still hoping people might be saved from the water. But hypothermia had its deadly effect, and all in the water had died within a matter of a few minutes from the terrible cold (Butler 145).

distraught men and women increased. All yesterday friends and relatives of the passengers had been prisoners of hope. Many of those who had left the offices during the day, encouraged by the optimistic reports given out by the company's officers, and smiling at the thought of the early arrival of dear ones, returned last night in tears. They remained patiently awaiting most of to-day, albeit the news received was only of a most fragmentary character, and, such as it was, confirming the worst fears.

The officers and clerks replied to thousands of inquiries during the day. Some of them had been at the offices since four a.m. yesterday. They believed at first that all was well with the passengers on the greatest steamship afloat; then came the staggering news that hundreds of souls had gone down in two miles of ocean depth. People hoped against hope that messages from the Virginian and Parisian would relieve the anxiety and diminish the list of fatalities, but when at last the brief, laconic messages came, reporting "Nobody rescued," everyone was despairing.

Not since the Slocum was burned to the water's-edge almost within sight of this city, with the sacrifice of 959 lives, chiefly women and Sunday-school children, had New York been so inexpressibly shocked. **18** All to-day long lines of motor-cars crawled along close to the kerb, and richly dressed men and women hurried in to the White Star Company's building and up to the offices on the second floor. Weeping women and staggering men returned to their machines and drove off to make way for others. The company could not give a ray of hope; it could only say that there was nothing to contradict the report that hundreds had gone down with the liner, and we must await the arrival of the Cunard's Carpathia late on Thursday or early on Friday for full details.

ANXIOUS INQUIRERS.

Among the first to reach the offices and ask for information was Mr. Vincent Astor, son of Colonel John Jacob Astor. He was accompanied by Mr. William Dobbyn, Colonel Astor's secretary. They were led to the private office of Mr. Franklin, vice-president of the International Mercantile Marine, and remained half an hour. Young Astor had heard a rumour that his father had gone down with the ship, but his step-mother was saved. When the party came out he was sobbing, supported by his father's secretary. Neither would say what information they had obtained.

Twice to-day young Astor drove to the offices, and when told that no complete list of the survivors had been received, he again left weeping, with his face in his hands. "Have you heard anything of your father?" he was asked. "Not a word," he replied; "I fear the worst."

Applicants for information came in scores throughout to-day. They had read

----

18. Before September 11, 2001, the loss of the steamship *General Slocum*, on the Hudson River, was the worst disaster in New York City history. The *Slocum* had been hired for a Sunday school outing. Many young people were lost (Richman).

the morning newspapers and seen the list of survivors, but still hoped that the name of some loved one had been only accidentally omitted. They came tremulous with hope and fear, and always left sobbing. Hardened reporters assembled all day in the lobby of the White Star offices refrained from questioning them.

Among those who made inquiry during the night and again to-day were Mr. William Force, father of Mrs. John Jacob Astor; Mr. Bradley Martin, jun., who would not tell for whom he was anxious; Mr. Pierpont Morgan, jun., who denied that the Morgans on the passenger list were relatives; and former Senator Clark, of Montana.

"DESPAIRING RELATIVES."

A young man and a young woman who refused to tell their names rushed into the offices before breakfast-time. "Is it true the Titanic is sunk?" asked the man. He was told it was. "My God," he exclaimed, "then we are ruined; they are all lost." The young woman became hysterical as she was led to the street.

In all the leading hotels rooms had been reserved for the Titanic's wealthy passengers. At the Ritz-Carlton Lord Rothes patiently waited all night for some tidings of Lady Rothes, who was on board the Titanic. Others on the Titanic who booked here were Mr. George Widener and his son Harry, and Mr. Bruce Ismay, chairman of the White Star Line…

THE "UNSINKABLE" SHIP.

To-day we learn that Captain Smith has

gone down with his unsinkable ship, and Mr. Franklin, greatly depressed, has only to say, "I must take upon myself the whole blame for that statement. I made it, and I believed it when I made it. The accident to the Olympic, when she collided with the cruiser Hawke, convinced me that these ships, the Olympic and Titanic, were built like battleships, able to resist almost any kind of accident, particularly a collision. I made that statement in good faith, and upon me must rest the error, since the fact has proved that it was not a correct description of the construction of the unfortunate Titanic."

Americans are appalled by the magnitude of the sea tragedy, and overwhelmed by the failure of the Titanic's safety devices. They are asking to-day: "Is there such a thing as an unsinkable ship?…"

GRAPHIC PICTURE
OF THE
GREAT WRECK.

HOURS OF ANGUISH.

A NIGHT IN THE BOATS.

NEW YORK, Tuesday.

New York and the nation generally awoke to-day to but a dull recognition of the appalling magnitude of the Titanic disaster. The truth of the catastrophe appeared at first too horrible to contemplate. Yesterday's reassuring advices had left the country unprepared to face a maritime disaster such as this, the proportions of which have only been made possible by that supreme triumph of construction and engineering which in itself was thought to have almost eliminated danger as a factor in ocean travel.

But slowly the accumulating evidence of the wireless messages shattered the popular faith in the indestructibility of the modern floating palace. The faltering wireless communications have as yet given but a bare outline of the harrowing tragedy, no details of which have so far been vouchsafed to the waiting public. What stands out is the fact that a gigantic mass of ice hopelessly crippled a supposedly unsinkable vessel, so tearing and rending her plates and steel beams as to send her within four hours bow foremost to the bottom.

Despite this respite, the despatches are regarded as indicating that the urgency of the occasion was considered so great that few were given time to return to their state-rooms for their clothes and belongings, but how far the transfer to the boats and rafts had progressed is not known, nor can anything be gathered from the information available to show whether it was lack of time or some other natural or material difficulty in the way of meeting such an emergency that sent two-thirds of the Titanic's human freight to the fathomless depths.

SELF-SACRIFICE.

But that order prevailed in conditions such as might well have been attended by chaos is eloquently shown by the proportion of women to men among the survivors, only seventy-nine men so far having been reported as aboard the Carpathia, out of a total of 248 souls whose names are as yet to hand. These

Survivors of the *Titanic* in one of the collapsible rescue boats.

figures tell their own story of heroism and self-sacrifice.

The Carpathia is now making for New York with the 868 survivors who alone can tell the tale of the midnight plunge into the angry whirlpool of ice wreckage and drowning men with which the great ship went to her burial. They alone can relate the bitter experiences of the wintry night spent in open boats on a lonely sea, of the waiting for morning, and of the hope of rescue, mingled with despair and anguish at the thought of the loved ones from whose embraces they had been suddenly torn.

The wireless messages have told how in the darkness their crews had to guide the boats with the greatest caution to prevent their being jammed in the ice or overturned by the swirling floes, so that the heavily-laden craft became widely separated from each other.

There followed hours of heartbreaking anguish before daylight came, and the first faint tones of the searching Carpathia's siren were heard through the dense fog. Even then their anxiety was not at an end, for the Carpathia proceeded cautiously, sounding her fogwhistle almost continuously until one after another she picked up the scattered lifeboats. No other ship was in the neighbourhood of the disaster, although before the Titanic disappeared wireless messages were pouring in telling of the approach of the Olympic, of the Baltic, of the Parisian, and of the Virginian, but they were still far away, and the Carpathia picked up all the survivors to be found long before they reached the scene.

Nothing is likely to be heard from the Carpathia until late to-night or early to-morrow, when she will be nearing Sable Island, as her wireless apparatus has a radius of only 150 miles.

HOPELESS SEARCH.

Meanwhile, a message from Halifax announces that the Parisian is approaching that port, and will arrive there in the morning. The captain reports that he steamed for hours among the masses of field-ice and floating wreckage looking for survivors, but sighted neither life, rafts, nor bodies. He adds that the weather was very cold, and that if any persons got away from the Titanic on pieces of wreckage they must have expired from exposure before help arrived. The Virginian has had no better luck, and is proceeding to Glasgow.

The White Star agents learned to-day from the Oceanic that all the Titanic's boats have been accounted for. This, together with the abandonment of the long-cherished idea that the Virginian or Parisian might have picked up some additional survivors, has dispelled most of the hopes that the number of those saved may be increased beyond the pitiful 868. Those friends and relatives still without tidings of those for whose safety they are so anxious are basing their last hopes on the publication of the names of the 483 survivors still to be sent by wireless telegraph from the Carpathia.

Many men of great prominence in the social, financial, and professional world are still missing. There is no word, for instance, of Colonel John Jacob Astor, whose youthful wife is among the saved, or of Mr. Isidor Straus, Major Butt, Mr. Benjamin Guggenheim, Mr. Francis D.

Millett, or of Mr. William T. Stead [19] tidings of whom are so anxiously awaited not in England alone...

Naval men and experienced navigators who have discussed the disaster in the light of all the news available agree that the present information all appears to support the theory that the Titanic struck an iceberg a glancing blow, not running into it "head on." Some hold that the liner ran on to a submerged floe that tore away the keel plates for the entire length of the vessel. The only alternative suggestion put forward is that the bulkheads failed to work, but this is an idea that is generally scouted.—*Reuter's Special Service.*

WAITING FOR NEWS.

SCENES IN THE WEST-END.

Throughout yesterday deeply pathetic scenes were witnessed at the West-end offices of the White Star Line, at Oceanic House, Cockspur-street. Even before the time for the commencement of business a little crowd had collected in front of the building, the majority being anxious relatives of passengers or members of the lost Titanic.

As soon as the doors were opened a sad procession began to pass in, and continued almost without a break until late in the evening. Over and over again the question was asked, "Who are saved?" and the answer was generally the same, "We cannot tell yet. Names are coming through slowly," and with this reply the distraught inquirer had to be content.

Hundreds of telegrams were received asking for news, and the telephones were kept going all the time, calls coming not only from London but from many parts of the country.

On the notice boards were placed copies of two wireless messages, and that grim announcement from Cape Race stating that the Carpathia had "found boats and wreckage only" held the attention of every caller. The officials had the scantiest information at their disposal, but they did what little was possible to relieve the distress of those who asked for further details of the disaster, and who sought with pitiful eagerness to hear if the first report that no lives had been lost might yet prove true. Hope was all too often extinguished by the reply that there was little doubt that very many had gone down with the great liner...

LISTS ON THE BOARDS.

Night brought little or no lightening of the load of tragic despair borne by the crowd of anxious relatives and friends, for the lists of survivors published in the newspapers during the day were painfully complete, so far, at least, as they went, and the lists which came at intervals over the wires to the officials of the company in the earlier part of the night were little more than confirmations of what was already known. There was a heart-rending pathos in the frantic rushes to the boards as the lists went up, the rapid scanning of the names, and the awful disappointment on people's faces as they turned away.

Save for one lady, who leant her head against the board and sobbed convulsively, most of the waiting crowd appeared to have reached that stunned condition where grief finds no visible outlet. Men tried to smoke, and, finding it a failure, walked a monotonous course up and down the hall. White-faced women clustered around the lists and read and re-read the names, as if fearful of having, in the excitement, missed the one name for which they were looking.

Soon after nine o'clock a whole batch of fresh names, this time of second-class passengers, was put on the board, and some people went away happy. This was quickly followed by a further first-class list, in which some, at least, of the names were new. It meant relief for a few. The others just settled—or tried to settle—to wait.

◆

SCENES AT LLOYD'S.

GIGANTIC LOSSES.

PEARLS INSURED FOR £150,000.

Our Marine Insurance Correspondence writes:

Monday at Lloyd's was a day full to the brim with excitement and anxiety on the part of members to know the amount of their holding on ship and cargo, and speculators were busy in taking or doing the risks against the Titanic getting into Halifax. Monday, in short, was the underwriters' day; yesterday the underwriter was completely overshadowed by the man, and all thoughts were turned to the appalling loss of human life.

As I stated yesterday, the amount insured on the vessel is £730,000. [20] More would no doubt have been done had sufficient market been available—on an insured value of £1,000,000 the rate for twelve months, which underwriters were paid, being 15s per cent., insurers to pay anything in excess of £150,000 on a single claim. The value of the Titanic in the present state of the shipbuilding market is £1,500,000. Compensation to the relatives of the crew does not fall on an ordinary marine insurance policy, but may be covered elsewhere.

It is so short a time since the Titanic left our shores that shippers have in many cases been able only this week to send the value of their shipments to their brokers to be endorsed on their floating policies, so that many underwriters have only now come to know

20. A pound was worth an estimated $5 in 1912 value (*Encyclopedia*).

the full amount of their loss. The market has heard of £18,000 on diamonds on one policy, and £25,000 on rubber on another; while insurances on bonds and registered post are plentifully spread over the market.

One insurance has caused a good deal of interest, that of £150,000 on three pearl necklaces, the property of Mrs. Widener, whose father-in-law, Mr. P. A. B. Widener, recently bought Rembrandt's "Mill" from Lord Lansdowne. Her name appears among the list of the saved. It is interesting to note that the policy stipulated that these three necklaces should be worn by her on the voyage. **21**

VALUE OF THE CARGO.

There is no possibility of stating positively the value of the cargo, but it may well run into £750,000. Merchandise to the United States has been lately coming forward in such bulk that steamer after steamer has had to sail leaving large quantities waiting on the quays.

Among the passengers is Mr. Christopher Head, recently Mayor of Chelsea, a member of a well-known firm of brokers and underwriters at Lloyd's. As his name does not appear among the list of the saved, it is to be feared he has gone down with the vessel. He was insured at Lloyd's against accident during the trip to America and back for £25,000. Mr. Head was well known and much respected by the marine insurance community, and his tragic death in the prime of life is deeply lamented. **22**

The loss of the Titanic eclipses anything that has been known at Lloyd's, and, coming on the top of a rapid succession of serious casualties, it must lead to a very considerable rise in rates even among the best steamers.

The White Star Company have been, considering their large fleet, very fortunate in the matter of wrecks. Since 1880 they have only lost the Naronic and the Republic. **23**

———◆———

TRAVELLERS ON THE LOST LINER.

PERSONAL SKETCHES.

21. The pearls survived the sinking (Geller 83).

22. Mrs. Charlotte Cardeza of Philadelphia made the largest claim by a passenger when she valued fourteen trunks, four bags, a jewel case, and three packing cases at $177,352.75. Her jewelry losses exceeded $80,000 (Eaton and Haas, *Titanic: Triumph* 285).

23. The *Republic* foundered after colliding with the *Florida* off Nantucket. The *Naronic* was carrying cattle and may have struck an iceberg in the approximate vicinity of where the *Titanic* went down years later (Nichol).

From Our Own Correspondent.

NEW YORK, Tuesday.

Colonel John Jacob Astor, the American head of the Astor family, held a prominent place in the life of New York for many years. Not alone has he been a conspicuous club member and leader of society, but he was engaged in vast business activities that gave him a place and rank apart from his immense fortune and social attainments.

Colonel Astor erected and owned more hotels and skyscrapers than any other New Yorker. **24** At one time he was a director in twenty or more large corporations, including railways. His fortune has been estimated between $20,000,000 and $40,000,000.

In July, 1911, an announcement was made of the engagement of Colonel Astor to Miss Madeleine Talmage Force, the 18-year-old daughter of Mr. William Force, of New York, with whom rumour had for some time associated his name. The engagement followed an acquaintanceship of less than a year. On Sept. 9, 1911, the two were married at Newport, Rhode Island, by Pastor Elmanood, of the Congregational Church, after several other ministers, in view of Colonel Astor's divorce, had refused to perform the ceremony. Soon after their marriage Colonel and Mrs. Astor went abroad.

MAJOR ARCHIBALD BUTT.

Major Archibald Butt, President Taft's military aide-de-camp, was returning on the Titanic after a visit to Rome, where he went to see the Pope and King Victor Emmanuel. He went to Rome as a personal messenger from President Taft, and one object of his visit was to discuss questions of precedence and other details in connection with the elevation of Archbishops Farley, of New York, and O'Donnell, of Boston, to the Cardinalate. It was reported from Rome lately that Major Butt was bringing home to Mr. Taft an important message from the Pope.

Major Butt has been one of the most popular officers in the army. Born in Georgia 41 years ago, he was for several years before the Spanish War a newspaper correspondent at Washington. From his first arrival in Washington he was popular in society. He accepted the position of First Secretary at the United States Legation in the City of Mexico, when former Senator Matthew Ransom, of North Carolina, was Minister, and remained there until the death of Mr. Ransom, when he returned to newspaper work in Washington.

In addition to newspaper work he also wrote for the magazines, and produced several novels based on his life in Mexico and the South, which rose to more than the ordinary level of finish and interest. His entry into the army was due to the late Major-General H. C. Corbin, who was Adjutant-General at the time of the Spanish War, and who selected Butt as one of twenty young officers to join fifteen new Volunteer Regiments and go

---

★ **24.** Most famously, he built the Astoria Hotel, which later became the Waldorf-Astoria. Its luxury set a standard that other hotels sought to emulate (Sinclair 205).

to the Philippines. While in the islands Major Butt wrote several reports on the handling of animals in the tropics which attracted attention. One of his military articles so pleased President Roosevelt **25** that he later asked him to become his military aide-de-camp.

On his return from the Philippines, Major Butt was given a commission in the regular army, and was sent to Cuba with the army of occupation. He was stationed at Havana, and did very good service there. Within a month after his return to duty in the Quartermaster's Department, President Roosevelt had him detailed to duty as his personal aide-de-camp. Major Butt kept up with Mr. Roosevelt in all his physical exercises, and made the famous ride to Warrenton and back in one afternoon. He climbed the heights of Rock Creek Canyon, with the President and Prince Henry, and at the same time reduced the handling of crowds at White House receptions to a fine art. He made the record there of remembering the names of, and introducing, 1,280 persons in an hour.

Major Butt was an ideal clubman. He knew everyone, and was liked by all. While in Manila he was secretary of the Army and Navy Club there. He was a bachelor, and lived in a fine old mansion at Washington, where he entertained old friends, including former reporter colleagues, in handsome style. His name was several times mentioned in rumours of his engagement to some of the prettiest and most popular young women in society, but one of the last things he did, just before sailing for home, was to deny in a jocular way the report that he was finally engaged, and to remark that he had been a bachelor for so long that he thought he had better stay so to the end of the chapter. Throughout Washington every comment on the disaster is followed by the expression, "I hope Butt is safe."

————

MR. HENRY B. HARRIS.

————

Mr. Henry B. Harris, who leaped into prominence in the New York theatrical field about half a dozen years ago, as a manager and producer, was nevertheless a veteran of many years' standing before Metropolitan fame came to him. He was a member of an old theatrical family. His father is Mr. William Harris, a theatrical manager of note, now associated with the firm of Klaw and Erlanger. Mr. Harris got his first training as a theatrical man in Boston, becoming connected with the famous old Howard Athaeneum there. He remained identified with that house for several years, leaving to become partner in the firm of Rich and Harris, for many years active in the theatrical history of Boston. During his association with the firm he laid the foundations of his future success by a number of highly successful ventures.

Among the stars he managed in a number of successful plays at this time were May Irwin, Pete Danley, and Mrs. Langtry. **26** He also produced "The

25. Theodore Roosevelt, of course.

26. Lily, the famous "Jersey Lily," and onetime mistress to King Edward VII, "the Caresser."

Climbers," with Amelia Bingham in the principal feminine role, and the success of this play went far towards paving the way for his coming to New York. After launching Robert Edison on a starring career, Mr. Henry B. Harris became manager of the Hudson Theatre, New York, in 1903, a position which he held continuously ever since. He acquired the Hackett Theatre in 1906, and soon after won one of the biggest victories of his whole career with Charles Klein's "Lion and the Mouse," which was played by several companies throughout the United States for several years and brought money and reputation to its producer.

Recently Mr. Harris had sixteen companies on tour during a single season. He was president of the Henry B. Harris Company and of the National Producing Managers of America, a director of the Theatre Managers' Association of Greater New York, treasurer of the Actors' Fund of America, and trustee of the Hebrew Infant Asylum, New York.

MR. CLARENCE MOORE.

Mr. Clarence Moore, a Washington banker, was one of the best-known sportsmen in the United States. He was a Master of Hounds, and on the visit to England from which he was returning, was said to have purchased twenty-five couple of hounds from the best packs in the North. His wife is a daughter of the late Mr. Swift, of Chicago. It is said that her husband's trip abroad had been for pleasure. Mr. Moore was a member of the New York Yacht Club and the Travellers' Club of Paris, besides the Metropolitan, Chevy Chase, and Alibi Clubs of Washington. Socially one of the best-known men in America, he was born at Clarksburg, Western Virginia, in 1865, and when he had finished his education at Dufferin College, Ontario, he interested himself in the development of the mineral wealth of that State.

Since 1890 Mr. Moore had lived at Washington, having business connections with the banking and brokerage firm of Hibbs and Co. Mr. Moore's first wife died in 1897, leaving two children. He married Miss Mabelle Swift in 1900, and by his second marriage has two children, Jasper and Clarence, jun.

MR. CHARLES M. HAYS.

Mr. Charles Melville Hays, president of the Grand Trunk and Grand Trunk Pacific Railway Companies, has been considered one of the most brilliant and successful railroad officials. He was born at Rock Island, Illinois, in 1856. His school education was completed when he was 17, and his first work in the railroad world was in the passenger department of the Atlantic and Pacific Railroad in St. Louis. He was soon promoted to an important position in the office of the auditor of the road, and was later transferred to the general superintendent's office, where he remained until 1877. In that year he was made secretary to the general manger of the Missouri-Pacific Railroad. In 1886 Mr. Hays became assistant general manager of the road, and one year later was appointed general manager of the Wabash, St. Louis, and Pacific, and later became manager of the Wabash Western. He had a complete grip of railway management and transport problems.

Upon the death of the late Collis Huntington, president of, and a large owner in, the Southern Pacific Company and steamship lines controlling upwards of 10,000 miles, Mr. Charles Hays was the first choice for his successor, and the appointment made on Jan. 1, 1901. In the autumn of the same year he resigned, and was recalled to take charge of the Grand Trunk Railway Company of Canada, becoming second vice-president and mineral manager on Jan. 1, 1902. In the same year Mr. Hays conceived the project of the Grand Trunk Pacific Railway, which Sir Wilfred Laurier and the Government made possible by the passage of the necessary legislation in 1903 and 1904. This line will be the only transcontinental railway wholly within Canadian territory. It will run from Moncton, New Brunswick, to Prince Rupert, British Columbia, a distance of about 3,000 miles. On Jan. 1, 1910, Mr. Hays was elected a member of the board of directors of the Grand Trunk Central Railway, and on that date was made president of the company and its consolidated lines, and subsidiary railroad and steamship companies. **27**

Mr. Hays has been in full charge of the company's affairs. In America a year ago Sir Wilfred Laurier, at a dinner of the Canadian Club in New York, said that Mr. Hays was beyond question the greatest railroad genius of Canada; as an executive genius he ranked second only to the late Edward H. Harriman.

MR. ISIDOR STRAUS.

Mr. Isidor Straus, who, with Mrs. Straus, was on board the Titanic, was the best-known American, next to Colonel Astor, among those reported to be missing. He was a trader, philanthropist, and educationalist of national fame. Mr. Straus's interest in political affairs was thoroughly aroused when Mr. Grover Cleveland became a Presidential possibility. It was then that he began to take an active part in legislation relating to sound currency and tariff reform.

In 1893, when the condition of business was desperate and grave doubts were entertained as to the position of Mr. Cleveland with reference to the expediency of convening Congress in extra session, Mr. Straus visited the President, and the proclamation convening Congress was issued. Every day Mr. Straus visited the White House, with the result that the extra session forms an important page in the history of the United States. Mr. Straus took an active part in the campaign which resulted in Mr. Cleveland's second election. He was later mentioned for the office of Postmaster-General, but made it understood that he had no desire to give up business pursuits for that position. He was later elected a member of Congress, and was a member of the Ways and Means Committee.

In the field of philanthropy Mr. Straus was as eminent as his two famous brothers, Nathan and Oscar, the former

★ **27.** As mentioned earlier, the company failed in 1919, already being deeply in debt while Hays was president.

celebrated for the splendid campaign in behalf of pure milk for babies. The Educational Alliance, the People's Palace of the congested tenement district of New York, of which he was president, owes its present position as one of the great factors in the solution of the sociological problem to his tireless work. Mr. Straus was a director in many, and a supporter of almost every, philanthropic and charitable institution of New York, regardless of creed.

He was a director of several banking and financial institutions, among which were the Hanover National Bank and the New York County National Bank, and vice-president of the Birkbeck Saving and Loan Company, vice-president of the Chamber of Commerce and Board of Trade.

MR. BENJAMIN GUGGENHEIM.

Mr. Benjamin Guggenheim, the millionaire president of the International Steam Pump Company, was born at Philadelphia in 1865. He was the fifth of the seven sons of Meyer Guggenheim, founder of the famous house of M. Guggenheim and Sons, who came to America from Switzerland in 1848. Mr. Benjamin Guggenheim married Miss Floretta Seligman, daughter of Mr. James Seligman, banker, of New York, and has three daughters. When Benjamin Guggenheim was 20 he was sent to Leadville, Colorado, by his father, to take charge of the elder Guggenheim's mining interests, which at that time began to be enormously productive. He had been in Leadville but a short time when he recognised the possibilities of the smelting business, and it was his keen foresight that started the Guggenheim family in that business, which made a greater part of their vast fortune, perhaps, than any other of the various branches of industry in which they were engaged. The first smelting plant was built at Pueblo, and Benjamin took charge, conducting it with such success that the family withdrew entirely from commercial business and devoted their energy to the smelting industry.

The success at Colorado led to the building of plants in Mexico and the immense refining plant at Perth Amboy, New Jersey. Mr. Benjamin Guggenheim managed the latter plant for several years. After the consolidation of the smelting industries was accomplished, the Guggenheim interests became so large that they were the ruling factor in the American Smelting and Refining Company, and, having seen his great object realised, Benjamin Guggenheim went to Europe for a well-earned rest. Two years later he returned to the United States, and in 1903 built a large plant at Milwaukee for the manufacture of mining machinery. Three years later it was merged into the International Steam-Pump Company, in which Mr. Guggenheim was a large stockholder. In 1909 the company had seven plants in this country and one in England. An army of 10,000 men draws it sustenance from these great industrial workshops, whose product is an infinite variety, from the smallest feed-pump to enormous pumping-engines capable of supplying cities' mains with 20,000,000 gallons of water daily.

LOST PASSENGERS. [28]

...Mr. Jacques Futrelle was one of the best known of the younger generation of busy American journalists, though he had of late left journalism to devote his talents to the writing of novels and short stories. Born in 1875, he engaged in newspaper work from 1902 to 1904. The theatre claimed his attention as manager for the next two years, after which he served in the office of the "Boston American" for a like period. Among the best known of the books he wrote are "The Chase of the Golden Plate," "The Thinking Machine," [29] "The Simple Case of Susan," "The Diamond Master," and "Elusive Isabel."...

Mr. Francis Davis Millet was not unknown in this country, both as artist and journalist. He was in his 67th year. He exhibited at several American exhibitions, and also at the Antwerp Academy of Fine Arts. He acted as correspondent of the *New York Herald*, the London *Daily News*, and the London "Graphic" in the Russo-Turkish War, 1877–8, and again as special correspondent of the *Times*, and "Harper's Weekly," at Manila, in 1898. He took an active part in connection with art exhibitions in various countries, receiving numerous decorations in appreciation of his services. Among his published works were "Capillary Crime and Other Stories," "The Danube," and "Expedition to the Philippines."

Mr. Washington A. Roebling, [30] who was in his 75th year, was one of the best known of American engineers. He joined his father in the construction of the Pittsburgh Suspension Bridge across the Allegheny River, but left to serve in the Union Army, where he rose from private to brevet-colonel. He resigned, to help his father to build the Cincinnati and Covington suspension bridge, the construction of the Brooklyn Bridge also being undertaken by the same firm. His father died, however, before the work was begun, the whole of the construction thus devolving upon the son, who, though only 32 years old, supervised the work till its completion.

Charles Williams, the racquet champion of the world, was a passenger on the Titanic. He was on his way to New York to play the first half of his home-and-home match with G. Standing on the 29th April.

---

28. The following list repeats information from other articles on a good many of those famously lost on the *Titanic*, but includes other names for the first time.

29. His most famous book creates the character of Professor S. F. X. Van Dusen, who solves cases by pure "ratiocination" (Steinbrunner and Penzler 162). A sequel was lost with the *Titanic*.

30. Ironically, this biography happens to be that of the uncle of Washington A. Roebling II, who went down with the *Titanic*. The lost nephew had nothing to do with the building of the Brooklyn Bridge (*Encyclopedia*, "Titanic Victims").

FRENCH LINER'S WARNING.

CAPTAIN SMITH'S THANKS.

From Our Own Correspondent.

PARIS, Tuesday Night.

News received from Havre since the arrival of the French steamer Touraine, of the French Line has a pathetic significance at this moment, as the captain of that steamer states that he warned the commander of the Titanic of the dangerous icefields which he had himself passed, and that he was in wireless communication with the ill-fated ship on Friday, April 12. The Touraine met an icefield on Wednesday, April 10, at midnight, and she was then in latitude 44.58 and longitude 50.40 W. The icefloes were numerous, and the vessel slowed down at once and kept a sharp look-out. The commander states that it took him an hour and a quarter to pass through the icefield, and that the floating masses were very low in the water.

In the morning, at six o'clock, the Touraine passed to the south of another icefield, which was in sight for three-quarters of an hour, and at the same time they saw two icebergs. The Touraine got into wireless communication with the Titanic at 9.0 p.m. on Friday, April 12, and informed her commander of the exact position and extent of the icefields. The captain of the Titanic wired back to M. Caussin, captain of the Touraine, thanking him sincerely for the information. The Touraine had left New York eight days ago, and arrived at Havre last night. She followed during the first part of her voyage the route taken by the Titanic, and passed almost the exact spot where the disaster took place.

THE FOUNDERING
OF THE
TITANIC.

SOUTHAMPTON MOURNING.

TEARFUL CROWDS.

From Our Own Correspondent.

SOUTHAMPTON, Tuesday.

Southampton is in mourning, for the loss of the Titanic has deprived many homes in the town of their breadwinners. When the hope, so warmly entertained and apparently justified yesterday, that there had been no loss of life, was dispelled by the news of this morning, the town flag was raised at half-mast at the Bargate and Audit House, and ensigns were similarly displayed at the yacht clubs and many other public buildings. Unfortunately Southampton is no stranger to marine casualties involving the loss of the lives of many residents who gain their livelihood in ships belonging to the port.

The present disaster, though more

appalling in its actual results, is in some respects similar to the loss of the Amazon, a fine new paddle steamer, belonging to the Royal Mail Company, which was burnt in the Bay of Biscay only two days after she left the port on her maiden voyage, many lives being lost. A fund which was raised for the bereaved came to an end only about two years ago, the small balance left being handed over to the Teuton fund, which was raised after the disastrous wreck of the Union Company's vessel Teuton. This fund is still running. So, too, is the West India Hurricane fund, the outcome of the loss of the Royal Mail Company's steamers Rhone and Wye in the hurricane at St. Thomas.

This by no means gives the full list of the vessels sailing from the port whose wreck has been attended with many fatalities, but of all that are or might be named the loss of the Titanic is the most appalling. To what actual extent families in Southampton are affected is not at present known, but it is certain that many of the crew and stewards belonged to this town, and some of the engineers and firemen also, those of the better class being, it is believed, chiefly men who came here from Liverpool when the White Star Line transferred its big Transatlantic liners from the Mersey to Southampton. **31**

During the day the offices of the White Star Line at the docks have been besieged by hundreds of anxious women, eager to learn the worst, though but little information could be given to them, and practically the first authentic news they received was from the following notice, which was posted outside the office:

"Titanic foundered about 2.30 a.m., April 15. About 675 crew and passengers picked up by ship's boats of the Carpathia and California, remaining and searching the position of the disaster. The names of those saved will be posted as soon as received."

The offices of the British Seafarers' Union, in Terminus-terrace, an organisation to which many of the crew belong, were also the centre of a tearful and anxious crowd. Many of the women had babies in arms and children clinging to their skirts. Mr. A. Cannon, the secretary of the union, stated that nearly all the deck and engineering staff of the Titanic were members of his union. The widow or dependents of each member are entitled to a death benefit of £5, and this the funds of the union were prepared to meet. "Of course," he added, "under the amended Workmen's Compensation Act, seamen, in which term are included all the hands working on a ship, come under the provisions of the Act, and their relatives will receive compensation in due course. At present the suspense is more awful than the actual truth,

---

31. Hyslop, Forsyth, and Jemima's book *Titanic Voices* states, "The vast majority of the crew of 898 were domiciled in the town and only 212 returned…" (4). Foster reports in his *The Titanic Reader* that "One teacher said to her elementary school class: 'Stand up any child who has a relative on the *Titanic*'— and the whole class stood up" (117).

however bad that may turn out to be. In one case a father, two sons, and a cousin are all firemen on the vessel."

The Mayor, Councillor H. Bowyer, R.N.R., is taking steps to open a relief fund, and goes to-morrow to London to confer with the Lord Mayor on the subject. His worship mentioned the matter at the meeting of the Southampton Harbour Board this afternoon, when it was suggested to him by several members. Alderman F. A. Dunsford urged that when further authentic details were received a public meeting should be called, and Councillor A. J. Cheverton said that all the citizens, from the highest to the lowest, would do all that was possible to support whatever step the Mayor might take.

Several of the passengers supposed to be lost were known locally, but there was only one who actually resided here, Mr. H. P. Hodges, a music-seller, and lately a member of the Town Council. He was going to Boston to visit a friend there. Mr. Hector Young, hon. secretary of a local Conservative Association, received a letter from Mr. H. P. Hodges, returning thanks for an expression of goodwill sent him on the eve of his departure. Mr. Hodges wrote that he had been having a fine time, the movement of the ship was unnoticed, and the weather was good. **32**

---

32. Mr. Hodges was lost.

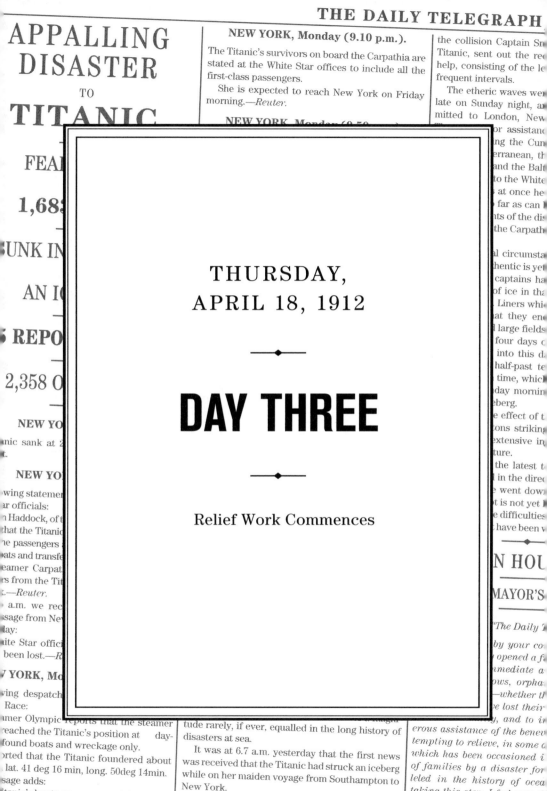

THE DAILY TELEGRAPH

APPALLING DISASTER

TO

TITANIC

FEAR

1,68

UNK IN

AN I

REPO

2,358 0

NEW YORK, Monday (9.10 p.m.).
The Titanic's survivors on board the Carpathia are stated at the White Star offices to include all the first-class passengers.
She is expected to reach New York on Friday morning.—*Reuter.*

NEW YORK, Monday (9.50

the collision Captain Sm
Titanic, sent out the re
help, consisting of the le
frequent intervals.
    The etheric waves wer
late on Sunday night, an
mitted to London, New

THURSDAY,
APRIL 18, 1912

DAY THREE

Relief Work Commences

NEW YO
nic sank at 2

NEW YO
wing statemen
ar officials:
Haddock, of t
that the Titanic
he passengers
ats and transfe
eamer Carpat
rs from the Tit
.—*Reuter.*
a.m. we rec
ssage from Ne
ay:
ite Star offic
been lost.—*R*

YORK, Mo
ving despatch
Race:
amer Olympic reports that the steamer
reached the Titanic's position at day-
found boats and wreckage only.
rted that the Titanic foundered about
lat. 41 deg 16 min, long. 50deg 14min.
sage adds:
itanic's boats are accounted for. About
ave been saved of the crew and passen-
tter are nearly all women and children.
and Liner California is remaining and
e vicinity of the disaster

tude rarely, if ever, equalled in the long history of
disasters at sea.
    It was at 6.7 a.m. yesterday that the first news
was received that the Titanic had struck an iceberg
while on her maiden voyage from Southampton to
New York.
    Both in shipping circles and among the general
public the utmost excitement and consternation
were caused.
    As has happened on several previous occa-

HOU

MAYOR'S

"The Daily 1
by your co
opened a f
mmediate a
ows, orpha
—whether th
e lost their
y, and to in
erous assistance of the benev
tempting to relieve, in some o
which has been occasioned i
of families by a disaster for
leled in the history of ocea
taking this step, I feel sure th
responding to the wishes of the
the keen sympathy universall
entertained for those who ha
been plunged into misery an

INTRODUCTION

———◆———

THE *DAILY TELEGRAPH* PROMOTES THE FUND-DRIVE IT HAS announced the day before for dependents of those who lost providers in the sinking of the *Titanic*. The fund is primarily for widows and orphans. In general male survivors of a certain age are expected to fend for themselves. Certainly, there is some money available to them, but all crewmen who survived were unemployed as of the moment the *Titanic* went down. Some crew members are even required to give testimony, further delaying their search for employment.

The sailor's lot is not a happy one.

Happily, the Lord Mayor of London also starts the Mansion House Fund, and it becomes the most successful of all charity drives, taking in over £400,000 before being closed down in 1958 (Bryceson 302). Even the City of Southampton sets up a fund that eventually pays out an astounding £41,000 by 1954 (Hyslop 262).

By the end of the 1950s, the Mansion House Council and Executive Committee converts remaining monies from all sources into annuities for surviving dependents. Although some £617,000 has been raised since 1912, very little is left to disperse at the end (Hyslop 262).

Millvina Dean, the last *Titanic* survivor, died in 2009 at the age of 97. She had been only nine weeks old when she was taken off the ship in the arms of her mother. Since she had no memories of the disaster, she did not originally participate in survivor reunions. But as the number of survivors dwindled to a precious few, she became more active, especially after the location of the wreck was found in 1985 by Robert Ballard (Burns).

Dean ended her days in a Southampton nursing home. Kate Winslet,

Leonardo DiCaprio, and producer James Cameron, of the fabulously successful movie *Titanic*, contributed funds to pay her final bills.

From an Unsigned Editorial

———◆———

This morning we publish the first list of subscriptions to *The Daily Telegraph* Fund for the widows and orphans of the heroic crew of the Titanic. The thought which is uppermost in the mind of the English-speaking world at the moment is not, "Why did this great liner which was unsinkable sink, how did the shipbuilders' elaboration of precautions—apparently so complete—prove so incomplete and unavailing? but How nobly did the men of the crew render up their lives on the high altar of humanity! When the crisis came, all, from the captain to the lowliest seaman and stoker, were transformed in the twinkling of an eye **1** into heroes of the sea, lineal descendants of those who in the past have given to our race its hall-mark of sterling worth. In the hour of peril, as of yore, the seaman's chant of sacrifice, "Women and children first!" was heard from stem to stern of the great leviathan; under the discipline of imminent death each man rendered back his life—his all—to his Maker, and did his part in buying safety for the weak and helpless.

For those of us who have watched the tragedy in imagination from afar, the instant effect of the disaster was to numb all thought; it was defeat of Man by Nature. But to-day, from the great berg-haunted waste of the Atlantic, there arises a new figure: it is not that of defeat, but of victory—man's triumph over the dumb giant forces in the hour of his overwhelming. This is the consolation which emerges from the tragedy enacted amid the icefloes in the darkness of that fatal Sunday night. We still have very scant details, but it seems that the doomed ship was steaming on her normal course when suddenly she ran into an iceberg, probably what is known as a "growler," one of those vast masses from the Greenland shores which float southward at this time of year, more than seven-eighths buried beneath the water. **2** What is seen in daylight is awesome, but it is the unseen, the sharp, razor-like, submerged ledges, whose terrors grip the heart of the sailor. The shock of impact probably demolished the towering decks forward, ripped open the side and the bulkheads, and split and shattered the bow. **3** It may further be conjectured that the huge liner mounted some distance up the glassy slopes and then reeled under the blow. Had she been less staunchly built all

---

★

1. Several allusions to biblical passages, such as this one to First Corinthians 15:52, are found throughout this editorial.

2. A "growler" is generally defined as a rather small chunk of ice that can still be dangerous to shipping. Of course, the *Titanic* struck a full-scale iceberg.

3. At this point, the editorialist has lost all contact with the facts and is sailing on his own. The ship grazed the iceberg and five or six holes were gouged into its side according to best reconstructions (Howells 23).

would have been over in a few minutes. A smaller ship would undoubtedly have gone down instantly. But the Titanic was made of stern stuff. Her powerful engines had thrust her deadweight of 60,000 tons **4** against this grim, unyielding enemy; a shiver ran from end to end of her decks when the impact came, the noise of the tearing of high-tensile steel rose above the sounds of human confusion, and then she recoiled and regained an even keel. With her bow torn to ribbons and her sides laid open to the sea, the water doubtless rushed with relentless force into compartment after compartment. Many of the bulkheads had gone and the ship's condition must have been hopeless almost from the first. Torn and wounded, the Titanic at once began to settle down at the head, while over her deck lay strewn fragments of the iceberg, which had become disengaged in the deadly duel. This is the tale of the disaster so far as it can be pieced together. It forms a picture of one of the greatest sea tragedies of history, the horror of which will chill the hearts of our children and of our children's children in the years to come.

The human mind is paralysed at the mere dim conception of the disaster. We know that after the great ship had sunk the steamship Carpathia, in the peaceful morning, reached the spot, to discover a group of the ship's boats heavily laden with human freight—"nearly all women and children." We cannot visualize the heartrending scenes which occurred as the crew set to work to launch the lifeboats—the partings between husbands and wives, between fathers and children. One was taken and the other left, for such is the law of the sailor-race; the strong sacrifices his strength in order that the weak may triumph in weakness. During the three or four hours before the moment of the ship's effacement, apart from the boats' crews, some 700 of the passengers—nearly all women and children—were placed in the boats. It is painful even to endeavour to adjust our mental vision to such a spectacle as the Titanic must have presented. In an incredibly short time, considering the conditions on board, women under the stress of the deepest emotion and children overwhelmed with terror were marshalled at the deck sides and transferred to the boats. The marvel is not that so few, but that so many could have been snatched from the vast living tomb. How the men of the crew must have worked in those last hours, as the first glimmering of day broke over the broad, desolate expanse of the Atlantic! Despite all the circumstances that conspired to fulfil the tragedy in awful completeness, some hundreds were saved—"nearly all women and children." Let this be the epitaph on the lives of these men: "Greater love hath no man than this, that a man lay down his life for his friend." The friends in this case were the chance companions of travel. The crew were not servants of the Crown, trained to the highest ideals

4. 46,000 tons

of a drilled service, but the servants of a company trading for profit—just ordinary men. In the moment when this world and the next are meeting all social distinctions, all disparities of wealth are forgotten. In the last act of such a tragedy, man may not be master of his fate, but he is captain of his soul. **5** This was a ship with a score of the wealthiest on board, travelling in all the luxury which only their great riches could buy. It was a ship with a score and more of masters of commerce—a ship with a group of men of great learning and great artistic powers. We mourn them all; we remember that the saved are "nearly all women and children." But beyond everything, Englishmen will remember the seamen and firemen—those hundreds whose strength might, in a frenzy of despair have borne down all opposition, who might, if they would, have seized the boats. The incident is only another illustration of the all-pervading influence of the Christian code, for can we doubt that each in his time had asked himself what shall it profit a man if he shall gain the whole world and lose his own soul? There is only one answer, and that answer was given on board the Titanic before she made her final plunge. Man triumphed, though his craftily-devised work perished.

It has been not infrequently declared that the essential virtues of man were becoming overlaid by the conventions of modern life—that in an age of luxury the heroic would disappear, swallowed up in selfishness. Yet the British and American peoples, as the King truly says in his sympathetic message to President Taft, are "so intimately allied by ties of friendship and brotherhood that any misfortune which affects the one must necessarily affect the other." To-day the two nations are drawn together by a common sorrow. As they stand in spirit beside the grave of those who have made the last sacrifice, they know that the age of heroes is not past. As the world circles round the sun, the light grows—the light of reason, of consideration for others, of kindly thought for the weak and needy. Beneath the armour which we all wear the old, and yet new, humanity is to be found for the seeking, and when the iceberg tore away the steel plates of the Titanic it laid bare the heroic spirit of the crew. Men untutored in worldly wisdom, men who had been content to do their duty in a humble sphere—mere working men— were revealed in the hour before the dawn of Monday morning as heroes of our century, drawing, all unconsciously, inspiration from their ancestry. They have gone before; Death has assuredly been swallowed up in Victory. It remains for us as a nation to remember those who mourn the dead, husband, father, son, or brother. When Nelson rendered up his life for the nation, bequeathing to it 100 years of peace, he left it also, as a trust, his daughter. These men of the Titanic have left us a sacred trust. There are wives who will never again see their husbands; children who will never

---

5. A reference to the poem "Invictus" by William Ernest Henley.

again know a father's love. They must not be forgotten. The breadwinner has been taken, and we who remain must be henceforward their breadwinners, making it our charge that no child shall suffer by the self-sacrifice of his father. We cannot pay our tribute of individual service in the humble homes—to be found for the most part in Southampton, a town of mourning. We cannot gather at the graveside to render our homage to these heroes of everyday life, but we can each make some sacrifice. We can raise a memorial in the secure future of their children. On Sunday these rude seamen heard a still, small voice uttering the words, "Women and children first." They responded with willing service. To us now comes the same challenge. The cold egoist may wrap himself in the stiff cloak of his self-complacency and refer to the benefits of the Workmen's Compensation Act, which may or may not flow to the dependents. This is not a matter of law; it is a matter of a debt which we as individuals and as a nation owe, a debt which cannot be set down in the formal phrase of an Act of Parliament. It is our responsibility to man the lifeboat which shall succour those whom the heroes of the Titanic have left. The immediate response to the appeal which was made in *The Daily Telegraph* yesterday on behalf of the widows and orphans has exceeded even the records of former funds. It is apparent that public feeling has been deeply stirred. To-day we publish an appeal from the Lord Mayor. There is a wide field for public benevolence in the results of this catastrophe, and every care will be taken to prevent overlapping in the work of relief. The same spirit will be observed as in 1897, when the Mansion House asked for contributions to the Prince of Wales's (now King Edward's) Hospital Fund, and *The Daily Telegraph* was invited to co-operate in order to commemorate the sixtieth anniversary of Queen Victoria's gracious reign. In the result over three-quarters of a million shillings were raised by this journal. On the present occasion we desire to raise a memorial not to a woman's work for her people, but to men's devotion to weak women in the hour of direst distress. **6** We are convinced that we have not overestimated the effect of the story of the loss of the Titanic on the public conscience, and the ever-ready sympathy of the theatrical profession is evinced once more. Money is needed, and money we are convinced will be forthcoming; but *The Daily Telegraph* Fund, we trust, will be something more than a record of subscriptions—a fitting memorial by the British people to the heroism of these sailors. They played their part in the hour of sudden tragic trial; it rests with us to put on record, in the only way open

---

★ **6.** Some feminists were outraged that women may have allowed themselves to be treated as helpless objects. Emma Goldman wrote: "With all the claims the present-day woman makes for her equality...she continues to be as weak and dependent...as if she were still in her baby age" (Foster 238).

to us, our heartfelt appreciation of their sacrifice and the honour which their acts reflect on the Anglo-Saxon race.

DISASTER TO THE TITANIC.

CARPATHIA'S RETURN.

EXPECTED AT NEW YORK LATE TO-NIGHT.

ONLY 705 SURVIVORS.

LATEST MARCONIGRAM...

CARPATHIA'S VOYAGE.

...Down to an early hour this morning very little further authentic information had been received in London with regard to the loss of the Titanic.

This mantra of "women and children first" has been repeated often enough by now that it is worth examining. According to John P. Eaton in a Foreword to Judith Geller's *Titanic: Women and Children First*, of the estimated 1,523 lost on the *Titanic*, only 158 were women and children. Taking 705 as the number Captain Rostron of the *Carpathia* counted as having survived, one comes up with a most startling statistic: women and children survivors, 370; men survivors, 335. There simply weren't all that many women and children on the ship in the first place! Some commentators were never able to become comfortable with the fact that so many men survived, as if the male survivors of the *Titanic* should have been issued an "Excuse Me for Living" badge. Major Arthur Peuchen was ordered into lifeboat No. 6 by Second Officer Lightoller to help with rowing. Later, on the *Carpathia*, Peuchen had Lightoller sign an affidavit to his innocence in case he was ever accused of having taken the place of a woman or child (Marcus 198).

Trying to make sense of a major tragedy is a challenge to the best of editorialists. Would the writer have felt a compulsion to make sense of the *Titanic*'s sinking if she had been a Japanese ship sailing in the Pacific? Probably not. But to many Englishmen and Americans, the *Titanic* was more than a ship: She was the advance of technology and science over the bleak forces of Nature.

If she could be sunk by a lowly iceberg, what did that say for modern human achievement? Surely, there must be a moral to this story, and so the editorialist searches for one and finds it. The *Titanic*'s sinking should be seen not just as a tragedy but also as a triumph for the Anglo-Saxon race.

The race's ethic of self-sacrifice has stood the test provided by tragedy. Women and children have been cared for first. Even common sailors have stepped aside and gone willingly to their deaths. Thus, Man, at least Anglo-Saxon man, has revealed himself in all his glory as still superior to the brute forces of indifferent Nature. Man has reaffirmed his place in the sun!

The most important telegram was the following, sent by Reuter's correspondent at New York, under date Wednesday (3.0 p.m.):

The Cunard Company has issued for publication a copy of a wireless message received from Mr. Winfield Thompson, of the *Boston Globe*, who is a passenger on board the Franconia. The message says:

"The Franconia established communication with the Carpathia at 6.10 this morning (New York time). The latter was more than 498 miles east of Ambrose Channel, and was in no need of assistance. She was steaming at thirteen knots, and expected to reach New York at eight o'clock on Thursday evening. She has a total of 705 survivors on board. The Franconia is relaying personal messages from the Carpathia to Sable Island."

It is pointed out that the number 705 given above may mean surviving passengers as distinguished from the crew, while the previous despatches, giving the total number of survivors as over 800, may include both passengers and crew. The officials of the Cunard Line do not expect the Carpathia to arrive earlier than midnight (London time) on Thursday.

The White Star Line have received from Marconi's statement that their wireless station at Camperdown, seven miles from Halifax, Nova Scotia, has got into communication with the Carpathia, and is able to announce officially that the Titanic struck an enormous iceberg and sank. Later, a cable from the White Star's New York house stated that no additional names of survivors had been received, the Carpathia evidently not being at present in communication with

the shore. They had chartered the steamer Mackey Bennett to leave Halifax this morning for the scene of the disaster, to remain there and recover bodies.

No further lists of survivors have come to hand to supplement those published in yesterday's *Daily Telegraph*. The gross total of these was 379, of whom 112 were men, 257 women, seven children, and three doubtful. But the exact number is less than this because an inspection of the lists shows that in several cases names have obviously been mentioned more than once. There is, for example, a Mr. Finnian Ormand, whose name appears as having travelled in all three classes of passenger.

A FALSE STORY.

A peculiarly glaring example of the utter worthlessness of the so-called descriptions of "How the Titanic met her end," which have been disseminated since the catastrophe occurred was afforded yesterday. Several New York papers published a telegram from St. John's, Newfoundland, which was alleged to have come by wireless from the British steamer Bruce, and to have been picked up from various steamers in the vicinity of the wreck of the Titanic.

This story, which was recabled from New York, and appeared in our evening contemporaries, professed to give a lurid account of the collision, the damage it caused, the scene on board, and so forth. It wound up saying:

"Within less than an hour the water had flooded the engine rooms. Wireless telegraphy was stopped, the dynamos ceased working, and the Titanic was plunged into darkness except for feeble gleams from lanterns and torches. The Bruce reports that all or nearly all the boats had cleared the vessel when the Titanic took her final plunge."

The whole of this "graphic narrative," as now appears, was a sheer fabrication from beginning to end. The Bruce, which arrived at St. John's on Monday, and left again yesterday, never was in touch with the Titanic, or any other steamer near the scene of the disaster. The only news she had of the wreck was a bulletin from the Cape Race Marconi station four hours before her arrival at St. John's. The Bruce's Marconi operator describes the stories printed in New York as "pure invention."

Until the Carpathia reaches New York, or gets into full wireless communication with the American coast; there cannot possibly be any authentic account of what took place when the Titanic struck the fatal iceberg. Therefore all premature statements may be dismissed as mere efforts of imagination on the part of those who practise a form of journalism highly discreditable to its authors, and calculated to inflict needless pain and sorrow on the friends and relatives of those who were aboard the ill-fated liner.

———◆———

"A PURE INVENTION."

———

ST. JOHN'S (Newfoundland), Wednesday.

The stories published in New York purporting to describe the actual scenes at the wreck of the Titanic, and to be based upon wireless messages from the British steamer Bruce, are pure invention. The Bruce arrived here at noon on Monday from Sydney, Cape Breton, and her Marconi operator informed the reporters of all the St. John's newspapers that the Bruce had not been in touch with the Titanic or any other steamer near the scene of the disaster.

Indeed, her only news of the wreck was a bulletin, which she received from the Cape Race station when passing that point, four hours before her arrival at St. John's.

The Bruce remained at St. John's until yesterday afternoon. Before she left to return to Sydney, all the steamers within the wreck zone were beyond touch of Cape Race.

The falsity of the descriptions, alleged to have been gathered by the Bruce from other steamers, is therefore obvious.

Like the Marconi operator, Mr. Henry Duff Reid, the vice-president of the Reid-Newfoundland Company, which owns the Bruce, also emphatically denies that any of the stories purporting to describe the scenes attending the loss of the Titanic were received by the Bruce either before reaching St. John's or while she was in the port. Mr. Reid says, moreover, that since she left here yesterday afternoon he has received but one message from the vessel, which read as follows:

"Midnight; twenty miles west of Cape Pine; weather stormy; nothing of Titanic tragedy."

Sir Ralph Williams, the Governor of Newfoundland, who has been exhausting every source of information during the past three days in endeavours to obtain details of the disaster, presumably for the British Government, states that he has not been able to learn anything beyond the meagre details which have been published in the St. John's papers.—*Reuter*.

The sinking of the *Titanic* was perhaps the first catastrophe to be recorded using modern communications technology, and the wireless was often used poorly. The practice of journalism had a long history of competition where one news outlet tried to beat other outlets to a scoop, and here was a great modern disaster to be reported. One just might get lucky and be right in reporting something overheard in a snatched conversation or by picking up something coming in over the wire but unconfirmed. A journalist's whole career could be made by a scoop. Fact-checking, as such, was rudely and haphazardly practiced. It was worth taking the risk.

Carr Van Anda, managing editor of the *New York Times*, decided to take such a risk. On the basis of the calculated hunch that the *Titanic* had gone down when her telegraph fell silent, he ran the following headline on the front page of the *Times* on April 16: NEW LINER TITANIC HITS AN ICEBERG; SINKING BY THE BOW AT MIDNIGHT; WOMEN PUT OFF IN LIFEBOATS; LAST WIRELESS AT 12:27 A.M. BLURRED. Van Anda wisely stopped short of saying the ship had already sunk, but he beat all other papers in making clear that the damage was fatal. He took a risk and gained a distinguished career (Wade 30–2).

★ ★

Titanic survivors are supplied with wraps aboard the *Carpathia*.

EARLY ARRIVAL OF THE SURVIVORS.

NEW YORK EXPECTANT

FIRST NEWS AT SEA.

'ALL THE WOMEN SAVED'

MESSAGE FROM OLYMPIC.

From Our Own Correspondent.

NEW YORK, Wednesday Night.

The Carpathia, with the survivors, is expected here about ten to-morrow night, and all arrangements have been made for their reception. Two Government cruisers despatched to escort the Cunarder have been in touch with her to-day, but their news by wireless merely confirms the sad details already known.

Newspaper men aboard the first cruiser to communicate with the Carpathia made desperate efforts to secure personal narratives and send them ashore. Up to a late hour to-day, however, they had not been successful, though their failure has not prevented the publication of some imaginary despatches based on details already reported in *The Daily Telegraph*.

That all the women on the Titanic have been rescued was the purport of one private wireless message from the Carpathia to-day. Another despatch, contradicting previous telegrams, but apparently transcribed carefully, gave the number of the survivors on the Carpathia as only 705, whereas the Cunard Line officers had previously relied upon despatches estimating the number at 800 odd. **7**

From the Franconia, of the Cunard Line, came the following:

Franconia established communication by wireless with Carpathia at 6.10 this morning, New York time. Carpathia was then 498 miles east of Ambrose Channel and in no need of assistance. She was steaming thirteen knots. She expects to reach New York at eight p.m. on Thursday. She has a total of 705 survivors aboard.

The Franconia is relaying personal messages from the Carpathia to Sable Island. This message was sent by Mr. Winfield Thompson, a member of the *Boston Globe* staff and a passenger on the Franconia.

7. Here the *Telegraph* begins to take the precaution of attempting to separate rumor from fact. In this way, the *Telegraph* can protect itself from being "scooped" on a big story, and yet show it is practicing cautious journalism.

"All the women saved; on the Carpathia."

This wireless despatch was received from Mrs. Caroline Bonnell, one of the Titanic's rescued passengers, now bound to New York on the Carpathia. The message came to her brother, who is stopping here, from Mrs. Bonnell's uncle on the Olympic. Before sailing it was agreed that Mrs. Bonnell, on the Titanic was to get in touch with her uncle on the Olympic as soon as possible on the voyage.

"All well!" was the conclusion of a wireless message received at the Cunard Line offices from the Carpathia. It was the first direct word from the vessel bringing to New York the survivors of the Titanic.

BODIES RECOVERED.

The following message from Mr. Roy Howard, general news manager of the United Press, was received at the company's New York office this morning:

"On board the steamship Olympic, eastbound, by wireless to Cape Race and land lines to New York, April 17.—Several bodies, some at least of the victims of the Titanic, will be brought, probably to Boston, on the Leyland liner Californian. Wireless advices reaching us from the scene of the disaster say that some have already been recovered. **8** They will be tenderly cared for, and we understand that they will be taken to port as soon as the Californian resumes her interrupted voyage; just when we do not know.

"The Olympic is proceeding. She could do nothing, though realising the tragedy, followed by the knowledge that the younger sister of the Olympic went to the bottom while this great vessel was rushing to her aid at top speed, and hoping against hope that she would get there on time.

"The captain's seat in the dining saloon, his cabin, and everything about the Olympic, are reminders that Captain Smith was the first commander of the Olympic, though he lost his life on the bridge of the sister-ship. There is little talking among the passengers. In hushed whispers they and the sailors alike discuss the tragedy, which is brought squarely home to everyone here.

"Since word was received that the Titanic had struck a berg the apprehension has been very great. As soon as Captain Haddock received the first wireless word of the disaster, he turned the Olympic's prow towards the scene and sent her ahead at full speed. There was some hope that we might arrive in time, but this hope was shattered when we got within wireless reach of the Carpathia, and the full news of the tragedy was received.

"The announcement of the tragedy shocked and appalled everyone. The Olympic's orchestra was hushed, and the instruments were put into their cases. They will not be heard again this voyage. The helplessness of all was apparent, and is best shown by the heavy contributions made to the fund for the sailor's dependents, which was immediately raised.

8. Captain Lord of the *Californian* testified he saw no bodies at all at the wreck scene. The *Californian* rescued no one (Davie 980).

"After remaining almost stationary most of Tuesday, relaying with melancholy exactitude the list of survivors received from the Carpathia, Captain Haddock was ordered to proceed on his voyage. Not until then was the use of the wireless permitted for any other purposes."

NOTABLE DEAD.

As the Carpathia nears port less wireless is received than yesterday, and the explanation is an electrical storm. Several "unofficial" messages are published here, which are interesting, but probably quite unauthentic, seeing that the Cunarder's operator is occupied almost completely with the company's official business, which is just now of great urgency. Besides Mr. W. T. Stead, other newspaper men are believed to be on board, but their names do not appear among the survivors, and they have probably missed journalistically the greatest chance of a lifetime…

WIRELESS CHAOS IN AMERICA.

SCANDALOUS SYSTEM.

IRRESPONSIBLE OPERATORS.

DEMAND FOR CONTROL.

ACTION BY MR. TAFT.

From Our Own Correspondent.

NEW YORK, Wednesday.

According to the American officials, the necessity for world-wide regulation of the wireless service to prevent interference in times of emergency has been abundantly proved by the Titanic disaster. There must be an international regulation, it is urged, which will effectively prevent confusion, tangle, and hopeless chaos, such as were witnessed on this side of the Atlantic during the last few days.

It is not too much to say that the national indignation has been aroused, and President Taft himself will take a leading part in order to bring the United States into line with other civilised countries in obtaining such regulation of the wireless service as may be necessary to secure accurate reports, and the greatest facilities for relief work in future.

To some extent America herself is to blame for the mob rule in wireless demonstrated on this side of the Atlantic in the case of the Titanic, because, as you will recall, the untiring efforts of the rival companies here were partly responsible for the defeat of the ratification of the Berlin Wireless Convention in 1906 in the Senate until two weeks ago, when the agreement was ratified.

A JUMBLE
OF MESSAGES.

The White House, like the American Press, received a series of wireless messages relating to the Titanic, but they were so fragmentary and so disconnected and often so contradictory that Mr. Taft, like everybody else, was at a loss to unravel their true meaning. These messages were constantly a source of much guesswork, and, as regards some newspapers, the efforts at embroidery, elaboration, and expansion, while they conveyed the "impressionist's" idea of graphic detail, resulted in making the confusion worse confounded...

Even American newspapers which desired to print the truth and nothing but the truth could not, in face of the hopeless jumble, refrain from the temptation of instructing a reporter to make "a connected story," based on the disconnected fragments, and to date the same from Cape Race, or some other wireless terminal. No description of the fatal shock had been wired, not a word about tragic escapes in the boats, no picture of the awful night-watch of the survivors in frail craft awaiting dawn, or of a rescue in the ice-encumbered sea, but a big section of the Press, nevertheless, encouraged by the existing conditions, and despairing of any immediate personal narratives, gave rein to their imagination and printed most realistic pictures of the disaster ever read.

NEED OF
REGULATIONS.

This kind of thing, it is urged, can be prevented, and should be prevented. Indeed, the officials here comment on the fact that hundreds of the lives aboard the Titanic were at the mercy of unscrupulous wireless operators, who might even have called off the vessels that started for her relief by adding to their list criminal messages, one saying that the ship was safe and needed no assistance at all. **9**

"If there ever was a demonstration that the regulation of wireless was necessary this is it," said Mr. Cone, at White House yesterday, just before the wireless conference.

"This wireless chaos that places human lives at the mercy of irresponsible operators who are beyond the control of the Government, or of any regulation, is particularly outrageous at such a time as this, but it is precisely what is bound to happen when we have no regulation by law, and it will happen again unless some means of regulation be prescribed."

Mr. Stimson, Secretary for War, reinforced this view, as he was leaving White House.

"This shows unmistakably what happens at a time when there is no control of wireless," said he, "and it demonstrates infallibly that the regulation of wireless is necessary."

Brigadier-General Allen holds the

9. The reporter is speaking theoretically. The problem was simply that there were no rules; the press had behaved badly itself by not waiting for the arrival of eyewitnesses before printing farfetched stories.

same view. He has been fighting for the regulation of wireless since 1906, when he signed the Berlin Convention, as one of the delegates of the United States.

DEFECTIVE LAWS.

Mr. Eugene Chamberlain, Commissioner of Navigation, in his annual report, printed yesterday, says:

"The need for regulation arises primarily from the fact that wireless messages interfere with one another, so that important despatches on public business may be obstructed by the mischievous efforts of a tyro. Land telegraph lines in America cannot be set in operation anywhere without some official sanction for the erection of poles and the stringing of wires, although one wire does not interfere with another. A fine of £200 or imprisonment for three years is provided by the penal code for interference with messages over the Government wires. The other is common property, and with the cheapest apparatus, unrestrained and trivial messages can create babel.

Again, bogus wireless messages may be sent by the reckless, and some have gone to the criminal length of faking the distress call of a passenger ship at sea."

The Senate has now ratified the Berlin Convention, and the United States will be represented at the International Radio-Telegraphic Conference in London on June 4, 1912…

SHIPS AND SHIPPING.

INFLUENCES OF DISASTER.

Public memory is proverbially short. It may be assumed, nevertheless, that for some little time to come the Titanic disaster will unfavourably affect ocean travel in general, and Atlantic travel in particular. The wreck of the Delhi and the sinking of the Oceana in deep water after collision were of themselves a

---

Passengers themselves also contributed to the problem by sending enigmatic information such as that contained in the previous article, "Early Arrival of the Survivors." The Marconigram "All women saved; on the Carpathia" was relayed by a survivor and became part of misinformation being circulated as authoritative. Marconi service was installed on ships as a benefit to passengers who wanted to send telegrams to their friends. For this privilege, they were charged a nice fat fee. That's how Marconi made money. Wireless service continued for passengers on the *Carpathia*, and *Titanic* survivors sent numerous, and in many cases confusing, messages to friends and family.

Eventually, America did enact laws to control amateur and professional wireless traffic, but this was more because of the investigation into the *Titanic*'s sinking than anything else. America's foreign policy was isolationist and remained so through the early part of World War I. In general, the country paid little attention to international committees and congresses of any kind. International relations were not a strong policy interest at this time.

reminder that the fleet even of the pre-
mier British steamship company is not
immune from disaster. But these casualties were fortunately accompanied by an
inconsiderable loss of life. There were
circumstances about each of them which
lifted them in point of interest above the
average of maritime misfortune, but the
vessels were by no means new ships,
and no special attributes were claimed
for them. The Titanic, on the other hand,
was the last word in naval architecture.
It was said of her that she was practically unsinkable, yet within a few hours
of collision with an iceberg she was two
miles under the sea. **10**

No sea tragedy has at all approached
this in magnitude or in impressiveness.
It is calculated to strike at the root of
public confidence, and one reads without surprise the rather definite assertion
that the loss of the Titanic seals the fate
of the leviathan ship. It might do so if
it could be proved that once a ship ex-
ceeds a certain size she is exposed to
special risks which make her construction inadvisable. But what has been the
teaching of the past? Assuredly that as
the world's ships have grown in dimensions they have not only become more
comfortable vehicles of transport, but
safer vehicles to boot. The Lusitania
and the Mauretania, of 32,000 tons, have
been running for five years without mishap. No one has ever suggested that they
represent the extreme limit of safety so
far as size is concerned.

BIG-SHIP POLICY.

It is quite likely that for a time the leviathan ship may, to some extent, remain
under a cloud. She may be distrusted
and avoided for a while. But it is worth
considering to what degree the leading
steamship lines of the world are delib-
erately committed to the policy of the
big ship. The Hamburg-American Line is
to launch the 50,000-ton Imperator next
month, and has two other mammoths
on the stocks. The Cunard Company is
building the Aquitania, whose dimensions will probably not be less than
those of the Imperator. The White Star
Line, the career of whose Olympic has
been chequered solely by the unfortunate collision in narrow waters with his
Majesty's ship Hawke, is understood to
be building another mammoth. It is evident, therefore, that the big-ship policy
is not likely to be stayed. Equally may it
be inferred that it would not have been
embarked upon if, in the opinion of the
world's leading naval architects, the
limit of safety had already been reached.

It was fashionable when even the
20,000-ton liner was non-existent to
speak of the big-ship craze. It was an un-
happy word to use. People do not build
boats costing a million and a half in pur-
suance of a craze. Their aim is to provide
the most economic form of transport.
We may assume that big boats are found
to pay. Clearly, if it were otherwise, the

---

10. Actually, there is little evidence that sea travel was impeded by the loss
of the *Titanic*. The overall safety record of passenger liners was so good that
it only made the sinking of this liner seem all the more arbitrary and mysterious.
People had to traverse the oceans anyway, and they had to go by ship.

advance in size of recent years would be inexplicable. Therefore, it is not a contest for mere superiority in dimensions in which the steamship companies have been engaged. They have been obeying an economic impulse, and by such obedience the public must obviously be the gainers. No boat that is not built for safety can truly be considered as economic. Hence all the skill which was applied to the Titanic to render her unsinkable. From what we already know it may be inferred that if she had stranded she would have floated long enough for every soul on board to have got ashore, and that if she had been damaged by collision with a ship, instead of an iceberg, everyone on board could have been got on that ship…

LORD MAYOR'S FUND.[11]

—◆—

GENEROUS DONATIONS BY THE KING AND QUEEN

AND QUEEN ALEXANDRA.

Speaking at the Easter banquet at the Mansion House last night, the Lord Mayor, Sir Thomas Boor Crosby, stated that, although he had only started the fund for the relief of the sufferers by the disaster to the Titanic since midday, he had already received several thousands of pounds. Amongst the donations were:

His Majesty the King—500 guineas.
Her Majesty the Queen—250 "
Queen Alexandra—£200

The telegrams accompanying these Royal gifts were as follows:

York Cottage, Sandringham.

I am commanded to inform your Lordship that the King subscribes 500 guineas and the Queen 250 guineas to the Mansion House Fund your Lordship is so kindly raising for the relief of those who are in need through the awful shipwreck of the Titanic.

WILLIAM CARINGTON,
Keeper of his Majesty's Privy Purse.
Sandringham.

Queen Alexandra will give £200 towards the Fund which your Lordship is raising for the relief of the relatives of those who lost their lives in the terrible disaster to the Titanic.

COL. STREATFEILD.

11. The *Daily Telegraph* encouraged its readers to contribute to a variety of funds for the relief of *Titanic* survivors. Its own fund was a significant source of help to destitute passengers, but the Lord Mayor's Fund, with contributions from the King and Queen and country, raised some £417,000. Other London and provincial papers were also raising funds (Hyslop 250). Not every *Daily Telegraph* appeal for contributions could be printed in this book because the names of those who contributed were also published by the paper and took up an enormous amount of column space. Queen Alexandra was the king's mother.

DOUBTFUL STORY.

HALIFAX (Nova Scotia), Wednesday.

The wireless operator of the cable steamer Minia reports having received a message announcing that 250 of the Titanic's passengers are on board the Baltic.

The message did not come from the Baltic direct, and the name of the steamer through which this news was re-transmitted is not known, but the same message states that the Carpathia had 760 survivors on board.

Captain de Carteret, of the Minia, confirms the operator's report about the picking up of the message, but does not vouch for its authenticity.—*Reuter.*

THE LISTS
OF
SURVIVORS.

WASHINGTON, Wednesday.

The scout-cruiser Chester sends the following wireless message:

"Established communication with Carpathia, which states list first, second-class, and crew survivors sent ashore. Chester will relay list steerage survivors as soon as convenient to Carpathia.—(Signed) Commander Decker."

Commander Decker's message is taken at the White Star offices to mean that there are no first or second-class survivors of the Titanic disaster beyond those whose names have already been published.—*Central News.*

PRESSMEN
NOT ALLOWED.

NEW YORK, Wednesday.

A significant development in connection with the arrival of the survivors is the notification of the Treasury Department by the Cunard Line that no reporters or newspaper men will be allowed on board the Carpathia until she reaches the pier. The object of this is to avoid disturbance to the survivors, many of whom are no doubt hysterical from grief.—*Reuter.*

12. The *Minia* may have been receiving a false message originating from amateur radio operators on the New England coast. The operators, seeking to be helpful, were reporting everything positive they could find either through rumor or sheer imagination.

GRAND TRUNK PRESIDENT.

From Our Own Correspondent.

MONTREAL, Wednesday.

Consternation is felt at the Grand Trunk offices at the absence of news as to the fate of Mr. Charles M. Hays. It is now considered almost certain that he is a victim of the Titanic disaster, together with Messrs. H. Markland Molson and Thornton Davidson, and several other prominent Canadians. Hope that future information may relieve the suspense has been almost abandoned. Should the fears prove correct it will be a serious blow to the Grand Trunk, as Mr. Hays has always been the master mind of that railway, as well as of the Grand Trunk Pacific, and he had intimate deals with many important matters, the settlement of which will be difficult should he have perished. **13**

Interest throughout Canada is feverish. In every city many special editions of the papers are published almost hourly and eagerly bought up. The general conclusion is reached that few men have been saved, but that most of the women and children are in safety, which is regarded with satisfaction as continuing the high traditions of the British marine.

WIDOWS AND ORPHANS.

COMPANY'S LIABILITIES.

By Our Legal Correspondent.

The owners of the Titanic, by virtue of Section 503 of the Merchant Shipping Act, 1894, are under a limited liability so far as the payment of damages is concerned. They can only be called upon to pay "in respect of loss of life or personal injury, either alone or together with loss of, or damage to, vessels, goods, merchandise, or other things, an aggregate amount not exceeding £15 for each ton of their ship's tonnage." **14**

From the original Workmen's Compensation Act of 1897, seamen and their dependents were excluded; but the rights enjoyed by other workmen were extended to them by the Workmen's Compensation Act of 1906. "This Act," says Section 7, "shall apply to masters, seamen, and apprentices to the sea service...provided that such persons are workmen within the meaning of this Act, and are members of the crew of any ship registered in the United Kingdom..."

In the opinion of experts in this branch

13. The Grand Trunk Railway debt stood at something like $100,000,000 when Hays drowned (*Encyclopedia* "Mr Charles Melville Hays").

14. Ship owners had very little liability at the time compared to the liability expected of businesses today.

of the law, the only members of the crew who would be held not to be "workmen" are the captain or other officer in receipt of more than £250 a year. Under the Workmen's Compensation Acts £300 is the maximum amount of compensation payable to the dependents of a deceased seaman, and the limitation of liability provided for by the Merchant Shipping Act might, of course, result in the payment of a proportionate part only of any compensation awarded. The nationality of the seamen employed on the Titanic would not be of any relevance if compensation were in question. Whatever their place of origin, they would be none the less "seamen."

£125,000 IN COMPENSATION.

The White Star Company will, it is estimated, have to pay a sum of about £125,000 of compensation to the widows of the seamen who went down in the Titanic...**15**

AT THE LONDON OFFICES.

A WEARY VIGIL.

Again all through yesterday there was a constant stream of anxious inquirers after missing relatives and friends at the offices of the White Star Line in Cockspur-street and Leadenhall-street, and many men and women remained hour after hour, scanning the notice-boards from time to time, in the hope of finding fresh names of survivors. But the hours dragged slowly on, and still no names were added to the lists which had reached London on the previous day and night. The only new announcement was a message which had been received from the Oceanic Company's Southampton offices in the early morning, in the following terms:

Titanic.—Have been pressing New York for names of crew survivors. Following cable just received: "Referring to your telegram of 16th, we have been pressing Olympic for this information, but regret so far have been unable to secure names crew survivors."

From this we conclude that previous messages were coming from Carpathia through the Olympic, and that the two ships have now got out of touch with each other.

Some of the watchers had remained in the office all through the night, had been aroused to hope by the posting of the last

---

15. It is difficult to ascertain what was paid in damages to widows only. The White Star's total liability after all suits were settled came to a little more than $660,000. This was a triumph for the White Star attorneys, but, of course, other funds were also paid to widows, children, and seamen from a variety of charities (Eaton and Haas, *Titanic: Triumph* 278–79).

list in the first hour of the morning, and had been depressed again by failure to find in it the names which they sought. The early omnibuses brought fresh arrivals, many of them City workers, who broke their journey in the hope of allaying their fears for the safety of loved ones. They were courteously received by officials of the company, many of whom had been working almost continuously for twenty-four hours. Though wan from want of sleep, the clerks were making a fresh start for another day's labours. "It is not the hours we are working which tell so much," said one, "but the painful scenes we have to witness."

PAINFUL SCENES.

As the day wore on, more than one of the watchers, worn out by the long vigil, fell asleep where they sat. Only once during the day was there anything like a sensational incident. A young woman, after scanning the list of surviving steerage passengers, burst into a fit of loud crying, and was with difficulty pacified by a sympathetic clerk. She explained that she was a native of Los Angeles, and that her mother and sister were among the Titanic's steerage passengers. She broke down again as she was leaving the office, and sobbed bitterly as she was led away.

For the rest the watchers sat sad-eyed and silent in the office or stood in the crowd outside—a crowd largely composed of merely curious sightseers, who throughout the day thronged the space between the statue of King George and the pavement in front of the Oceanic House, watching the stream of people passing in and out, and occasionally glancing up at the half-masted flags which floated from the roofs of all the steamship offices in Cockspur-street.

A young steward of the White Star Line named Taylor, whose father and brother were on the Titanic—the former as a steward and the latter in the engine-room—stated that on being discharged from the Oceanic last week he was approached with a view to signing on for the Titanic, but declined because he wanted a few days' holiday before going to sea again. His brother, he said, had already experienced the terrors of shipwreck, as he was on board the Republic when she foundered three years ago.

Questions put to the officials elicited always the same response. They were awaiting as anxiously as the inquirers the arrival of further lists of survivors; but the Carpathia, whose radio-telegraphic installation is only of moderate power, was not yet near enough to the American coast to communicate with a shore station, and presumably she had for the time got out of range of wireless communication with other ships.

Eight o'clock came with not a name to add to the list which was posted on the boards when last the clock announced midnight. The strain of the twenty hours' vigil was obviously telling terribly on the waiters. There was always hope, of course, for, according to the very lowest computation of the number of survivors, there was still a list of 350 or 400 names to come. And surely the loved ones of some of the lingering crowd would be among them. But hope deferred, even for an hour, under such circumstances, brought a terrible sickness of heart, **16** and there was a black depression brooding over everybody. It was a typically English assembly—save for one thing. There were no scenes, no excitement, very little weeping. But the kinship of grief broke down English reserve, did away with the necessity for introductions, and forced people to commiserate with others whom they had never seen before…

MORE LIFEBOATS.

◆

STERN AMERICAN CAMPAIGN

INADEQUATE PROVISION.

From Our Own Correspondent.

NEW YORK, Wednesday.

The American campaign for more lifeboats, which began when the news of the loss of the Titanic was first received, proceeds vigorously. As explained already in my despatches, it is not suggested that the big steamship companies do not provide all that the law requires, but it is urged that they should do more to encourage and develop mechanical inventions designed to save life, which would give most of the people on board at least a chance of safety, such as was impossible in the case of the Titanic. Americans are being urged to sign the following pledge, which is distributed broadcast:

> Appalled by the disaster to the Titanic, and believing that the great and lamentable loss of life was directly due to the failure of ocean liners to provide a sufficient number of boats and life-rafts to save the passengers in disasters of this kind, we hereby pledge ourselves not to take passage in future upon any ocean liner which does not carry sufficient boats and life-rafts to save every human being on board in case of a dire disaster such as befell the White Star liner Titanic.

Mr. Hearst's newspapers, in particular, and many others, support the campaign for more lifeboats. As usual, when any big corporation is concerned, the *New York American* is especially bitter, and, after attacking steamboat officials in general, it adds:

DEMAND FOR LEGISLATION.

"The *American* speaks for millions of Americans in urging Congress and the State Department to make adequate

---

★ **16.** Proverbs 13:12: "Hope deferred maketh the heart sick; but when the desire cometh, it is a tree of life."

laws for the safety of passengers at sea. The heart of the whole nation has been wrung with sympathy for those who are suffering, and with anxiety lest such agonies be repeated. At the instance of this newspaper, a bill will be introduced both in the House and in the Senate dealing with this matter. The bill will prescribe that no seagoing vessel shall be permitted to clear from any American port, under any flag, without being equipped in such a manner that every human being on board can leave the ship and live afloat in the water for many hours. Even the whole International Shipping Trust is not big enough to drown 1,200 picked and proven men, and escape punishment."

There is much more of the same sort, all calculated to inflame the minds of people against Transatlantic shipping companies, and to stimulate the measures already taken by the Government to "swat the Shipping Trust," meaning the members of the Atlantic Shipping Conference, who are now accused of pooling rebates, and other alleged infringements of the Sherman Anti-Trust Law. It is agreed by all sections here that the lifeboat scarcity alone was responsible for the appalling loss of life. To quote the *New York Herald*, "the appalling fact to-day stands revealed, when the last departing lifeboats swung away with the last of the 800 who had been chosen to live, the Titanic's life-saving devices had been exhausted. When those last heart-rending farewells had been said from the darkened decks in the midnight gloom and Polar cold, 1,400 doomed ones who had been elected for death had no alternative but to leap into the sea, clinging to a lifebelt or buoy, or wait, in manly fortitude, to be swallowed in the vortex with the sinking ship."…

————

MANSION HOUSE FUND.

◆

LORD MAYOR'S ACTION.

————

To The Editor of "The Daily Telegraph."

Sir—I desire, by your courtesy, to intimate that I have to-day opened a fund at the Mansion House for the immediate aid and permanent relief of the widows, orphans, and dependent relatives of those—whether they be crew or passengers—who have lost their lives in this great national calamity, and to invite the ever-generous assistance of the benevolent public in attempting to relieve, in some degree, the distress which has been occasioned in many hundreds of families by a disaster fortunately unparalleled in the history of ocean navigation. In taking this step, I feel sure that I am promptly responding to the wishes of those who urge that the keen sympathy universally and unstintedly entertained for those who have thus suddenly been plunged into misery and distress should assume some practical shape, for the future advantage of the bereaved families. Of the real extent of the calamity it is too soon to expect reliable details. Some time must necessarily elapse before information can be obtained as to the number of those lost, and their wives and families, and their circumstances; but sufficient is known to make it evident that a very large sum will be required to adequately provide for those in distress, apart from their claims under the Workmen's Compensation Act.

In raising a Manion House Fund, I am assured of the hearty and active co-operation of the Mayor of Southampton, to whose town the great bulk of the crew and their families belonged, and of others who are raising subscriptions; and I should especially welcome the assistance of The Daily Telegraph and London and provincial Press in making known the existence of the Fund, and, if possible, in collecting, acknowledging, and remitting donations in response to this appeal.

Donations may be sent to the Mansion House, or to the Bank of England, where an account, "The Titanic Disaster Fund," has been opened. I am, Sir, your obedient servant,

THOS. BOOR CROSBY, Lord Mayor.
The Mansion House, April 17…

SOME PERSONAL NOTES.

Mr. J. P. Moody, the sixth officer of the Titanic, of whom no information has been received, is a son of Mr. J. H. Moody, solicitor and a former member of the Scarborough Town Council. Mr. Moody left Scarborough some fifteen or twenty years ago, and though the son, like the father, is a native of Scarborough, he is practically unknown in the town, from which he was taken in his infancy or early boyhood. Mr. J. P. Moody's grandfather was town clerk of Scarborough up till a little over thirty years ago. **17**

Mrs[.] Barkworth, mother of Mr. Algernon H. Barkworth, J.P., of Tranby House, Hessle, near Hull, whose name appears in the list of the survivors travelling first class, was merely staying in Scarborough as a visitor. Mrs. Barkworth informed our Scarborough Correspondent yesterday that the wireless telegram which she had from her son on Monday saying "All well," not "Safe," as previously reported, must have been despatched before the collision, and not afterwards. She had since heard from the White Star Line, however, that her son was on board the Carpathia on his way to New York.

Mrs. M. K. Roberts, one of the stewardesses of the Titanic, who, it is feared is lost, is the wife of the principal of the West Bridgford Motor Company, 9, Chestnut-grove, West Bridgford, and has been in the service of the White Star Line for some years. She was transferred to the Titanic from the Olympic, upon which she made her last voyage. Mrs. Roberts was at home with her husband and family only a few weeks ago for a brief stay before proceeding to Southampton. **18**

★ **17.** Mr. Moody did not survive.

18. Mrs. M. K. Roberts was saved.

One of the first-class stewardesses of the Titanic was Mrs. J. Gould [K. Gold], of Burton-on-Trent, who has had an astonishing record of shipwrecks. She was on board the Suevic when the boat was cut in two, and was also on the Olympic when that vessel was rammed by the Hawke in the Solent. It is not known whether she is among those rescued. [19]

Two residents of Ilfracombe, Mr. Phillips and his daughter, were among the passengers of the Titanic. [20]

Among the third-class passengers on the Titanic were three brothers from West Bromwich and their uncle. The latter leaves a widow and one son, and one of the brothers leaves a widow, he having been married the day before his departure, the arrangement being that his wife should later join him in Canada. It is stated that these four men nearly missed the train to Southampton.

A statement that Mr. Thomas Pears, of the well-known soap firm, and Mrs. Thomas Pears had been saved seems, unfortunately, to have been based upon a misunderstanding. It appears that on Monday afternoon a message was received from Mr. Pears, "All's well," dated from Potsdam. As there is a town on the American coast of that name, it was believed that Mr. Pears had communicated with the wireless station there. Subsequent inquiries, however, show that the message was read by the steamship Potsdam in mid-Atlantic on Sunday before the disaster occurred, and was passed on to England on Monday. [21]

Mr. Lawrence Beesley, one of the passengers drowned, [22] was the son of the late Mr. H. Beesley, bank manager, of Wirksworth. He was a widower, and leaves a young boy. Mr. Beesley was a science master at Dulwich College, and resigned his position to go for a holiday in the United States and to visit his brother at Toronto.

19. Mrs. K. Gold was saved (Tibballs 504).

20. The daughter was saved.

21. Mr. Pears was lost.

22. He was not drowned, but later went on to write a famous book about the Titanic's sinking. See Bibliography.

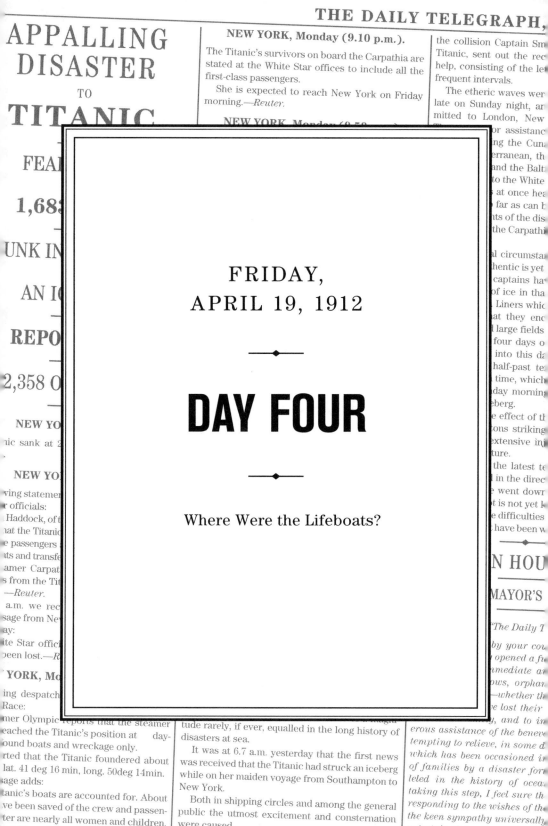

FRIDAY,
APRIL 19, 1912

◆

DAY FOUR

◆

Where Were the Lifeboats?

INTRODUCTION

———◆———

PASSENGER LINERS AND THE BOARD OF TRADE JUMPED ON the bandwagon for more lifeboats and safety gear primarily because the media and the public shocked them into action.

The Board of Trade's position on regulating the shipping industry had been, on the whole, a defensive one. So, from the beginning of the *Titanic*'s disaster, the Board took the side of British industrial concerns. Shipboard safety, they said, was a complicated matter and deserved intense study, committee work, and a final report after a period of reflection. Nothing hasty must be done. Some of their experts were not entirely sure that the Board of Trade need do anything. As for passenger liners, they only became enthusiastic about more lifeboats as they were led to consider how they would fare before a jury in trying to explain the lack of them to unsympathetic laymen.

The truth is that passengers, until now, had been pretty complacent about lifeboat accommodations. Shipping experts were supposed to know how to best protect passenger interests. Hence the shock at the realization that there were not enough lifeboats on board *Titanic*! Surely such an elementary safety precaution would seem to be fundamental.

It is not surprising then that one of the more important statements ever made about the priority of safety first for passengers came from none other than second-class passenger Lawrence Beesley, a science teacher who escaped the sinking to write his classic, *The Loss of the S. S. Titanic*.

In a letter to the *Times* of London, published on April 20, he wrote, in part:

As one of the few surviving Englishmen from the steamship Titanic, which sank in mid-Atlantic on Monday morning last, I am asking you to lay before your readers a few facts concerning the disaster, in the hope that something may be done in the near future to ensure the safety of that portion of the travelling public who use the Atlantic highway for business or pleasure...

The accommodation for saving the passengers and crew was totally inadequate, being sufficient only for a total of about 950. This gave, with the highest possible complement of 3400, a less than one in three chance of being saved in the case of an accident...

I have neither knowledge nor experience to say what remedies I consider should be applied; but, perhaps, the following suggestions may serve as a help:—

First, that no vessel should be allowed to leave a British port without sufficient boat and other accommodation to allow each passenger and member of the crew a seat; and that at the time of booking this fact should be pointed out to a passenger, and the number of the seat in the particular boat allotted to him then.

Second, that as soon as is practicable after sailing each passenger should go through boat drill in company with the crew assigned to his boat...(147–48).

Beesley's suggestions were enacted by consensus as the Board of Trade and the British Wreck Commission finally saw the wisdom of doing what the press and the public had already concluded were commonsense things to do.

———◆———

BOATS
AND
BULKHEADS.

———

TITANIC'S EQUIPMENT.

———

MATTERS FOR INQUIRY.

———

In due course a Court of Inquiry will conduct a searching investigation into the loss of the Titanic, and, out of conclusions arrived at, recommendations will be made. **1** At this stage, even before the full story of the disaster is known, it is perfectly safe to prophesy that the rules of the Board of Trade governing life-saving appliances in merchant shipping will be drastically overhauled. For the facts are so very plain. The rules of the governing authorities are so hopelessly out of date with the march of progress and enterprise in steamship construction that they might just as well be non-existent where ships are four or five times larger than the largest provided for. The other cold fact is that the boats carried by the Titanic were only equal to saving about a third of the passengers and crew, **2** and the two-thirds had to accept death by drowning. It was their only dread alternative, even although the sea was calm, and a place in a small boat under such conditions might be considered as safe as on a liner intact.

It is nothing less than amazing that the discovery of the inadequacy of the rules should only have become generally known through this world-shaking catastrophe. Truly the awakening could not have been more appalling and violent. Mr. Buxton, the President of the Board of Trade, was called upon to answer a question bearing on this point in the House of Commons in December last. In his reply he made no direct reference to the vast increase in tonnage since the rules were made nearly twenty years ago, but added: "The Board of Trade are carefully considering at present the question of the number of boats required to be carried by large passenger

---

1. The British Wreck Commission would be chaired by John Charles Bigham, Lord Mersey. He would hear some ninety-six witnesses over thirty-six days in a highly organized examination into what went wrong on the *Titanic*. His great problem would be that of credibility. He was part of a team put together by the Board of Trade to investigate itself. Lord Mersey's actual knowledge of maritime law was quite good, for he had practiced in the area of business law for more than twenty years. His weak point lay in the area of technical matters with regard to ship construction. Yet any other judge would have had the same problem (Butler 193–94).

2. That is, if the boats had been loaded to capacity, a highly unlikely situation in a disaster where time to do this would have been short.

and emigrant steamers, and also the question of the seaworthiness of ships' boats." In the House of Commons yesterday Mr. Buxton referred to a matter which the peoples of other nations, as well as ours, are viewing with the deepest concern and anxiety. As will be gathered from the report of his speech, which we print elsewhere, his Board, during the last few days, have been considering a report of the Advisory Committee which was appointed last year to investigate the matter. Apparently, before the news of the Titanic disaster became known, those recommendations, which are now made public, were not considered adequate, and the whole matter was referred back to the committee for further investigation.

QUESTION OF BOATS.

There is an idea that the problem would be solved by a rule stipulating that each ship must carry sufficient boats to hold all passengers and crew in case of emergency. Experts, however—and a number were seen yesterday by a representative of *The Daily Telegraph*—are far from agreeing that this would be a solution. It would mean, at a rough estimate, about eighty boats for a ship of the size of the Titanic. **3** Where, say the experts,

would this fleet be accommodated without adding to the top-hamper so seriously as to make the ship unseaworthy? Where would the officers be found to man these boats? Would it be possible to keep all these boats provisioned? Was it likely that eighty boats could be lowered from a great height—it might be the ship would have a dangerous list—in the time elapsing between a disastrous collision and sinking?

These are questions to which the man in the street finds no difficulty in supplying answers. He will say that everything must be sacrificed in securing the safety of human life by all possible means. If the building of great ships to carry masses of people means thus reducing the margin of safety, then they must be restricted. If with Olympics and Titanics accommodation cannot be found on the boat deck for eighty boats, then the design must be altered. These are the answers of the man in the street. **4** But he must bear in mind one or two necessary facts. One is that only in case of collision are boats likely to be required. They would be valueless in a gale which had imperilled the ship. Another is that from the high deck where they must be kept, if they are not to be swept by the devastating winter gales in the Atlantic, only a certain number could be handled in the time between collision and sinking.

3. Eighty boats at roughly sixty persons per boat would carry 4,800 people—well more than what the *Titanic* needed.

4. The paper seems to be indicating that "the man in the street" is being too simpleminded with regard to the lifeboat question. Indeed, the question of how best to use lifeboats is under constant review to the present day.

TWO WATER-TIGHT SYSTEMS.

Allowing for this, however, it is agreed on all hands that though the White Star liner more than complied with the antiquated Board of Trade rules, she, nevertheless, was allowed to leave port hopelessly unprepared to deal with such an awful emergency as actually arose. The suggestion is seriously made that the bulkhead water-tight system discounts the value of boats, since up to this week it has been regarded as equal to practically any emergency. We know now that it was not. It has failed, though failure no doubt was inevitable in the terrible circumstances. It is conceivable that the authorities, both in the shipyards and Government offices, have been placing too high a value on the bulkhead water-tight doors...

PARLIAMENT
AND THE
CATASTROPHE.

IMPORTANT STATEMENT BY MR. BUXTON.

BOATS FOR 1,178 PERSONS.

In the House of Commons yesterday, in reply to questions addressed to him by various members, Mr. Sydney Buxton, President of the Board of Trade, made an important statement in regard to the regulations respecting life-saving appliances on British ships, and in regard to the equipment of the Titanic in that matter.

Mr. Wedgwood (R., Newcastle-under-Lyme), on behalf of Mr. Martin (R., St. Pancras, E.): I beg to ask the President of the Board of Trade if there is any law which gives his Board power to compel the owners of passenger steamers to provide sufficient lifeboats to give a place in them to every human being on the boat in case of a disaster like the loss of the Titanic; whether, as often alleged, there is no passenger steamer leaving a British port with lifeboats sufficient for that purpose; whether in many cases the lifeboat accommodation is only about

Simply put, investigative inquiry revealed that the *Titanic*'s watertight bulkheads did not reach high enough to prevent the ship from rapidly sinking. True: all bulkheads reached above the waterline, but just barely. If one bulkhead should fill with water, it would spill water into the next compartment, and thus, the ship would fill. The weight of the water in the sinking *Titanic* pulled the front of the ship down in the bow and caused the ocean to cascade into successive bulkheads, dooming the ship. The Cunard Line had two ships, the *Lusitania* and the *Mauretania*, with covered bulkheads that prevented water from spilling from one compartment to another. This feature might well have saved the *Titanic* (Marriott 35).

one-third of that required; and, if there is no such law, will the Government introduce a bill for that purpose?

Mr. Fred. Hall (U., Dulwich): I wish to ask the President of the Board of Trade whether, taking into consideration the reported loss of life which has recently occurred to the passengers of the steamer Titanic, he will take steps that regulations may be made to compel all steamers to carry boats, rafts, or other life-saving apparatus sufficient to accommodate the whole of those on board?

Mr. Bottomley (R., Hackney, S.): I beg to ask the President of the Board of Trade whether he will consider the propriety of framing a regulation for the purpose of preventing British passenger liners for New York, during the spring season, taking the Northern Atlantic route, with a view to establishing crossing records, and, further, whether he can state the exact lifeboat accommodation which was provided on the Titanic, and what proportion it bore to the authorised number of passengers and crew.

Mr. Buxton: I think it will be convenient if I deal in a single statement with all the questions relating to the boat accommodation of the Titanic, and the Board of Trade regulations relating to boats and other life-saving appliances. I would ask the indulgence of the House in making rather a long answer. (Cheers.) **5**

The Board of Trade are empowered, by Section 427 of the Merchant Shipping Act, 1894, to make rules for life-saving appliances on British ships, and Section 428 requires the owner and master to give effect to the rules.

The rules now in force were originally drawn up in 1890, and revised in 1894 and subsequently, and prescribe a scale indicating the minimum number of boats to be provided in accordance with the gross tonnage of the ship. The highest provision made in this scale is for vessels of 10,000 tons and upwards.

In view of the increased size of modern passenger steamers, the Board of Trade early last year referred to the Advisory Committee on Merchant Shipping the question of the revision of the rules, and in particular of the provision to be made in the case of steamers of very large size.

In view of the public interest aroused by the recent lamentable disaster, I am having the report of this committee printed with the Votes.

After considering this report, together with the views of their expert advisers, the Board of Trade were not satisfied that the increased provision recommended by the Advisory Committee was altogether adequate. After additional investigations and tests in regard to the best type and proportions of lifeboats, the Board within the last few days referred the question back to the Committee for further examination.

★ **5.** This paper was conservative and almost always approved of whatever the government said or did. The ruling party was always right or mostly right. (Cheers) indicates that most of parliament was cheering the government response. (Jeers) would have meant that he had failed to be convincing.

I mention this in order that the House may understand that before the recent terrible disaster occurred the Board of Trade, in concert with the best expert authorities available, had been carefully and practically considering the question of the revision of the scale of boat accommodation prescribed for large ships.

I do not, of course, desire to forecast in any way the result of the inquiry which will be held into the loss of the Titanic, or any modification of policy that may be necessitated by the findings of the inquiry, or by the new situation created by the present disaster. I wish the House, however, to understand quite clearly that up to the present it has never been the intention of the Board of Trade regulations, and, so far as I know, it has not been suggested by any responsible expert authority, that every vessel, however large, and however well equipped as regards watertight compartments, should necessarily carry lifeboats adequate to accommodate all on board.

It has always been considered up to the present, by all expert authorities, that subdivision by watertight compartments is a safeguard to be taken into account in considering the minimum number of boats required.

The Board of Trade rules (following in this respect the report of the Life-Saving Appliances Committee of 1890) expressly allow a deduction in the case of vessels so equipped, and the recent report of the Merchant Shipping Advisory Committee makes further recommendations in the same sense.

No doubt the present disaster creates a new situation, which will need to be considered most carefully—I hope, however, not in a panic—in the light of all the information which the inquiry will disclose.

Coming to the actual facts of the case, the present rule of the Board of Trade with regard to a ship of 10,000 tons and upwards, requires a minimum boat accommodation of 9,625 cubic feet—i.e., sixteen boats under davits, with a capacity of 5,500 cubic feet, and an addition of 75 per cent. in the shape of other boats, rafts, &c. This would provide for about 960 persons.

The Titanic actually carried sixteen boats under davits, with accommodation for 990 persons, and four Engelhardt boats **6** accommodating 188 persons, in addition; that is, altogether accommodation for 1,178 persons. Besides these there were forty-eight lifebuoys **7** and 3,560 lifebelts.

The total number of passengers and crew which the vessel was certified to carry was 3,547, and on the recent voyage the actual number on board when the vessel left Queenstown was 2,208.

With reference to the question of framing a regulation to prevent British passenger steamers for North American ports during the spring season from taking the Northern Atlantic route, I am not prepared at the moment to express

6. Known as collapsibles because their sides were canvas and could be raised and lowered.

7. A floating device in the shape of a ring; not very effective in frigid water.

any opinion. This and all other relevant questions will be submitted to searching inquiry...

Mr. Buxton: My desire, and that of my Department, will be to facilitate the inquiry as far as possible, but there must necessarily be an inquiry into the loss of the Titanic, and it is quite clear that until we have such information as is available with regard to the disaster, we shall not be in such a strong position as to know what to do. I can assure the House we fully feel the great responsibility the Board of Trade bears in the matter, but I really think it is far better that we should give a little longer time, and come to a really satisfactory conclusion, than act rapidly, and be possibly led into other evils.

Mr. Lough (R., West Islington): Having regard to the rapid growth in the size of vessels in recent years, does not the right hon. gentleman consider that it is a long time to wait from 1894 to 1911 without making any regulation for vessels over 10,000 tons?

Mr. Cooper (U., Walsall): Is it not a fact that Atlantic liners of German and United States nationality to-day actually carry close on double the lifeboat accommodation required by the Board of Trade regulations in this country?

Mr. Buxton: I do not think that is so, as a matter of fact. Perhaps the hon. gentleman will give me notice of that question. **8**

Mr. Bottomley (R., S. Hackney): Does not the right hon. gentleman really think it is an established fact that this unfortunate vessel was right in the zone of the icebergs during the season when they are a well-known and established danger, and that the Board of Trade should take immediate steps to prevent a recurrence of such a thing?

Mr. Buxton: I really think it is a matter in regard to which some consideration should be shown by the hon. member. Hon. members must remember that if this great disaster has given a great shock to public opinion, it will also be fully taken into account by the managers and directors of these great lines, who are naturally anxious for the safety of their vessels and their passengers. But I really do not think I ought to be asked to give an answer to such a question just now.

Mr. Bottomley: I beg to give notice that at the end of questions I shall ask

---

8. This is a written request for information which allows the government minister time to prepare an answer (Wikipedia "Question Time").

★ ★

Buxton artfully defends the Board of Trade, but it isn't easy. Neither Germany nor America had laws that specifically required enough lifeboats to carry all persons on a ship. Ship owners generally used their own discretion in deciding how best to serve passenger safety, but that was before the Titanic sank. Nearly all maritime nations required improved standards for passenger safety in the wake of the Titanic calamity. One vast improvement, involving the Atlantic trade, was the establishment of the International Ice Patrol, which still tracks the routes of icebergs coming down from Newfoundland. Eighteen countries support this service to all Atlantic shipping.

leave to move the adjournment of the House on this subject.

Mr. Wilkie (Lab., Dundee): Do I understand the right hon. gentleman to say that these vesels only carry lifeboats and life rafts in accordance with the tonnage, and not in accordance with the number of passengers carried, and further, is he aware that there is no difficulty whatever in naval architecture in having a sufficient number of lifeboats to carry all the passengers?

Mr. Buxton: The boat accommodation is founded on tonnage. That may or may not be a good plan...

——◆——

BRITISH REGULATIONS.

————

SAFETY OF PASSENGERS.

————

BULKHEADS NOT RELIABLE.

————

On the motion for the adjournment of the House of Commons, made shortly after eleven o clock last night,

Mr. Bottomley said: I crave the indulgence of the House for a few moments to refer to a subject which occupied some time at questions to-day, and the importance and urgency of which are my excuse for trespassing on the House. I refer to the inadequate provision made by the Board of Trade for the safety of passengers on ocean liners.

I do not wish to make a single observation against Mr. Buxton. There is no more industrious or conscientious Minister, and no one appreciates more than I the tremendous strain which has been put upon him in recent months. But I want to say that it does not seem to be fully appreciated by the public that the sole responsibility for the safety of passengers on these liners rests upon the Board of Trade. **9**

Under the Merchant Shipping Act the whole regulations as to lifeboat accommodation and so on have to be dealt with by rules made by the Board of Trade.

I want to call the attention of the House to the extraordinary fact that, according to an answer given by Mr. Buxton to-day (assuming his premisses to be correct, which I say they are not), the utmost requirements the present rules of the Board of Trade for the life-saving accommodation of a vessel like the Titanic amounted to accommodation for 960 people.

The vessel was authorised to carry, in round figures, 3,500 passengers, though on this particular voyage she carried some 2,200. The President of the Board of Trade mentioned that, beyond boats, the total life-saving accommodation was for 1,178.

I submit that the Board of Trade—I make no charge against any particular Minister or party—are to be censured severely for allowing obsolete rules to remain in force which legalise such inadequate accommodation.

Any cargo-boat has more than double that protection.

Under the same rules of the Board of Trade, the smallest cargo-vessel has to have lifeboat accommodation equal to the entire number of people on board on each side of the vessel. The same rule applies to men-of-war and troopships, and apparently to every vessel except these great ocean leviathans. The President of the Board of Trade was good enough to tell me that there has been inquiry by the Advisory Committee of the Board of Trade into these matters. In November, 1910, I called the attention of the President of the Board of Trade to what I conceived to be the inadequate lifeboat accommodation of the sister vessel, the Olympic. The answer I then received was in the same official character as that which I got to-day. It ignored that fact that when the regulations of the Board of Trade were made in 1890, and revised in 1894, the largest tonnage of any of these liners was something under 14,000 tons, and that there had been no serious revision since...

I have here an official plan of the boat-deck of the Titanic. I want the President to give his serious attention to the important fact that there is room on that boat-deck, even with the system of single boats, for at least twelve more lifeboats.

Not only that, but when I come to read a sort of prospectus by the White Star Line of this particular vessel, they point out that the entrance to the boat-deck is for the convenience of those who desire to promenade in the central part of the ship at this high level, and the notable feature of that is that the lifeboats are so disposed that for over 200ft of the promenade there is an uninterrupted view.

When you have the owners of the boat telling you that, for the purpose of giving a promenade with an uninterrupted view of 200ft, they have failed to utilise a space sufficient to provide at least twelve further lifeboats, I say it is a very serious thing indeed.

These rules are altogether out-of-date, and I hope the President of the Board of Trade, in the inquiry he is about to institute, will have full regard to the new conditions...

Mr. Cooper (U., Walsall): I desire to support Mr. Bottomley in pressing the Board of Trade to take immediate action for the protection of liners crossing the Atlantic. We are led to understand through the Press—which I think in this matter may be trusted—that the American Senate and Congress have already dealt in rather strong manner with this matter, and it is suggested that they are even considering the necessity for abrogating certain treaties between the United States and this country in order to enable them to remain free to make their own regulations concerning vessels of all nationalities that touch their ports. They can only be doing that because they regard the competency of our Board of Trade as insufficient to meet what they consider necessary for their own people travelling upon those boats.

I would urge the right hon. gentleman seriously to consider whether he ought not at once to issue regulations to compel all steamers to take the southern course without delay.

MR. BUXTON'S REPLY.

Mr. Buxton: As I said at question time, it does appear to me that without further information than I have at my disposal, and without further inquiry and consultation with those who have expert knowledge, it would be idle for me at this moment to lay down a proposition such as Mr. Bottomley asks. It is clearly a case which must be considered in connection with the great disaster which has befallen this country, and it clearly could not be of any advantage to the shipping community or the community at large if I were suddenly to step in without knowledge. **10** (Hear, hear.)

I take full responsibility, as President of the Board, for what the Board of Trade may have done or for what it may have left undone in past years, but we have been of late at all events alive to the necessity of taking further action in regard to this very matter and we have been spending some time past in making most careful inquiry with the officers of the advisory committee, who represent the best expert knowledge.

With our own expert advisers, we have come to the conclusion that, apart from this calamity, we should have suggested more stringent provisions even than the Advisory Committee themselves had recommended.

Mr. Bottomley seemed to suggest that there had been delay between the date of the report of the Advisory Committee last July and the present time. That is not so. The delay has arisen from this cause: That our expert advisers throughout the country have been having experiments made in regard to lifeboats, the carrying capacity of ships, and other matters of that sort of the most practical character. They have had this done on the sea with boats and so on.

That has all taken time. In this matter we were anxious in moving to move with certainty, to move with knowledge, and to move in the right direction. Mr. Bottemley insinuates that this matter was referred back to the Advisory Committee in consequence of the sinking of the Titanic. There is no truth in that. These matters have been considered, and we have been in consultation with the Advisory Committee and the experts to see how soon, in what direction, and how far we should move.

WATERTIGHT COMPARTMENTS.

I venture also to say that I think we must in this matter also wait—not wait in the sense of not doing anything—but I think we also require to have before us such evidence as we can obtain with reference to the calamity itself. (Cheers.) I pointed this out to the House to-day—and I think they assented—that, while, I admit, we were gong to propose greater boat

10. This is one of the first statements by an official that the very reputation of the country is at stake in this national, not just corporate, disaster. To some observers, British self-confidence in its industrial technology would never be the same.

accommodation for these larger ships, I will undertake to say that not a single expert throughout the country, nobody who has given the matter any consideration at all, would for a moment have said that the fact of a large ship of this sort being built in watertight compartments was not a factor in its safety, and therefore that such a ship as that would really require, in proportion to its size, a smaller proportion of boats than those without watertight bulkheads.

Unfortunately this calamity has shown that these watertight bulkheads cannot be relied upon.

Therefore the question becomes a new one, but it is not the desire of the Board of Trade to shirk either their responsibility, or the care that they intend to give to it. I hope the House will be satisfied with that assurance on behalf of the Board of Trade. (Cheers.)…

LOSS OF THE TITANIC.

THE BRAVE CREW.

HELP FOR THE WIDOWS.

DISTRIBUTION TO-DAY.

From Our Special Correspondent.

SOUTHAMPTON, Thursday.

The wives and children of the Titanic's heroes expect to know the worst to-morrow morning. Most of them believe that their breadwinners are gone; but their fears for the future are relieved by the generous response of their grateful fellow-countrymen to the funds for the relief of dependents. I have had the pleasure of handing a cheque for £500, as the first instalment of *The Daily Telegraph* Fund, to the Mayor of Southampton to-day. Mr. Councillor Henry Bowyer, R.N.R., the Mayor, was thankful to receive it, for distress is already acute, and the immediate necessities of the sufferers demand instant attention. **11** The first distribution from *The Daily Telegraph* Fund will be made by his worship at ten o'clock to-morrow morning. By that hour the names of the survivors of the crew will have reached the borough, and the needy among those who have lost husbands, sons, and fathers will receive temporary relief, until a scheme of a permanent character has been prepared.

The Mayor anticipates that between 600 and 700 families will come on this fund, and counting three persons to

---

★ **11.** "The immediate necessities of the sufferers" probably refers to their emotional needs. The loss of male "providers" was great, and many women were soon to know of their financial peril. The money of common laborers lasted from week to week, not from month to month.

each family, the subscriptions of the philanthropic will have to provide for the maintenance of 2,000 women and children—a huge total truly, and one which demands that the people shall recognise their national duty to put beyond the possibility of want those who have so worthily upheld the traditions of the sea...

STORIES OF DISTRESS.

...In the Town Ward an alderman, who, like his father, has performed civic duties for many years, told me that the condition of some families in the ward he represented is extremely pitiable. To-day he had inquired into the wants of twelve mothers, who between them have nearly sixty children. One of them, the wife of a steward, had seven young children, and was absolutely penniless. Another had six youngsters and was expecting another—there will be a large number of posthumous children of men who observed the "Women and children first" rule on the Titanic—and she had not one farthing. The money on advance notes had all gone in rent and discharging debts.

Most of the women were wives of firemen and trimmers, **12** and the good alderman's words of comfort and hope fell on deaf ears. "There may be 100 of the crew saved," say they; "but not a fireman or a trimmer will be among them." They, poor forlorn creatures, know the story. They describe to you how a seaman or two were ordered in each boat, while the firemen toiled in the Titanic's bowels till they had to rush from the stoke-holds when water reached the furnaces. Then they had to "stand stock still to the Birkenhead drill," and to take their places with millionaires and die like white men. **13**

"There's no hope for a fireman's wife," they tell you, "nor stewards' wives either." The engine-room staff has gone, they insist, and they point to the decreased number of survivors signalled by the Carpathia to prove their point, that only the minimum number of seamen required for manning the boats have escaped. And who can answer their arguments? The only reply is to tell them to hope on, and to promise that some help on the morrow will relieve the anxiety, which is weighing all these brave mothers down, of how to feed their hungry children.

This difficulty has been removed by the instalment of *The Daily Telegraph* Fund now in the Mayor's hands, and if the mothers to-morrow learn that they have become widows, they will at least know that their sorrow is not to be increased by witnessing the effects of hunger upon their children. The distribution of the Fund will be in the hands of the Mayor, who, being a sailor, is

---

12. Firemen shoveled the coal into the furnaces, and trimmers brought the coal to the firemen from the coal bunkers.

13. It appears there was only one black man on board the *Titanic*, who, we suppose, died as well or as ill as the others (Aldridge 42–3).

full of sympathy for the dependants of the gallant men Southampton has lost... **14**

———◆———

AMERICAN AID FOR SURVIVORS.

———

PROMPT MEASURES.

———

CARING FOR THE DESTITUTE.

———

From Our Own Correspondent.

NEW YORK, Thursday.

Money, shelter, food, and clothing have been provided at New York by a committee of society women for the destitute survivors of the wreck. It is known already that the first and second-class passengers of the Titanic are arriving here in most cases just as destitute as the poor folk of the steerage, and for them also the necessary arrangements have been made. There is no lack of money and a sufficient number of American philanthropists have come forward to guarantee payment, whatever cost may be necessary, pending the receipt of collections from all parts of the country.

The American Government will house the steerage passengers, as usual, at Ellis Island, the great clearing house for all steerage passengers, and where hospital wards are now being prepared with a staff of volunteer nurses to commence work immediately. As soon as the unfortunate passengers have recovered from the effects of their shock and are in a condition to leave Ellis Island they will be taken in hand by the ladies' committee, who will furnish them with clothes and money, and expedite their journey to places in the United States where labour organisations exist to secure employment. **15**

———

LAWS RELAXED.

———

New York is already surfeited with European aliens, and the congested districts of the East side are no whit better

14. Actual statistics are that twenty-one of thirty-one seamen, forty-eight of 176 firemen, and twenty of seventy-three trimmers were saved. Only one of twenty-five engineers lived, and none of the musicians, but all seven of the quartermasters and all six lookout men survived (Tibballs 496–500).

15. Someone in authority, no one is quite sure who, thought better of this separate and unequal treatment of the steerage passengers, and all survivors were welcomed at the New York pier where the *Carpathia* docked (Marcus 202).

situated than the corresponding district of the East-end of London. It is the rule of the American Government that no persons shall be allowed to land here from abroad unless they possess £5 in cash and have friends or relatives on shore to make themselves responsible for their custody, so that the country may be furnished with some guarantee that they will not become charges on the public authorities. President Taft has suggested that the Immigration Laws shall be interpreted as liberally as possible in behalf of the sufferers, and the wave of sympathy which extended across the continent from ocean to ocean would hardly permit the Customs authorities here, except in the rarest instances, where the aliens proved to be criminal lunatics or suffering from an incurable disease, to be deported, as is usually the case, to the place whence they sailed. **16**

The White Star officials here are co-operating in every way possible to aid the public authorities and the committee of philanthropists in fulfilling their humane intention. As to the first and second-class passengers, hundreds of motor-cars lent by New Yorkers will be waiting at the landing-pier to-night to convey them to the homes of friends, where they will stay, receiving every solace possible, until they have made their own arrangements for the immediate future...

16. Mercifully, *Titanic* passengers escaped this examination (Geller 149).

★ ★

The ad hoc network of aid societies that sprang up to help *Titanic* survivors was remarkably successful. One case, in particular, demonstrates a remarkable efficiency.

Michel Navratil, age three, and his brother, Edmond, age two, were stolen from their mother, Marcelle, by their father. No one knows what was wrong with the marriage. Calling himself Mr. Hoffman, the senior Michel Navratil took his children on board the *Titanic* to try for a new life in America. As the ship was sinking, Mr. Navratil gave his children over to women in Collapsible D to save their lives. He perished in the sinking.

Since the children arrived in America under the name Hoffman, there was a great deal of confusion over what to do with them. At this point, Margaret Hays, a first-class survivor, stepped forward and offered to take care of the children rather than let them go into an orphanage. That could have been the end of the story except that Miss Hays spoke fluent French and suspected the boys were not German.

Eventually, a story about the plight of these orphans was circulated widely in Europe, and Mrs. Navratil recognized them as her own children. The White Star Line then furnished passage to New York for Mrs. Navratil, and the family was reunited. Michel Navratil Junior lived to be ninety-one. Edmond died at the age of forty-three from injuries suffered during World War II (Geller 91–4).

POSTING THE NAMES.

From Our Special Correspondent.

SOUTHAMPTON, Thursday (10.0 p.m.).

At twilight word was passed from the White Star offices to the waiting crowd that a cablegram had arrived giving the names of some of the survivors among the third-class passengers and crew. There was an immediate stir among the crowd, which pressed forward towards the pavement to secure a good position from which to read the names as they were posted on the blackboard. The men gave way to the women, who occupied every place several rows deep. The back of the crowd was exclusively composed of workmen and sailors from ships in the docks who had joined the throng to see if they could recognise former messmates among the saved.

At first a few names were put up. They evoked not a murmur from the crowd. Clearly among them was not a single member of the crew. Then a couple of dozen names of fortunate survivors were posted. Again the list was eagerly scanned, and once more there was dead silence. A third list, longer than the other two, appeared. Not a movement in the crowd resulted. The suspense was awful, and one awaited the shriek of a hysterical woman. It came not, but there was a sigh of anxiety when, after the fourth list was posted, there came a message that the United States cruiser could not gather any more names owing to the bad atmosphere and "fierce disturbance."

So far not a single name of a member of the crew has been signalled. The crowd know no passengers, and though there has been no demonstration the people are bitterly disappointed that the cablegram should break off just when they were beginning to expect news of supreme interest to Southampton.

Up to the present 453 names have been received. There are 252 still to come, and for these the people are waiting. One poster on the board excited the curiosity of the crowd. It ran, "Jimmy, please call at 93, Millbrook-road, for information." The parents of

---

★ More than two hundred crew members did survive, but passenger listings, mostly of first- and second-class travelers, came first. Keep in mind that one could not simply pick up the cell phone and get answers "straight from the source." The relay of survivors' names had so many confusing aspects: Sometimes initials were used for a survivor instead of his proper first name; some men went by nicknames; maids and other servants were often referred to by naming whom they worked for; and various relay telegraphers garbled names and misspelled them. In the case of third-class passengers, some could not speak English or could not write. The wonder is that the lists were as accurate as they were.

a seaman on the Titanic knew their son had an old friend whose first name was Jimmy. They were not aware of his surname, but wished to tell him that Patsey was on the Titanic. Jimmy saw the poster, called at Millbrook-road, and learned for the first time that his old chum was missing.

BOATS
ON LINERS.

EQUIPMENT QUESTIONS.

DISPARITY IN
PRACTICE.

By OUR SHIPPING
CORRESPONDENT.

On every liner that goes to sea there is posted in a prominent place—usually somewhere on the principal staircase—a Board of Trade certificate of the extent of the vessel's accommodation for passengers and crew. There is also exhibited a certificate as to the life-saving appliances, including boats, which the ship carries. The number of persons a vessel is certified to transport is arrived at by a consideration of cubic space. In determining the life-saving equipment other considerations, including the provision of watertight compartments, come into play.

In general, it may be taken that boats are provided in excess of official requirements. This further goes to explain why there is no precise ratio between the passengers and crew and the boat accommodation. Once the official minimum is assured, the matter rests with the steamship line.

NORTH ATLANTIC
CONTRASTS.

That there is a strange diversity of practice is apparent from the equipments of various North Atlantic liners. The following comparison may be given, with the perhaps necessary remark that rarely do passengers and crew reach the certified figure, and usually fall considerably below it:

Steamer	Passenger and crew accommodation	Boats	Boat accommodation
Titanic	3,547	20	1,178
Mauretania	2,972	16	976
Adriatic	2,225	18	1,038
Laurentic	2,147	16	992
Empress of Britain	1,914	21	1,045

It is difficult to understand the reasoning on which such figures are based. **17** The White Star's Adriatic has far more

★ **17.** Ship regulations on both sides of the Atlantic were way behind the times. There had been little loss of life in the previous two decades. One source claims only eighty-two passengers out of over nine million lost their lives crossing the Atlantic in British ships during that time (Cox 47).

boat accommodation in proportion to her passenger accommodation than had the Titanic. The Laurentic's boat accommodation is in relatively the same proportion as that of the Adriatic, although she is in the White Star's Canadian trade, and therefore goes further north. The Canadian Pacific liner Empress of Britain is, in proportion to the life at stake, the best provided with boats of this representative group of five. Of her twenty-one boats, five are collapsible, as were four of the Titanic's. The sixteen boats carried on the Mauretania are all lifeboats. **18**

OTHER COMPANIES' ARRANGEMENTS.

The North Atlantic liner's passage is a comparatively short one. Liners in many other trades may also travel on routes that are well laid down, but these frequently involve the traversing of very long stretches of lonely sea. The circumstance may possibly affect the number of boats carried. Anyhow, whether we take vessels in the Australian, South African, or South American trade, the proportion of boat accommodation to the certified passenger and crew accommodation represents a much higher average.

The Royal Mail Steam Packet Company's Asturias has boats for 1,395 out of a possible maximum of 1,511 persons. The Union-Castle liner Balmoral Castle can carry 1,099 people, and has boats for all but seventy-one of them. The new P. and O. liner Medina, which does not carry third-class passengers is credited with twenty-three boats, and has a considerable margin of boat accommodation to spare. The new Orient liner could carry in her boats 972 out of 1,261, and the Aberdeen-White Star liner, which takes the Cape route to Australia, has boats for 1,023 people.

Inevitably, the moral seems to be that in the longer voyage trades the boat provision, although not wholly free from eccentricity, is much more generous than in the North Atlantic trade.

COMMITTEE'S SUGGESTIONS.

In his statement in the House of Commons yesterday with reference to the boat accommodation on the Titanic, Mr. Buxton referred to the report of the Merchant Shipping Advisory Committee on the subject of the boats carried on large liners, and added that the Board of Trade was not satisfied that the Committee's recommendations were adequate, and had referred the matter back for further consideration. Later in the day the right hon. gentleman issued the Committee's report, which has not hitherto been made public.

18. Individual shipbuilders had a remarkable amount of freedom as to how many lifeboats they put on their ships. The *Titanic*'s own builders had originally planned for thirty-two lifeboats but settled for twenty because Managing Director Ismay thought too many lifeboats might clutter up the looks of the ship. Perhaps in Ismay's mind the *Titanic* was more of a floating hotel than a mere ship.

In April of last year the Advisory Committee was asked by the Board of Trade to report with reference to the minimum number of lifeboats to be carried on vessels of 10,000 tons gross tonnage and upwards. The matter was carefully gone into by a sub-committee, and the following report was forwarded to the Board of Trade on July 4, 1911:

The Committee were asked to advise:

1. As to the manner in which the table in the appendix to the Life-Saving Appliances Rules should be extended so as to provide for vessels of tonnage up to 50,000 tons gross and upwards, and

2. As to whether Rule 12 should, or should not, be revised, so as to exempt altogether from the requirement of additional boats and (or) rafts those vessels which are divided into efficient watertight compartments to the satisfaction of the Board of Trade.

In considering these questions, we have had specially in mind the fact that the number of passengers carried does not necessarily increase in proportion to the increase in the tonnage of a vessel. This is particularly true in the case of vessels exceeding 10,000 tons—a type of vessel which is practically only built to provide special accommodation for large numbers of first and second class passengers.

Similarly, there is no fixed relation between the tonnage of vessels and the deck space available for the carrying of lifeboats under davits. Increase in the length of a vessel is only one of the factors, and often not the most material factor contributing to the increase in its tonnage, and it should also be remembered, in estimating the space available for the launching of lifeboats, that it is impossible to place davits forward of the bridge and very undesirable to have them on the quarters of the vessel.

We are strongly of opinion that every encouragement should be given to secure the provision of vessels which by their construction have been rendered as unsinkable as possible, and which are provided with efficient means for communicating with the shore or with other vessels in case of disaster.

RECOMMENDATIONS.

In view of these considerations we have agreed upon the following recommendations:

1. That it is questionable whether it is practicable to increase the number of davits.

2. That any increase in the number of lifeboats to be carried can probably be best effected by providing for the launching of further boats from the existing davits.

3. That the table should be extended in the manner indicated below:

1	2	3	4
Gross Tonnage.	Minimum number of boats to be placed und'r davits.	Minimum number of additional boats to be readily available for attachment to davits.	Total minimum cubic contents of boats required by Columns 2 and 3.
10,000 and under 12,000......	16	—	5,500
12,000 and under 20,000......	16	2	6,200
20,000 and under 35,000......	16	4	6,900
35,000 and under 45,000......	16	6	7,600
45,000 and upwards	16	8	8,300

It is further recommended that all passenger vessels of 10,000 tons gross tonnage and upwards should be required to be fitted with wireless telegraph apparatus.

4. That the rules should be amended so as to admit of decked lifeboats of an approved type being stowed on top of one another, or under an open lifeboat, subject to suitable arrangements being made for launching promptly the boats so stowed.

5. That the additional boats and rafts required under the provisions of Division (a) Class 1 (d) of the Life-Saving Appliances Rules shall be of at least such carrying capacity that they and the boats required by Columns 2 and 3 of the above table provide together three-fourths more than the minimum cubic contents required by Column 4 of that table.

6. That vessels divided into efficient water-tight compartments to the satisfaction of the Board of Trade should (provided they are fitted with wireless telegraphy apparatus) be exempt from the requirements of additional boats and (or) rafts. The committee suggest in this connection that the Board of Trade should review the requirements designed to attain the standards as to watertight compartments at present enforced by them under Rule 12, having regard to the developments of shipbuilding since the report of the Committee on the Spacing and Construction of Watertight Bulkheads.

WALL STREET.

◆

BIG RISE IN MARCONIS.

MARKETS STEADY.

From Our Financial Correspondent.

NEW YORK, Thursday.

The feeling of depression increases in financial circles as the Carpathia, bearing the Titanic's survivors, crawls to port beneath a shroud of fog. Even professional speculators are so appalled by the disaster that they remain in a state of stupor, and allow prices to drift aimlessly. The market is at half-mast, and will doubtless remain so until there is a rift in the gloom…

★ As yet under no pressure from the public or the papers, the Board of Trade relies on the concept of unsinkable construction as the main way to make passengers safe. The old hubris of Man over Nature remains. But the Board of Trade was not being entirely arbitrary. Lifeboats are useful only if they can be safely placed into the water. The scandal of the *Titanic* was that more boats could actually have been launched than were available because the sea was absolutely calm, a condition that was noted as extraordinarily rare. If the *Titanic* had struck the iceberg in rough weather, there would have been great difficulty in launching any boats. Wind would have made it more difficult to load the boats in the first place, and waves would have made it more likely for the boats themselves to take on water. The Board of Trade had no easy task in making recommendations about lifeboats.

International Mercantile Marines declined only slightly. The Common on small transactions broke 5 ⅛ to 4 ⅞, and Preferred 21 ½ to 20 ¼. The absurd report that the worst phase of the disaster was held back on Monday to allow insiders to raid Marine stocks was disproved by facts. Fewer than 10,000 shares of each class of stock were traded in during the first three days of the week, and only 3,000 shares were borrowed in loan, indicating that the short interest had been trivial.

The Titanic catastrophe called the attention of the public to the utility of wireless telegraphy to such an extent as further to augment the speculative craze for Marconi stocks. American Marconis, which several months ago were going a-begging at $2 a share, advanced to-day on the kerb from $170 a share to $220. Conservative brokers regard this as an absurd price in view of the company's earning potentialities under the best conditions…

ARRIVAL OF THE PARISIAN.

CAPTAIN'S STATEMENT.

HALIFAX, Wednesday.

The Allan liner Parisian arrived to-night with no news of the Titanic beyond what it obtained at second hand by cross-messages. Captain Hains declined to make a statement as to the purport of these messages, but gave other facts which he felt at liberty to disclose. An interesting thing, he said, was that at half-past ten on Sunday night his Marconi operator was in touch with the Titanic, and got that ship to relay a message via Cape Race to his owners. That message was forwarded by the Titanic.

The Parisian never heard the signal from the Titanic for help, the reason being that the operator, having been busy all day, had retired for the night. The Parisian, Californian, and Masaba had all been trying to pick up another steamer which was adrift without coal, but she was eventually picked up by the Asian from New York…—*Reuter's Special Service.*

WIDOWS AND ORPHANS.

STATE AND PRIVATE AID.

It is yet too early to enable any estimate to be made as to the number of widows and orphans of the crew of the Titanic

Conditions for buying Marconi stocks were only going to improve. Eventually, legislation passed on both sides of the Atlantic that required ships to carry Marconi operators around the clock, so the sets could be manned at all hours. Also, more types of ships were required to have sets than was previously the case before new laws went into effect. For a while Marconi enjoyed a practical monopoly that, while short-lived, was immensely profitable.

that have been left destitute by the appalling disaster in the Atlantic. So far as is known the ship carried a crew of 903, all told. Of these only the officers and men who manned the lifeboats were saved. The latest reports place the total of the sailors so employed at 163, leaving 740 who went down with their vessel. **19** The men saved will, as a matter of course, be almost entirely confined to men rated as able-bodied seamen, as practically none of the firemen, stewards, electricians, cooks, or other classes of the crew would be qualified for boat work, and would all be left on board. It is a tradition with the White Star Line to employ only the very highest class of British seamen, a fact which readily explains the splendid discipline that must have prevailed on board the lost Titanic when so large a proportion of women and children were saved. The other grades on board the company's ships are of an equally good type. It is evident that one and all were inspired by the highest degree of self-sacrifice, and it is the duty of the public to see that the dependents of these heroic men do not become destitute as the result of the courage and devotion displayed by them in the moment of trial. It is becoming a common argument in these days when an appeal is made for those who are bereaved by some great national calamity like the wreck of the Titanic, or a dreadful colliery explosion, that under recent legislation compensation is provided compulsorily at the expense of the employer, and a certain class of persons are unwilling to loose their purse-strings in consequence. Happily in the present distressing instance, which has deeply touched the public sentiment, this attitude is not so apparent. But at the same time, lest a mistaken notion should prevail as to the amount which the dependents of those who have given their lives for others are entitled to receive it is well to make the matter clear.

COMPENSATION ACT.

Under the Workmen's Compensation Act of 1906, the widows of seamen who are drowned are entitled to compensation. The terms of the Act and the decisions of the Courts have established this principle. Up to the present the sums awarded under the Act in such cases vary from about £250 to £300. It need hardly be pointed out how inadequate is this sum to provide for the wants of a widow and family whose breadwinner has been taken away. Even if the larger sum is awarded, and the whole of it invested at, say, 4 per cent—which is about the highest interest obtainable consistent with complete security—it will not allow the bereaved family more than 4s 7d per week, or barely enough to provide the very poorest class of lodging. Nothing will be left for food or clothing, and absolute destitution and starvation must be their lot. It seldom happens, however, that the compensation is awarded in one sum. The man is rare who has only one person dependent

---

19. The White Star Line list released on May 9, 1912 had 210 crew members surviving out of 908 (Eaton and Haas, *Titanic: Journey* 233).

upon him. When money is recovered under the Workmen's Compensation Act in case of death, it is paid into the county court. If the various claimants entitled to a share agree as to the distribution of the compensation, an order is made by the county court judge accordingly. But where the dependents of the deceased cannot agree, an arbitrator is appointed, and the money is allotted in accordance with his award. The matter is usually decided on the question of fact as to how far each claimant was dependent upon the deceased. In certain cases the amount awarded is paid over to the Public Trustee for administration, but these rarely arise in connection with claims on the death of seamen. The compensation, therefore, rarely reaches the widow or orphans intact. Law costs absorb a certain amount, and what is left is distributed as the judge or arbitrator may direct...

SURVIVORS OF THE TITANIC.

CARPATHIA ARRIVES IN NEW YORK HARBOUR.

VOYAGE DELAYED BY FOG.

DOCKING THIS MORNING.[20]

OFFICIAL PREPARATIONS.

NEW YORK, Thursday (7.50 p.m.)

The Carpathia reached the quarantine station at 7.30 this evening.—*Reuter*.

NEW YORK, April 18 (8.15 p.m.).

The Carpathia did not stop at the quarantine station. She continued her voyage up the bay, and should reach the pier within an hour—*Reuter*.

NEW YORK, Thursday.

The Carpathia docked at 8.27 p.m.— *Central News*.

The Duke of Connaught, Governor-General of Canada, has wired as follows to President Taft:

"I have delayed telegraphing to you in the hope that Major Butt (President Taft's Aide de Camp) might still be among the saved, but I fear that there is now no hope. Accept the expression of my deepest sympathy in this gallant officer's tragic end, and the loss to yourself of a devoted member of your staff. I also take the opportunity of assuring you of my heartfelt sympathy with the United States in the loss of so many of its citizens through the awful

---

20. To Londoners the ship docked on Friday morning, but Reuter's time is from New York. London time for the liner's arrival is 12:45 a.m., Friday.

catastrophe of the sinking of the Titanic.(Signed) ARTHUR."

His Royal Highness has also subscribed $500 to the fund for the relief of the sufferers.

Among the donors to the Mansion House Fund yesterday was the Princess Royal [Princess Louise], who forwarded £100...

It is now expected, according to a bulletin posted up in New York by the White Star officials last evening, that the Carpathia, conveying the survivors of the Titanic, will arrive at New York about 11.0 p.m. American time, or four o'clock this morning, London time. Fog, however, is always a factor to be reckoned with in New York Harbour, hence the vessel may not dock until even later.

Stringent precautions have been adopted by the authorities to secure the comfort of the unfortunate travellers, many of whom it is realised will be in a pitiable mental and physical condition. **21**

In the meantime there is still an entire absence of information as to the circumstances of the disaster, and the stories published in New York must be accepted with caution. The Carpathia made no reply to a message of inquiry from President Taft as to the fate of his aide-de-camp, Major Butt. **22**

★ **21.** The *Carpathia*'s passengers disembarked first, to get them out of the way. Then the reporters surged in on the survivors who were let off the boat last (Butler 172).

22. By the time this accusation came before the U.S. inquiry run by Senator Alden Smith, Captain Rostron of the *Carpathia* was in Gibraltar. He cabled: "...I did not forbid relaying message[s] to any ship...Only message I prevented sending were further press messages. I desire full investigation my actions" (*Titanic Reports* 33).

★ ★ ★ ★ ★ ★ ★

Clearly telegraphers Cottam and Bride were not trying to conceal names of the *Titanic* survivors. Therefore, the difficulties of their task must be kept in mind when evaluating their performance. Bride was in pain from frostbite to his feet through the whole ordeal, and neither

Rescued *Titanic* passengers aboard the *Carpathia*.

operator was able to get adequate sleep. Bride would have been in better shape if he had gotten into Collapsible B. Instead, he clung to it while still in the water until his feet were numb (Cox 86).

A rumour reached White House yesterday morning that the steamship Baltic had picked up 250 survivors of the Titanic disaster, but little credence is placed in this report.

A supplementary list of survivors, apparently including members of the crew and third-class passengers, was received by the White Star Line in London last night. It gives the names of 130 persons.

According to a statement in the House of Commons by Mr. Sydney Buxton, yesterday afternoon, the total number of persons on board was 2,208 when the Titanic left Queenstown. About 140 passengers embarked at Queenstown, making the total 2,350, or thereabouts.

A revised list of first and second class passengers issued last night gives 320 names. To these must be added 57 third-class passengers whose safety had previously been notified, and the 130 fresh names furnished yesterday. Hence the total of survivors whose names have heretofore been wired is 497, which leaves 1,853 to be accounted for.

CRAWLING IN A FOG.

—◆—

From Our Own Correspondent.

NEW YORK, Thursday Evening.

The Carpathia, delayed by fog, is creeping towards New York at a snail's pace, with apparently no chance of landing the Titanic's survivor's until early on Friday morning.

In the meantime, another day of mingled suspense and despair has nearly ended, with the disheartening probability that the roll of those rescued from the lost Titanic has been closed, and that the total may not be more than 705 persons, instead of the 868 indicated in previous marconigrams.

The last hope that the number of the saved might be increased with more complete knowledge vanished when the scout-cruiser Chester flashed ashore a wireless yesterday that she had been in communication with the Carpathia, and had learned that the rescue ship had no names to add to those already transmitted by means of the Olympic's relay.

The Carpathia was met at sea by little steamers, some with relatives and friends aboard, others with officials and reporters. Flags on every ship in port and outside the port are half-masted, and the little flotilla slowly steaming towards the city skyscrapers recalled a strangely weird funeral procession.

———

WAITING CROWDS.

———

Terrific scenes are anticipated on the landing-pier, where a big crowd of privileged people, mostly relatives and friends, is assembling. Outside is a long line of carriages and ambulances. The world's greatest sea tragedy has stirred all America, from the Atlantic to the Pacific, let alone New York, to the uttermost depths, and the police recognised from the first that the only method of preserving order when the Cunarder, with her burden of human agony, should warp alongside the pier, would be to issue passes only to those entitled to them. Tens of thousands applied for permits, but only a few hundreds were granted.

People of all ranks and conditions in life have assembled at the pier, but the first place will be given to the relatives, some of whom are dressed in deep mourning, who arrived several hours too early, weeping all the time.

Government officials from Washington, and Mr. Gaynor, the Mayor of New York, intend to be present at the Carpathia's arrival in their official capacity, and amongst the visitors to receive a permit was Mr. Henry Arthur Jones, **23** the English dramatist, who will describe the pathetic scene in *The Daily Telegraph*.

During the greater part of the day the Carpathia's wireless apparatus has spoken with the shore, indicating the probable time of arrival, but in view of the approaching disembarkation of the very people who had so recently looked death in the face, and who would soon tell a story of unprecedented tragedy in their own words, these details attracted only the smallest attention. As a rule reporters here board the liners in harbour, and interview the passengers before they land. In this case, however, the port authorities, desiring to show national respect to the sufferers, refused them permission to board the Cunarder in harbour or at sea, and they also waived the right of the Customs for the examination of passengers. It was felt that a Customs examination, in view of the fact that the majority of the Titanic's rescued had escaped only in the clothes

they were wearing at the time of the catastrophe, and that some were only in their night-robes, with overcoats hastily donned would have been a sorry farce indeed, and if any stricken passenger possessed dutiable articles in his pocket, it was held that he would surely be entitled to keep the same as a sad souvenir of an awful experience without paying the usual financial tribute to the Treasury. **24**

MEETING THE CARPATHIA.

American reporters are not easily repressed, and they chartered a boat, in fact, several boats, which put forth to sea in the early hours of a most dismal and rainy morning, and met the Carpathia as she slowed down on the last lap of the sad journey preparatory to threading the path through the long and narrow channel which leads into New York Harbour, some hours distant. It was dusk then, and very raw and cheerless, but the lights on the steerage deck showed silent, pathetic groups, chiefly of women, who had come up from their cabins to obtain a glimpse of the distant glare reflected in the sky, indicating the myriad illuminations of New York City.

One little craft, with the New York interviewers aboard, pegged alongside the liner with the evident intention of landing

---

23. Jones was one of the leading lights of the London theater, and it was thought that only his skilled dramatic talents could do justice to the *Titanic*'s story.

24. Normally, all immigrants would be checked for contraband, disease, and for complete documentation.

its occupants aboard the Carpathia, but the liner refused permission, and the interviewers, seeing the risk of shipwreck involved by the suction of the vessel, and the mighty wash from her propellers, finally desisted. The passengers on deck were too preoccupied to answer questions bawled through megaphones. "Wait till we land," was the reply usually vouchsafed in reproachful tones...

A GLOOMY SHIP.

Slowly, and with her speed continually decreasing as New York came nearer, the Carpathia advanced to port. The reporters refrained from the futile task of hurling questions at the silent and sorrowful ship, and were soon left behind in the gloom. They lingered long enough, however, to see the rescuing ship before the rest of New York, and also to see the weeping and sobbing women on deck.

Some of the Carpathia's saloon passengers had left the upper deck, and were visiting the disconsolate steerage passengers from the Titanic. To some, however, who had lost their husbands, and others who had lost brothers or children, human consolation just then seemed little worth while. One had a glimpse of a richly-clad lady trying to cheer up a poor stricken woman from the Titanic with words of sympathy, and herself breaking down and sobbing.

Strangers in a strange land, it is hard for emigrants to disembark at New York cheerfully at the best of times, and the sorrows of the Titanic's rescued passengers had accumulated beyond measure. Men who saw the Slocum burn to the water's edge in the East River, New York, and heard the cries of burning women and children were present in the newspaper boat at the meeting with the Carpathia at sea to-day, and the first glance of the stricken people on the lower deck revived the same pangs of anguish and feelings of helpless commiseration. One consolation remains. New York has risen to the emergency in a manly way, and the survivors of all ranks will find themselves amongst a host of earnest friends and generous helpers as soon as they put foot on American soil.

That the Carpathia is practically a hospital ship is indicated by the scraps of information caught indirectly by the wireless operator at Norfolk, Virginia, early to-day. Some 175 women rescued from the Titanic, according to the report, are confined to their cabins, and had not left the same since they were picked up frantic terror-stricken, and suffering from exposure in the Titanic's lifeboats. Many of the survivors were in an hysterical state from being bereft of their husbands or other loved ones, and were constantly under the care of the ship's surgeons, some in delirium, while others had not recovered from the rigours of eight hours **25** in the lifeboats on a cold and foggy sea. Cases of pneumonia are mentioned, and children lying almost at death's-door.

★ **25.** Eight hours would have been about the longest that any survivor would have had to have been in a lifeboat (Lord, *A Night* 176).

DELAYED MARCONIGRAMS.

The Cunard officials here are rather confused regarding the best possible decisions under all the circumstances. They are being assailed on all sides for not allowing a complete account to be wirelessed here long before the arrival of the Carpathia, but the private necessities of the survivors and their friends come first, and the two operators aboard the Cunarder are quite unable to cope with the enormous burden of the messages. Early to-day thousands of Marconigrams addressed to the Carpathia since Monday were still undelivered, and probably will not be read by the addressees until they are handed to them at the landing-pier late to-night.

One of the scout cruisers reported to Washington that the Carpathia had failed to answer the request for information sent by President Taft, and if this proves to be true there will be trouble for someone to-morrow.

Newspaper proprietors with expensive arrangements made to handle the first wirelessed account received here, and, with tugs chartered and equipped for the purpose, were in a state of exasperation all yesterday, and at the time of cabling this afternoon they are still fuming. On behalf of *The Daily Telegraph* I have co-operated with others in chartering a wireless tug of the ocean-going variety to intercept the Carpathia before her arrival, but if the distracted operators, acting probably on the principle of "a square deal for everyone and no preference," declined, as is alleged, to answer Mr. Taft's question relating to the fate of his missing aide-de-camp, Major Butt, to whom the President was deeply attached, the prospect of others, it was thought, was not cheerful. 26

THE WIRELESS SCANDAL.

Notwithstanding the plea to amateur Marconigraphers to suspend their scientific amusements as the Cunarder approaches port and allow the liner every preference in the way of air waves, there has been disturbance by irresponsible operators all day, and another lesson, in fact, has been taught the Government regarding the necessity of regulating wireless telegraphy, as is done in England. It

26. Cottam and Bride could not have imagined the intensity of interest that had built up around the *Titanic* story. After sending out the list of survivors and numerous messages from survivors to waiting family members, what more could they have relayed to President Taft other than that Archibald Butt was, indeed, dead? He may have been important; he may have been the president's advisor; but he did not make the survivors' list, and there was nothing more to say about him. Some papers reported that Major Butt behaved heroically in his last hours, but virtually all news reports were inconsistent as to what, if anything, he actually did. It is just possible that the major retired to the saloon to calmly await his fate as so many other men did (Marcus 285).

is believed that the Carpathia probably would have sent a story shortly after midnight yesterday, telling the essential details of the world's greatest marine disaster, but for the apprehension that the messages would, on account of interruptions, be distorted and confused, perhaps even meaningless, and this fear, we know, has already been abundantly justified by actual occurrences.

"UNJUST REPORTS."

At the offices of the White Star Line, the vice-president, Mr. [Philip A. S.] Franklin, was much disturbed because of the insistent reports that the White Star agents knew of the sinking of the Titanic many hours before they allowed the news to become public. In most emphatic terms Mr. Franklin declared that such reports were unqualifiedly false and unjust, and he begged *The Daily Telegraph* to impress the force of his denial upon the public on your side of the Atlantic. Still the rumours would not be allayed, and Mr. Franklin was at last informed that a minor official of the Cunard Line, whose name I refrain from mentioning, told several newspaper men that the sinking of the Titanic was known at New York as early as ten o'clock on Monday morning, though it was not announced at the White Star offices until seven o'clock that evening. Mr. Franklin asked the general agent, Mr. Sumner, of the Cunard Line, to send the official indicated to his office.

There reporters confronted the minor official, and, with pale face and trembling lips, he admitted that he told the newspaper men that the sinking of the ship was known, but denied that he said or intimated that the White Star officials knew it.

"A very close friend of mine whose name I cannot reveal, a man of high standing in the business world," he said, "told me on Tuesday morning that at ten o'clock on Monday he received definite word that the Titanic had sunk several hours before. I asked him if he knew that the information was authentic, and he said he did. Because of his standing and of his affiliations, I had, and still have, every reason to believe that he spoke the truth, and so I told these gentlemen," pointing to the reporters. "But I did not say that the White Star line knew it. My friend is not connected with the line," added the man hurriedly, while Mr. Franklin transfixed him with a glare. "I would not think of saying that the White Star line deceived the public." **27**

I am able to say that from the time the Carpathia rescued the survivors until late this afternoon practically nothing has come from the Cunarder relating to

27. Franklin testified at the American inquiry that he did not receive direct telegraphic information that the *Titanic* had sunk until about 6:30 in the evening of April 15. Before that time all had been mere rumor and conjecture. But Franklin had received information from an unknown reporter from the Associated Press that the *Titanic* might be in trouble as early as 2:00 a.m., New York time. Yet for all that time in suspense, he still couldn't bring himself to believe that the "unsinkable" ship was in danger (Kuntz 110–20).

the precise details of the accident, and that her wireless dealt almost exclusively with the names and corrections of names. By the time this despatch is printed in London the man will have a chance of giving the official version before the Congressional Committee of Inquiry…

CROWDED BOATS AND LIFE-RAFTS.

It is believed by American shipping men that there are enough indications from the start to warrant the assumption that not only every lifeboat, but every raft, from the Titanic was crowded before the crumpled Leviathan sank to her grave, and that undoubtedly the liner went down bow first. **28** Scores are believed to have been injured, either in entering the lifeboats or by mishaps on the sinking Titanic before the boats were swung out for launching.

Another story, purporting to be wireless news from the Carpathia, last night, says that after the crash the officers of the Titanic refused to believe that the vessel could sink, and that the first wireless distress call sent out was merely a precautionary measure. When the menace became apparent, the boats

were launched, and in the rush for them many held back to save the boats being swamped. When the passengers rushed on deck, about equal proportions were in evening gowns and in the utmost negligée. The boats were endangered by a choppy sea, which continually drenched the occupants. **29** The temperature was freezing, and the hands of four or five members of the crew who manned the small boats were numbed with cold. The Titanic, by this account, slid up on the ice, and buckled amidships after the crash. **30**

Much had been expected in the way of news from the scout-cruisers Chester and Salem, which started at full speed for the Carpathia's wireless zone on Tuesday night, hurrying at twenty-four-knot speed. The Chester reached out with her powerful wireless for the Cunard liner. The shore stations heard the cruiser's insistent call. A perfect storm of messages troubled the air, and blotted out the possibility of the Marconi people connecting with the Carpathia.

The Chester finally succeeded in establishing communication with the liner about 8.30 o'clock last evening. When this was known the Marconi Company sent orders to have all commercial messages stopped, in order to enable the Carpathia to get news through.

28. For the sake of clarity, the term "raft" and the term "collapsible" refer to the same type of boat so far as the *Titanic* was concerned.

29. This is not accurate. Testimony from both American and British inquiries established that the ocean was unusually calm (Kuntz 47).

30. The *Titanic* hit the iceberg a glancing blow near the bow on the starboard side and did not slide up on the iceberg at all (Marcus 129).

WIRELESS CHAOS.

The captain of the cruiser asked for a full list of the Titanic's survivors, and then for such information as would throw light on the disaster. At the Boston Navy Yard the wireless operator heard the Carpathia tell the cruiser to "keep out," that she would not work with the Chester, but only with the station at Siasconsett. **31** Landward came the disappointing news that the Carpathia was telling none of the secrets of the Titanic's loss. The Chester kept trying, as the Marconi people discovered when they tried to talk with the Carpathia, and the cruiser's waves blocked their efforts to listen to what the Carpathia was endeavouring to say to the Siasconsett station. The Chester then relayed to the Salem, which was nearer shore, four messages to the Carpathia, but on account of the atmospheric conditions they could not be made out ashore.

If the complete list of first and second cabin passengers has been made known there remains to be told a story of woman's devotion perhaps unparalleled, for the list now here does not contain the names of seventy-eight women who are known to have been in the first and second cabins. Thirty-eight of this number were first-class passengers and forty second-class. The omission of their names means that most likely seventy-eight women chose rather to perish with husband, father, or brother than part from them in their last earthly moments. **32**

Little could be gleaned about the message that the Leyland liner Californian, due at Boston to-day, had been to the scene of the wreck and picked up some of the bodies of the drowned.

HEROES OF THE TITANIC.

◆

PUBLIC APPEAL.

THE DAILY TELEGRAPH FUND FOR THE WIDOWS & ORPHANS.

---

31. Strong rivalries did exist among wireless companies, and Marconi operators did not always cooperate with the competition. It is quite possible that both Cottam and Bride were simply acting as company men. Testimony to the U.S. Senate Inquiry does not clarify whether they had made their exclusive arrangement with the *New York Times* before or after their contact with the *Chester*, but the deal with the *Times* seems to have come after the *Chester* incident (Kuntz 245).

32. By one counting, the approximate number of first- and second-class women who were lost stands at only sixteen (Lord, *A Night* 189–98). Actually, an amazing 97 percent of first-class women survived. Eighty-six percent of second-class women survived (British Parliamentary 42).

MAGNIFICENT RESPONSE

———

£2,659 : 1s. : 8d.
IN
TWO DAYS.

———

RELIEF WORK STARTS
THIS MORNING.

———

The generosity of the readers of *The Daily Telegraph* has often made history—private history, that is, in thousands of sorrowing and anxious homes. It is doing again to-day service which will long be remembered in the annals of the poor. The second day's contribution to our Fund for the relief of those dependent upon the men who died at their posts on the Titanic amounts to £1,507 15s 11d, upwards of £350 more than the amount collected on the first day.

Our correspondence to-day shows still further how deep and widespread—and how practical—is the sympathy with the bereaved families of the crew of the lost liner. Letters reach us from all classes—including sailors—enclosing contributions, and making suggestions for meeting the needs of the bereaved...

———

ATLANTIC
TRACKS.

◆

CHANGES OF ROUTE.

OFFICIAL EXPLANATION.

———

From Our Own Correspondent.

LIVERPOOL, Thursday.

From an authoritative source, and with a view to removing some misapprehension in the public mind as to the tracks followed by the great Atlantic liners, I have been supplied with the following statement:

"These tracks have been in vogue for many years now, and were arranged by agreement between the various Atlantic lines after very careful thought and study, and with a view to the safe navigation of their steamers.

"Liners bound to America proceed on one track, while, with the object of avoiding collisions, steamers homeward bound from America proceed on a track to the southward of the outward one, the maximum distance between them being fifty to sixty miles.

"There are two sets of tracks in operation, covering two distinct periods of the year. From August to January, which is the period of the year when that part of the Atlantic is free from ice, and navigation is not impeded, the shorter, or northerly, track is followed.

"Between January and August, when it is usual for ice to come down from the northerly latitudes, a change of route is made, a track being steered between 200 and 300 miles south of the more northerly track, and calculated to take the steamers well clear of ice floes or bergs. This season ice has made its appearance in the Atlantic much earlier than was expected, and is consequently being directed further to the southward than usual. To avoid altogether the possibility of their steamers meeting ice, the Atlantic lines have decided that their steamers shall take a course which is still more southerly, and where the chances of ice being seen are reduced to an absolute minimum.

"This is the change which was indicated in the Press a couple of days ago, but possibly the general public hardly realise from the technical description of the positions mentioned the steps which the Atlantic lines had taken. It has always been a cardinal feature of the policy of the Atlantic companies to keep the captains of their steamers fully and promptly posted of any obstructions observed on the tracks. This has been greatly facilitated since the introduction of wireless telegraphy. In addition, the commanders of all liners are constantly exchanging information by the Marconi system as to obstructions of any kind which may be observed, and the travelling public may rely upon it that no question receives closer attention from the steamship companies. It is considered desirable to make this explanation with the view of reassuring intending passengers who may not be quite clear as to the present situation. The observance of the tracks is strictly enforced, the paramount object being to ensure at all times the safe navigation of the liners, regardless of distance." **33**

With reference to previous announcements as to changes in the tracks in the Atlantic, the Cunard Line and other lines announce a still further amendment in the west-bound track, which will come into force right away. All the steamers at present on their way to America will now take the course which will place them quite clear of ice. As far as homeward steamers are concerned, their track is much to the south of the outward track, and does not take them anywhere near the ice regions.

MR. ISMAY'S ORDER.

NEW YORK, Thursday.

Mr. Bruce Ismay has sent a wireless message from the Carpathia signed "Yamsi," **34** instructing the White Star officials here to postpone the departure of the s.s. Cedric until to-morrow, in

---

33. Hence, all the more mystery as to why the *Titanic* should have taken so little notice of numerous iceberg warnings received the day of the collision (Howells 22). Claims that the freighter *Rappahannock* even signaled a warning to the *Titanic* by Morse lamp have never been substantiated. The captain of the *Rappahannock* did make such a claim, but only some fifty years after U.S. and British investigations (*Encyclopedia* message board).

34. Code name: Ismay spelled backward.

order that she may take the survivors of the Titanic's crew. **35**

Mr. Franklin, the vice-president of the International Mercantile Marine Company, has authorised the following announcement: "The Cedric will sail as scheduled, at noon to-day."

The following wireless message was picked up from the Carpathia early this morning, addressed to "Islfrank, New York" (probably the White Star Line):

"Send responsible ship's officer fourteen White Star sailors on two tugs take charge thirteen Titanic's boats at quarantine.—(Signed) Yamsi" (probably Ismay).—*Reuter.*

SENATE'S INQUIRY.

—◆—

COMMITTEE APPOINTED.

WASHINGTON, Wednesday.

Mr. Martine introduced a resolution in the Senate to-day to the effect that President Taft be advised that the Senate would favour treaties with maritime nations to regulate the safety of ocean craft and passengers and crews. **36**

Mr. Perkins presented a resolution providing for the equipment of steamers with adequate life-saving apparatus, so that every steamer shall have a sufficient number of seaworthy lifeboats to carry "at one time every passenger and every member of the crew," the same to be certified in the presence of a Federal inspector before any vessel be allowed to clear from any American port.—*Reuter.*

WASHINGTON, Thursday.

The sombre task of investigating the Titanic wreck began to-day in the Senate. **37** The Commerce Committee has appointed a sub-committee of seven to take testimony. The committee, of which Mr. William Alden Smith, Senator for Michigan, is chairman, will leave immediately for New York, accompanied by the Sergeant-at-Arms of the Senate, to procure witnesses.

Mr. Ismay will be among the first asked to give evidence.

Much comment has been aroused here by the curt acknowledgements received

---

35. Bruce Ismay, managing director of the White Star Line, may have been trying to escape back to England in order not to appear at American hearings, or he may have been thinking, perhaps uncharacteristically, about the crew, which had become suddenly unemployed on the sinking of their ship (Kuntz xvii–xviii).

36. Here the British shipping industry is enduring the sting of United States' criticism. The implication was that maybe America should take the lead in reforming safety regulations and shipping law in the face of a British failure.

37. The U.S. Senate had a legitimate concern in the matter of the *Titanic*'s sinking. The ship was, after all, American owned. Therefore, liability issues needed to be resolved in America as well as in Britain, where the ship was built.

from the Carpathia in response to messages from Government officials, including President Taft, transmitted through the war vessels Salem and Chester, and by the refusal to reply to the requests for information conveyed in them.

Whether the responsibility rests with the Captain of the Carpathia or with Mr. Bruce Ismay, the chairman of the White Star Line, who is reported to be among the survivors on board, is a matter of conjecture, and the officials of the Navy Department are accordingly withholding judgment upon the matter. Naval officials, however, indignantly reject the insinuation that the naval wireless operators are not handling messages with due celerity.

A joint investigation, in which both the Senate and House of Representatives would be represented, is favoured by Mr. Alexander, chairman of the House Committee for the Merchant Marine, and a suggestion for such an investigation will be made. Meanwhile, Mr. Alexander has presented to the House a joint resolution proposing a conference to "consider uniform laws and regulations for merchant vessels at sea," the subjects specified for discussion to include regulations in regard to the efficiency of crews, the construction of vessels, the equipment of lifeboats, wireless apparatus, searchlights, submarine bells, and life-saving and fire-extinguishing apparatus. While the Titanic never entered an American port, the investigation is expected to show the extent to which other great lines meet the American safety regulations. Many members of Congress are openly opposed to the idea of holding an investigation into the disaster.

Mr. MacVeagh, Secretary of the Treasury, has instructed a revenue cutter to take the Senate Committee of Investigation out to the Carpathia tonight. The Carpathia will be stopped by the Customs officers and the committee set on board before the vessel reaches port. She will then be within American Customs jurisdiction, and authority to stop her is lodged in the Secretary of the Treasury.—*Reuter.* **38**▸

★▸ **38.** In fact, Chairman Smith was content to arrive by train at dockside and there secure Ismay's and the White Star Line's cooperation for the investigation (Kuntz xviii).

★ ★

British naval historian Geoffrey Marcus writes: "William Alden Smith was a man of humble origins, who, starting his political career as a page-boy in the Michigan House of Representatives, had arrived in the Senate by way of the bar and the lower House." Bryce (British Ambassador to America) described him in a dispatch to Sir Edward Gray (British Secretary for Foreign Affairs) as "one of the most unsuitable persons who could have been charged with an investigation of this nature" (Marcus 211). Bryce's chief concern may have been over Smith's utter ignorance of naval matters. He once asked a *Titanic* officer what an iceberg was made of. Fifth Officer Harold Lowe's droll reply: "Ice."

Ignorant of naval procedure and terminology Smith was. An ignoramus he was not. At the conclusion of his U.S. hearings, all the following committee recommendations were passed into law:

— Passenger ships must carry enough lifeboats to accommodate every passenger and crew member.
— At least four members of the ship's crew, "skilled in handling boats," should be assigned to each lifeboat.
— Lifeboat drills should be practiced at least twice a month and entered into the ship's logbook.
— Ocean steamships carrying more than one hundred passengers should carry two electric searchlights.

Additional requirements were also passed and the freewheeling approach that had applied to oceangoing safety came to an end (*Titanic Reports* 35–6).

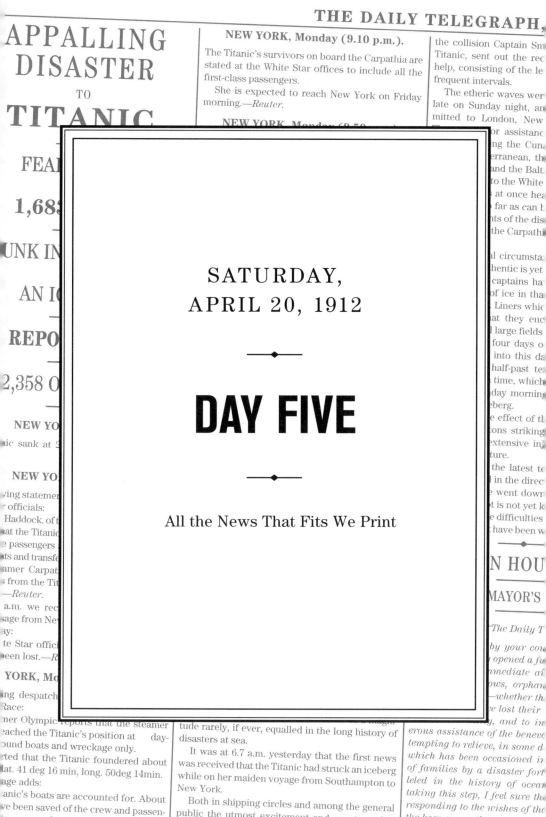

APPALLING DISASTER

TO

TITANIC

FEAR

1,685

UNK IN

AN IC

REPO

2,358 O

NEW YO

ic sank at 2

NEW YO

ving statemer
officials:
Haddock, of t
at the Titanic
e passengers
ts and transfe
amer Carpat
s from the Tit
—*Reuter.*
a.m. we rec
sage from Ne
ay:
te Star offic
een lost.—*R*

YORK, Mc

ing despatch
Race:
ner Olympic reports that the steamer
eached the Titanic's position at day-
ound boats and wreckage only.
rted that the Titanic foundered about
at. 41 deg 16 min, long. 50deg 14min.
age adds:
anic's boats are accounted for. About
ve been saved of the crew and passen-
er are nearly all women and children.
nd Liner California is remaining and
e vicinity of the disaster

NEW YORK, Monday (9.10 p.m.).

The Titanic's survivors on board the Carpathia are
stated at the White Star offices to include all the
first-class passengers.

She is expected to reach New York on Friday
morning.—*Reuter.*

NEW YORK, Monday (9.50

tude rarely, if ever, equalled in the long history of
disasters at sea.

It was at 6.7 a.m. yesterday that the first news
was received that the Titanic had struck an iceberg
while on her maiden voyage from Southampton to
New York.

Both in shipping circles and among the general
public the utmost excitement and consternation
were caused.

As has happened on several previous occa-

the collision Captain Sm
Titanic, sent out the rec
help, consisting of the le
frequent intervals.

The etheric waves wer
late on Sunday night, an
mitted to London, New
or assistanc
ing the Cun
erranean, th
and the Balt
to the White
at once hea
far as can b
ts of the dis
the Carpathi

l circumsta
hentic is yet
captains ha
of ice in tha
Liners whic
at they enc
l large fields
four days o
into this da
half-past te
time, which
day mornin
eberg.
e effect of tl
ons striking
extensive in
ture.
the latest te
l in the direc
e went down
t is not yet k
e difficulties
have been w

N HOU

MAYOR'S

The Daily T

by your cou
opened a fu
mmediate ai
ows, orphan
—whether th
e lost their
y, and to in
erous assistance of the benevo
tempting to relieve, in some d
which has been occasioned in
of families by a disaster fort
leled in the history of ocean
taking this step, I feel sure the
responding to the wishes of the
the keen sympathy universally
entertained for those who ha
been plunged into misery an

SATURDAY,
APRIL 20, 1912

DAY FIVE

All the News That Fits We Print

INTRODUCTION

———◆———

IF EVER THERE WAS A PANIC CONNECTED TO THE SINKING OF the *Titanic*, it came the day the rescue ship *Carpathia* arrived in New York Harbor. Deadline-driven reporters were panicked by the thought that they might miss the scoop of their lives and left no survivor uninterrupted in his or her grief. The sinking of the *Titanic* was the greatest story of the new century, and it would be a crime not to make one's mark by getting the best stories possible at the scene of the docking. It was a time of very creative storytelling by reporters overwhelmed by the dramatic possibilities of this once-in-a-lifetime moment.

For passengers, too, there was a kind of pressure—but not a pressure to get attention. Male passengers found themselves having to justify how they had survived, when "women-and-children-first" orders had purportedly gone out, and reports indicated that women and children made up the bulk of those saved. This theme had been so drummed into the public consciousness that there was genuine consternation when survivors' lists began showing that 48 percent of those saved had been men. How could these men justify their selfishness and good fortune?

On the other hand, even surviving women weren't safe from scrutiny. Some of them had supposedly gone mad. Where were these mad women? Why hadn't more women stayed loyally with their husbands on deck, as Mrs. Isidor Straus had done? Some suffragettes were ashamed at women who had taken to the boats *first*. And why hadn't both men and women done more to rescue those floating and freezing in the water?

The collective situation for both survivors and news gatherers was, by way of mitigation, unprecedented, and there were several limitations under which they were operating. Reporters had to take down their stories using longhand, either with the unreliable fountain pen or the faint lead pencil. Lighting had to have been bad and the noise excessive at the pier, since the *Carpathia* hadn't docked until Thursday evening. And the press would have had to deal with Captain Rostron's deep antipathy toward them. He was a man concerned for passenger welfare only; the press was too willing to intrude and make its reputation on private grief. In fact, he was so concerned for the survivors that he let them depart last, so they wouldn't immediately be besieged by eager reporters.

As for the survivors, they had already endured several days at sea as they sailed for New York. They were fretful and impatient to return to a normal life. They had shared their stories among themselves. Now, who could quite remember who had seen what firsthand or had only heard about it? What had been present experience, freshly remembered, now became mingled with the words and expressions used by others.

The most glaring of survivor inaccuracies are noted in this chapter, and explanatory comments are provided to clarify what actually happened when it is known for a fact that an account is wrong or improbable. The day's accounts do not read all that tidily because a wreck at sea is not a tidy story. There had been some 190 feet separating the first and last lifeboats on either side of the ship. Because there was no moon to provide visibility, it is a wonder the survivors' tales aren't more convoluted than they are.

Hence, the immortal Captain Smith is reported to be all over the ship and in several different places in the water after the *Titanic* sank. The fact is, many people loved Captain Smith and wanted to tell some heroic story about him, but to this day investigators are unsure of what happened to him and how he met his end.

So some mysteries concerning the events of that "night to remember" will always remain mysteries, not because the real truth can't be told, but because the real truth can't be known.

SUMMARY.

Yesterday, after a most agonising suspense of four days, details of the loss of the Titanic were received.

The Carpathia, with 705 survivors, arrived at New York in the early hours of the morning.

It now appears that there were 1,400 passengers on board the Titanic. The crew numbered 940, making a total of 2,340 persons. **1**

On a clear starlight night, the monster liner going, it is alleged, at full speed, struck an iceberg[.]

A great hole was made on the starboard side below the waterline.

Two hours and forty-five minutes later the Titanic sank, going down head first.

With a view to allaying panic, Captain Smith ordered the ship's band to muster, "rag time," tunes being played.

Meanwhile the wireless operator, J. Phillips, was despatching the danger signals "C.Q.D." and then "S.O.S." in every direction.

Up to the last moment the loud buzzing of the sending instrument was heard by the occupants of the boats.

All accounts agree that throughout, except for some disturbances among the steerage passengers, there was no signs of panic. **2**

"Woman and children first" was the order. **3** Many of the men who were saved were picked up by the lifeboats after the Titanic had gone down.

Mr. Bride, assistant Marconi operator on the Titanic, gives a graphic description of the way his colleague remained

1. Stowaways on board the ship make a definitive count impossible. Hardly any two books agree on this issue. The *Encyclopedia-Titanica* website lists 2,207 passengers on the liner with 712 being saved.

2. Few steerage passengers ever made it to a place where they could be seen to cause panic. They died inside the ship or on the stern as the ship went down, bow first (Lord, *A Night* 133–34).

3. On the port side only. Officer Murdoch let men into the lifeboats on the starboard side. It was women and children first, then men if there was room (Lord, *A Night* 45).

A *Titanic* lifeboat is hoisted aboard the *Carpathia*.

at his post long after the captain had advised the rest of the passengers and crew to look after themselves.

Many of the survivors state that as the Titanic sank the band was rendering "Nearer, my God, to Thee." **4**

The story that Captain Smith committed suicide before the lifeboats were launched is denied by survivors.

Lady Duff-Gordon, who was in one of the last boats to leave, describes how the captain shot a "boat-rusher." **5**

The Daily Telegraph Fund in aid of the dependents of the crew, amounts to £5,777, £3,118, having been received during the day.

———◆———

From an Unsigned Editorial.

———

Yesterday, when the Carpathia reached New York, carrying the survivors from the Titanic, the first authentic news of the terrible disaster was divulged to a thrilled and expectant world. Little by little, from the incidents as told by the survivors, the various details of the tremendous tragedy are being pieced together. We do not yet know the whole of the story, but what we have learnt provides materials for one of the most stupendous records of mingled heroism and agony which the pages of history have to show. We cannot dissociate the two elements which were inseparable in the tragedy itself. There is the awful, prolonged tension and terror, where every minute, as it passed on leaden feet, seemed to be an hour to overburdened nerves; and, side by side with this, the cool, indomitable patience, the unflinching valour, the unconquerable spirit of man. Long ago we were certain that whatever records leapt to light, the memories of the victims of one of the supreme disasters in our modern world would not be shamed; and every fresh piece of news, as it is communicated to the wires, give us additional facts to show that, however crushed by the overwhelming powers of Nature, man can still confront his doom with calm eyes and a heart that never falters. Amidst all the horror and pathos, the enormous loss of life, the misery of those who went down with the ill-fated ship, the possibly greater misery of those who survive, there rings one clear note of triumph,

4. Many survivors denied this reported incident ever happened. Colonel Archibald Gracie, who was on the boat deck to the very end, stated emphatically that no such hymn was played as it would have caused panic. The colonel swam free from the ship and joined Second Officer Lightoller on overturned Collapsible B (Gracie 20).

5. Lady Duff-Gordon was in one of the first boats to leave and was in no position to see the captain. Indeed, her testimony before the British Wreck Commission is vague and riddled with inconsistency. She seems to have suffered a nervous collapse ("British Wreck" Day 11).

which remains as a proud boast for us, who belong to the same race as the sufferers—the discovery that, when the trial comes, human nerves and human courage are equal to the test, and that men and women confronted with the supreme peril of their fate do not disgrace their native worth. It is, doubtless, well that we should be reminded now and again, in the long struggle which we wage with the grandiose, inhuman forces of Nature, that while brute strength prevails to dash into misery and oblivion all our highest hopes, there is something more unconquerable still in the dauntless spirit of our common human race.

Rarely, perhaps, has a more piteous history been unrolled before our eyes. Some of the scenes burn themselves into our imagination with unforgettable strength, as though, indeed, we were not merely readers of a narrative telegraphed to us from the ends of the earth, but were actual eye-witnesses of, or even participants in, the appalling catastrophe. There is the usual daily and nightly round of ordinary amusements going on in a floating hotel, which harbours two thousand souls. Upon them falls the first rude stroke of Destiny— the shock, the scattering of the ice on the decks, the sudden stopping of the engines. For a moment or two no one realises what has occurred. It is impossible to conceive that so well-built a ship— practically unsinkable, as its designers proudly boasted—could possibly suffer any harm, whatever the dangers with

which it was encompassed. The half-interrupted avocations were resumed. Men and women return to their cabins, almost reassured. And then slowly there passes throughout the ship the ghastly whisper that the evil is something more than had been supposed. The whole of the fore part of the vessel seems to be slowly settling down into the waters. There is a feeling that the slippery decks no longer can be trusted for safety. Each traveller looks his neighbor in the face, and wonders whether the maiden voyage of the Titanic is ever to be realised. Soon uncertainty is dispelled by the quick order to man the lifeboats...First, all the women and children are stowed in the boats—no, not all, for some of the wives refuse to leave their husbands, feeling that personal safety is too dearly purchased by the loss of all they hold most dear. One by one the boats put off from the side of the doomed vessel. Now and again some man finds a place, not because he has pushed his way there, but because his turn had come. **6** And there are left on board only those for whom no further room can be found—a thousand heroes waiting for the end. And what are the last scenes imprinted on the brain of the few hundred who are slowly rowed away in the darkness? There is, first, the picture of Captain Smith, alone on the bridge, washed off once and swimming back again, now standing with arms folded, facing the inevitable doom. The captain of the vessel saw his destiny, and confronted the

6. The *Daily Telegraph* has not yet begun to deal with the fact that an astonishing 48 percent of the survivors were men, and many of those men will spend the rest of their lives trying to justify how they survived when so many others were lost.

oncoming figure of Death without fear. Then across that cold waste of waters, strewn with the treacherous floes of ice, and full of deadly peril for the frail boats thus cast adrift, there came the sound of the ship's band playing the last requiem for the souls that were rendering up their account to their Maker—"Nearer, my God, to Thee!" The pity and pathos of it is almost more than human heart can bear…We cannot get out of our heads the short, sharp silhouettes which the telegraph wires have revealed to us— the husband bidding his wife goodbye, and telling her that they would meet in New York; the wife resolved to stay by her husband's side; a derelict child suddenly found, and handed down to one of the last boats to leave the side of the vessel; the chief officers of the ship doing all the tasks that their position demanded with inimitable calmness; here and there one or two passengers themselves helping in the work of discipline, although they knew that their last hour had come; the noble end of the Marconi operator; the captain standing proudly alone before he rendered up his life to the hungry waves. Nor ought we to forget how these stories will be received in our English seaports, and especially in

Southampton, whence most of the crew came—how many widows there are there, how many fatherless children, for whose sake we are organising *The Daily Telegraph* Fund, which has already been so magnificently responded to by the public. In a disaster which affects them alike in common, the two nations, the English and the American, join hands, for we have both been bereft of lives we could ill spare; men and women who have proved themselves to be some of the noblest of our race. Nevertheless, we have no mind to end on a note of despair. However miserable the loss of life, however awful the last agony of the doomed Titanic, we still cherish the impression of human strength and courage, the splendid audacity of human souls who know that they are something higher and better than all the material forces of the natural world. We are proud to read how they, having done their duty to the utmost of their power, consign themselves, with sublime confidence, into the hands of that Providence who, though we cannot understand all the complicated patterns of His design, ordereth, in His inscrutable wisdom, "all things well." **7**

7. Mark 7:37: "And were beyond measure astonished, saying, He hath done all things well: he maketh both the deaf to hear, and the dumb to speak."

Even now in the current era, when there is an astonishing disaster of the magnitude of an earthquake or volcanic eruption or unexpected flood, the human mind seeks for an explanation of how Fate, Providence, God, and unexpected catastrophe work together for some meaningful end.

Two of the most representative examples of how survivors themselves dealt with these themes are found in the works of Archibald Gracie, an amateur American historian, and Lawrence Beesley, a retired British science teacher who had planned to spend a holiday in America.

First, here is what Colonel Gracie had to say:

"…I had no time to contemplate danger when there was continuous need of quick thought, action and composure withal. Had I become rattled for a moment, or in the slightest degree been undecided during the several emergencies presently cited, I am certain that I never should have lived to tell the tale of my miraculous escape. For it is eminently fitting, in gratitude to my Maker, that I should make the acknowledgment that I know of no recorded instance of Providential deliverance more directly attributable to cause and effect, illustrating the efficacy of prayer and how 'God helps those who help themselves.' I should have only courted the fate of many hundreds of others had I supinely made no effort to supplement my prayers with all the strength and power which He has granted to me. While I said to myself, 'Goodbye to all at home,' I hoped and prayed for escape. My mind was nerved to do the duty of the moment, and my muscles seemed to be hardened in preparation for any struggle that might come…" (Gracie 43–4).

Beesley adds a slightly different but still characteristic point of view:

"…[I]n moments of urgent need men and women turn for help to something entirely outside themselves…To those men standing on the top deck with the boats all lowered, and still more so when the boats had all left, there came the realization that human resources were exhausted and human avenues of escape closed. With it came the appeal to whatever consciousness each had of a Power that had created the universe…When the boats had left and it was seen the ship was going down rapidly, men stood in groups on the deck engaged in prayer, and later, as some of them lay on the overturned collapsible boat, they repeated together over and over again the Lord's Prayer—irrespective of religious beliefs, some, perhaps, without religious beliefs, united in a common appeal for deliverance from their surroundings…Men do practical things in times like that: they would not waste a moment on mere words if those words were not an expression of the most intensely real conviction of which they were capable. Again, like the feeling of heroism, this appeal is innate and intuitive, and it certainly has its foundation on the knowledge—largely concealed, no doubt—of immortality…" (Beesley, *Loss* 196–8).

◆———

THE TRAGEDY
OF THE **TITANIC**.

———

AN EPIC OF DAUNTLESS HEROISM.

———

ONLY 705 PERSONS SAVED: 1,635 LIVES LOST.

———

THE SURVIVORS AT NEW YORK.

———

STORIES OF HEROISM AND SELF-SACRIFICE.

———

TITANIC'S FATAL SHOCK

———

AFLOAT FOR 2 ¾ HOURS.

———

SPECIAL CABLE FROM OUR OWN CORRESPONDENT

NEW YORK, Friday (3.47 a.m.).

In America the unexampled world's tragedy of the Titanic will always be remembered as the one great incident of the century, when it was impossible, I won't say to exaggerate, but even to render partial justice to the terrific story of death and woe.

It is a story which can hardly be told in a single chapter, but must be painfully unfolded page by page in all its dramatic and piteous detail and agony, in order to be fully understood and adequately pictured.

———

SALIENT FACTS OF THE TRAGEDGY. ▶8

———

From the stories told by the survivors, these salient facts stand out:

The Titanic struck an iceberg from 50ft to 100ft high.

The blow was not a head-on, but rather a glancing one.

It thus ripped the great ship's side, and made useless the most essential watertight compartments.

★▶ **8.** Actually, testimony later revealed a more complex story of the hours after *Titanic* struck the iceberg, but to be fair to this correspondent, separating fact from fiction with regard to the *Titanic* has been going on for one hundred years and will, no doubt, continue to go on for years to come. Historian Walter Lord explains: "The survivors added their own myths and fables to the fiction conjured up on shore. For some the heartbreaking trip back was too much. Others were simply carried away by the excitement. The more expansive found themselves making a good story even better. The laconic had their experiences improved by reporters" (Lord, *A Night* 169).

The Titanic, it is alleged, was going full speed at the time.

Promises had been made to the passengers that no attempt would be made to break the record in crossing the Atlantic; but the passengers declare, and the officers deny, that the ship was urged ahead at full speed from the time she left Daunt's Rock.

No ice had been seen during the day.

It was a clear, starlight night.

The ship's searchlights were not in use.

Captain Smith was not on the bridge when the ship struck the iceberg. The first officer was in charge.

Fifteen minutes after the ship struck the iceberg disappeared from view.

The Titanic struck the iceberg on the starboard bow, and a great hole was ripped in her side.

The passengers were at first assured the ship was in no danger, and was unsinkable.

The ice was struck at 11.35 p.m.

Fifteen minutes later the passengers were called on deck and told to don life-belts.

Forty minutes after the collision the passengers were told to take to the lifeboats.

Passengers in bed were aroused not by the collision, but by the stopping of the engines.

The men in the first and second cabins made no attempt to save themselves, but remained to sink with the ship and watched the women being put off in the lifeboats.

Some men in the steerage tried to storm the lifeboats, and half a dozen Italians were shot to protect the women in the boats. **9**

The Titanic sank two hours and forty-five minutes after she struck the iceberg.

The boilers blew up a few minutes before she sank.

The bow went first, and the stern reared high in the air, and the great ship plunged into the depths of the sea.

Just before she sank several of the men on board jumped into the sea, and these were for the most part the male survivors brought by the Carpathia.

The electric lights of the Titanic burned until the boilers gave out.

The lifeboats carrying the women waited a mile from the ship until she sank, and then drew in and picked up the men found floating in the sea. **10**

9. It is generally believed now that no one was shot, though some feel that First Officer Murdoch may have taken his own life. No one knows for sure (Lord, *A Night* 99-105).

10. Alas, no; not in a single case. After the *Titanic* went down, Fifth Officer Harold Lowe did organize several boats to more evenly distribute survivors in each boat. Then he took a boat filled only with crewmen back to the wreck site, but only after he had waited for the screaming of those in the water to die down. Four men were found in the water alive, but later one died of the effects of exposure; so only three survivors total were saved out of the water by a direct effort from the lifeboats. This fact astonished both American and British investigators (Lord, *A Night* 155).

Four of those saved died as the result of exposure before the Carpathia reached New York, others were badly maimed, some were temporarily insane, many had to be taken to the hospitals, while private ambulances and physicians met many more.

The Carpathia arrived on the scene at eight a.m. on Monday, and picked up the lifeboats.

One lifeboat was filled with stokers. **11**

It is some hours now since I left the Carpathia's side, and heard at first hand from the survivors some account of one of the greatest marine tragedies ever related, and one's imagination still stands appalled at the amazing revelations of the shock, suffering, horror, torture, and injury to limb, and the monstrous loss of life attending the collision of the Titanic with a giant iceberg off the banks of Newfoundland. **12**

Passengers	Saved	Lost	Total
First Class	202	128	330
Second Class	115	205	320
Third Class	178	572	750
Officers & Crew	210	730	940
Total	705	1,635	2,340

Out of the ship's total complement, therefore, less than one-third were rescued. The remainder went down to a watery grave in the icy depths of the North Atlantic.

The maximum capacity of the lifeboats was less than one-third of the passengers and crew, and they carried away from the sinking ship only 80 per cent. of their full capacity.

MRS. STRAUS'S DEVOTION.

Among the many tragic and heroic incidents of the wreck, that of the heroism of Mrs. Isidor Straus, who refused to be saved and leave her husband to drown, stands out conspicuously. Mrs. Straus was in one of the lifeboats which was about to put off from the Titanic. She called for her husband to join her. He waved his hand in good-bye, and smilingly refused to take the place of a woman who might be saved. Before the boat could be lowered into the water Mrs. Straus scrambled out and half fell

THE DEATH ROLL.

In my last despatch to the *Daily Telegraph* I described how we met the Carpathia at sea, and how the Cunarder, with an escort of small boats, warped alongside the pier at 9.35 p.m. It was not until then we knew authoritatively the appalling results of the disaster. The figures of the actual numbers involved in the catastrophe may be tabulated as follows:

11. Stokers tended the furnace fires that heated the boilers.

12. By approximately 450 miles.

at the feet of her husband. No urging could make her take a place in another boat, and she went down in the Titanic with Mr. Straus.

Colonel John Jacob Astor and Major Archibald Butt stood side by side as the Titanic sank, and waved good-bye to the small boats hardly to be seen a mile away on the starlit sea. When the order was first given for the passengers to take to the lifeboats, Major Butt defended the passage from the steerage against a rush of the panic-stricken men, and helped to save the lifeboats for the women and children.

FIRST SURVIVORS ASHORE.

Five minutes after the Carpathia tied up at her pier last night the first survivors came ashore.

Two men walked out, the first one in oilskins and the other in a raincoat. They looked around in a dazed manner. From the great crowd waiting there was a faint cheer, and the two jumped over the rail holding back the crowd.

A man and a woman came next. There seemed none to meet them.

Mr. Bruce Ismay remained closeted with Mr. Franklin, vice-president of the White Star Line, on board the Carpathia until 11.5 o'clock. When the two came ashore Mr. Ismay issued a statement saying the White Star Line would do everything possible to alleviate the sufferings of the survivors; that the ship had complied with all the regulations, and that the inquiry by the Senate Committee would be welcomed.

The Customs officers on the pier opened up a lane through the crowd, and then the survivors of the Titanic came straggling out. They seemed only anxious to get away, and few were willing to talk. Those first to come said the passengers had agreed not to talk, but that the Line would issue a statement.

As the number of those who came ashore grew larger, however, many were found to tell the story of the loss of the great liner.

COLONEL ASTOR'S SACRIFICE.

All agreed that Colonel John Jacob Astor met death heroically. According to one story, told by Miss Margaret Hays, of New York, Colonel Astor chose death for himself to save an unknown woman who came along just as the lifeboat in which he had a place, because of the absence of any more women, was about to be lowered.

It was a grim lottery, in which Colonel Astor had drawn a fortunate number, and which he later freely surrendered to a woman, whose name is unknown.

The story, as told by Miss Hays, was as follows:

When the Titanic struck I did not feel the shock very much. I made my way to the deck, where everything was excitement, and was assisted into a lifeboat that was waiting to be lowered. Colonel Astor, with his wife, came out on deck at that moment, and both got into another boat. Colonel Astor had his arms about his wife, and assisted her into the boat. At the time there were no women waiting to get into the boats, and the ship's officer at that point invited Colonel Astor to enter the boat with his wife. The colonel, after looking around, and seeing no women, got into the boat, and his wife threw her arms about him.

The boat in which Colonel Astor and his wife were sitting was about to be lowered, when a woman came running out of the companionway. Raising his hand, the colonel stopped the preparation to lower his boat, and, stepping out, assisted the woman into the seat he had occupied. Mrs. Astor cried out, and wanted to get out of the boat with her husband, but the colonel patted her on the back, and said something in a low tone of voice.

As the boat was being lowered we heard him say, "Ladies will have to go first."… **13**

CHIVALRY OF THE SEA.

I have interviewed scores of passengers, and they are all agreed regarding the splendid heroism of the captain and crew, and the men who heroically gave their lives to save others.

Duty was the watchword of the crew, and discipline was maintained to the last.

A few Italians in the steerage were apparently panic-stricken, and threatened to cause trouble, but the firmness of the crew repressed them. There is nothing in the story of the Titanic so far as it has developed which need bring a blush of shame to an English cheek. All told me the same story—the discipline of the crew, the coolness of the captain, and from beginning to end there was the same keynote, "Women and children first."

This chivalrous law of the sea was applied so rigorously that men with wives and families were turned back in some cases from boats only partly filled with women. Some few boats thus lowered were soon filled with sailors and stewards who were picked out of the water, and helped to man them.

It seems proved that the bulkhead system, though probably working in the manner intended, availed only to delay the ship's sinking. The position and length of the ship's injury on the starboard side admitted icy water, which caused the boilers to explode, and these explosions practically broke the ship in two. Had the ship struck the iceberg head on, at whatever speed and with whatever resultant shock, the officers

13. Actually, according to Colonel Gracie, who was standing nearby, Colonel Astor asked if he could go on board the lifeboat with his wife because she was in "a delicate condition." The officer in charge said "no," women and children must go first. And that is the last that is really known about John Jacob Astor until his body was recovered from the sea, days later. In his wallet was enough cash for sixteen years' wages for a common ship's telegrapher. A rumor of that time had it that Astor's body was marred beyond recognition because the forward funnel had fallen on it, but others claim the colonel simply died from the cold (Eaton and Haas, *Titanic: Destination* 101–02).

say the bulkhead system and water-tight compartments would probably have saved the vessel. **14**

To quote one man: "It was the impossible that happened, when, with a shock unbelievably mild, the ship's side was torn for a length which made the bulkhead system ineffective."

The Titanic was 1,799 miles from Queenstown, and 1,191 miles from New York, speeding for a maiden voyage record. The night was starlit and the sea glassy. Lights were out in most of the state-rooms, and only two or three congenial groups remained in the public rooms, and a few playing cards in the restaurant. In the crow's-nest on the look-out, and on the bridge the officers and members of the crew were at their places, awaiting relief at midnight from their two hours' watch.

At 11.45 came the sudden sound of two gongs, a warning of immediate danger. The crash against the iceberg, which had been sighted at only a quarter-mile distance, came almost simultaneously with the click of the levers operated by those on the bridge, which stopped the engines and closed the watertight doors. Captain Smith was on the bridge a moment later, giving orders for summoning all on board and for putting on lifebelts and lowering the lifeboats.

REVOLVERS DRAWN.

The first boats lowered contained more male passengers than the later ones, as the men were on deck first, and there were not enough women there to fill them. When, a moment later, the rush of frightened women and crying children to the deck began, the enforcement of the "Women first" rule became rigid. **15** Officers loading some of the boats drew revolvers, but in most cases the men, both passengers and crew, behaved in a way which reflected glory on their humanity.

Revolver shots were heard by many persons shortly before the end of the Titanic, and caused many rumours. **16** One was that Captain Smith had shot himself. Another was that the first officer, Mr. Murdock [Murdoch], had ended his life.

It is known that Captain Smith, Mr.

---

14. This view is, in fact, supported by a host of authorities who also note that crew and third-class passengers in the bow section would have been killed on impact, but only two or three hundred would have died instead of more than 1,500 (McDonnell 53–4).

15. Second Officer Lightoller enforced the "women and children rule" and commented on it in his testimony to the U.S. Senate Inquiry, but First Officer Murdoch, who perished in the sinking, merely tried to see that starboard lifeboats were full. As has been noted, only slightly more women than men were saved.

16. These would be shots from Officer Lowe's revolver. He shot down the side of the ship so that he wouldn't hit anyone. By firing his gun he kept men from jumping aboard the already crowded boat (Aldridge 55).

Murdock, and the sixth officer, Mr. Moody, have been lost. The surviving officers, Messrs. Lightoller, Pitman, Boxhall, and Lowe, made no statement.

THE CAPTAIN'S DEATH.

The members of the crew and others aboard the Titanic whom I have interviewed discredit all reports of suicide, and say Captain Smith remained on the bridge until just before the ship sank, leaping into the sea only after those on the decks had been washed away. It is also related that when a cook, later, sought to pull him aboard a lifeboat, he exclaimed, "Let me go," and jerking himself away, went down.

What became of the men with life-belts? is a question asked since the disaster by many. The belts did their work of supporting their wearers in the water until the ship went down. Many of those were drawn into the vortex, despite the belts, and did not come up again until their dead bodies floated to the surface.

As the last boats moved away the ship's band was playing the ragtime air, "Autumn." I find there is a lack of agreement in this report with the wireless operator's statement reported elsewhere, that "Autumn" was still being played when the Titanic was on the verge of her fatal plunge below.

The captain, it is said, ordered the band to play to allay the excitement, and there is a general agreements that when the last boat pulled away—some time after the wireless operator got safely over the ship's side—the strains of the band most closely resembled those of "Nearer, my God, to Thee."

This is only one of the hundred details on which the interviewers find a conflict of statement; a conflict which, as you would realise after chatting with the stricken passengers, was almost inevitable.

On such important matters as the speed of the ship, the capacity of the lifeboats, wireless disturbance, and so forth, there is so far very little authoritative statement worth cabling. All these things will be examined shortly by a Congressional Committee before which Mr. Ismay and the officers are to appear...

COMPLETE ABSENCE OF PANIC.

To most passengers the midnight crash against the ice mountain seemed of very trifling force. Many were so little disturbed by it that they hesitated to dress and put on lifebelts even when summoned by the thundering knocks and shouts of the stewards. The bridge players in the smoking-room kept on with their game.

The alleged wireless messages describing "the terrific impact, a roar like thunder, an avalanche of ice falling on the vessel, 200 sailors in their sleeping berths killed in the forecastle," were sheer fiction.

Once on deck many hesitated to enter the swinging lifeboats. The glassy sea, the starlit sky, the absence, in the first few moments, of intense excitement, gave them a feeling that here was only some slight mishap, and that those who got into the boats would have a chilly half-hour below, and might later be laughed at. It was such a feeling as this, from all accounts, which caused Colonel Astor and his wife to refuse the places offered to them in the first boat, and to retire to the gymnasium. In the same way Mr. H. J. Allison, a Montreal banker, laughed at the warning, and his wife, reassured by him, took her time about dressing. They and their daughters did not reach the Carpathia. Their son, less than two years old, was carried into a lifeboat by a nurse, and was taken in charge by Major Arthur Peuchen.

The admiration felt by passengers and crew for the matchlessly appointed vessel was translated in those first few moments into a confidence which for some proved deadly. In loading the first boat the restrictions of sex were not made, and it seemed to the men who piled in beside the women there would be boats enough for all. But the ship's officers knew better than this, and as the spreading fear caused an earnest advance toward the suspended craft, the order, "Women first," was heard, and the men were pushed aside...

THE FINAL MOMENTS.

As the end of the Titanic became manifestly but a matter of moments the oarsmen pulled the boats away, and the chilly waters round the ship began to echo splash after splash as passengers and sailors in life-preservers leaped over and started swimming to escape the expected suction.

Only the hardiest constitutions could endure for more than a few moments

such a numbing bath. The first vigorous strokes gave way to heartbreaking cries of "Help, help," and soon stiffening forms were seen floating, the faces relaxed in death.

The last of the boats, a collapsible, was launched too late to get away, and was overturned by the ship's sinking. In the Marconi tower almost to the last the loud buzz of the sending instrument was heard over the waters. Who was receiving the messages? Those in the boats did not know, and they least of all supposed that a Mediterranean-bound ship, on the distant eastward steamer track, would be their rescuer.

Led by the thoughtful steward's green lamp under the light of the stars, the boats drew away and watched with tearful eyes the vast black bulk of the Titanic. But not for long. First the bow, then the forward decks, then the funnels, and last the stern of the marvel-ship of a few hours before passed beneath the waters for evermore. The dreaded suction of the sinking ship was not so great as had been feared, and rocked but gently the group of boats now a quarter of a mile distant from the spot where "smeared with ash and streaked with oil, the lukewarm whirlpool dies." [17]

THE WORK OF RESCUE.

On the sixteen boats which, in forlorn procession, entered on the terrible hours of rowing, and drifting, and suspense, women wept for their lost husbands and sons, sailors grieved for the ship which

17. From the poem "The Destroyers" by Rudyard Kipling.

had been their pride, men choked back tears and sought to comfort the widowed and the fatherless. "Perhaps," they said, "other boats might have put off in another direction towards the last." They strove, though none too sure themselves, to convince the women of the certainty that a rescue-ship would appear.

Early dawn brought no ship, but not long after five a.m. the Carpathia, far out of her path, and making eighteen knots instead of her wonted fifteen, showed her single red and black smokestack upon the horizon. In the joy of that moment the heaviest griefs were forgotten. Soon afterwards Captain Rostrom and Chief Steward Hughes were welcoming the chilled and water-soaked arrivals over the Carpathia's side.

Mr. Carlos Hurd, one of the passengers aboard the Carpathia, thus describes the arrival of the survivors aboard:

"The silence of the Carpathia's engines caused me to dress hurriedly and awaken my wife at 5.40 a.m. Our stewardess, meeting me outside, pointed to a wailing host in the rear dining-room, and said, 'From the Titanic; she's at the bottom of the ocean.'

"At the ship's side a moment later I saw the last of the line of boats discharge their loads, and saw women, some with cheap shawls about their heads, some with the costliest fur cloaks, ascending to our decks. Such joy as the first sight of our ship may have given them had disappeared from their faces, and there were tears and signs of faltering as the women were helped up the ladders or hoisted aboard in slings.

"For lack of room to stow them, several of the Titanic's boats, after unloading, were set adrift. At our north was a broad icefield the length of hundreds of Carpathias. Around us on other sides were sharp and glistening peaks; one black berg seen about ten a.m. was said to be that which had sunk the Titanic.

IN THE WIRELESS ROOM.

"In his tiny house over the second cabin smoking-room was Harold Cotton [Cottam], the Marconi operator, a ruddy English youth, whose work at his post on what seemed ordinary duty until almost midnight had probably saved the lives of the huddling hundreds below. Already he was knitting his brows over the problem of handling the messages which were coming in batches from the purser's office. The haste with which these Marconigrams were prepared by their senders was needless in view of the wait of two days and two nights for a land connection.

"'Safe' was the word with which most of the messages began. Then in many of them came the word 'Missing.' Dishevelled women, who the night before could have drawn thousands from their husbands' letters of credit, or from the Titanic's safe, stood penniless before the Carpathia's purser, asking for their messages to be forwarded 'Collect.' Their messages were taken with the rest. The Californian, a cattle ship, came near us, and though she gave no sign of having any of the Titanic's survivors on board, her presence in the vicinity gave hope to many women, who were encouraged in the belief that the Californian might have picked up their loved ones.

"Captain Rostrom's [Rostron's] decision to abandon the Mediterranean course was made on the Thursday, **18** and the return to an American port was soon known to the passengers. At first it was reported that Halifax or Boston would be the destination, but at noon a notice of intended arrival at New York three days later was posted. At that time the Carpathia, at an increase over her usual moderate speed, was westward bound, and her passengers were deferring their hopes of Gibraltar, Naples, and Trieste, and were sharing their rooms with the newcomers.

CAPTAIN'S CABIN AS HOSPITAL.

"Few men on the Carpathia's passenger list slept in bed in any night that followed. They and the men from the Titanic lay on chairs, on the deck, on dining tables, or smoking-room couches, or on the floors of the rooms which held their hand-baggage and their curtained-off guests.

"The captain was the first to vacate his room, which was used as a hospital.

"In the first cabin library," says Mr. Hurd, concluding his narrative, "Women of wealth and refinement mingled their grief, and asked eagerly for news of the possible arrival of a belated boat or a message from some other steamer telling of the safety of their husbands. Mrs. Henry B. Harris, wife of the New York theatrical manager, checked her tears long enough to beg that some message of hope be sent to her father-in-law.

"Mrs. Ella Thor, Miss Marie Young, Mrs. Emil Taussig, and her daughter Ruth, Mrs. Martin Rothschild, Mrs. William Augustus Spencer, Mrs. J. Stuart White, and Mrs. Walter M. Clark, all well known here, were a few of those who lay back exhausted on the Carpathia's leather cushions and told in shuddering sentences of their experiences.

"Mrs. John Jacob Astor and the Countess Rothes had been taken to state rooms soon after their arrival on board the Carpathia. Those who talked with Mrs. Astor said she spoke often of her husband's ability as an oarsman, and said he could save himself if he had a chance; that he could have had such a chance she seemed hardly to hope."

SURVIVOR'S COMMITTEE.

GRAVE ALLEGATIONS.

INSUFFICIENCY OF BOATS.

NEW YORK, Thursday (10.10 p.m.).

The following statement, issued by a committee of the surviving passengers, has been given to the Press:

"We the undersigned surviving passengers of the Titanic, in order to forestall any sensational and exaggerated statements, deem it our duty to give to the Press a statement of the facts which

---

★ **18.** Perhaps Monday was meant.

have come to our knowledge, and which we believe to be true.

"On Sunday, April 14, 1912, at about 11.40 on a cold starlit night, the ship struck an iceberg, which had been reported to the bridge by the look-out, but not early enough to avoid collision. Steps were taken to ascertain the damage and save the passengers and the ship. Orders were given to put on lifebelts, the boats were lowered, and the usual distress signals were sent out by wireless telegraphy, and rockets were fired at intervals.

"Fortunately, a wireless message was received by the Carpathia about midnight. She arrived on the scene of the disaster about four a.m. on Monday. The officers and crew of the Carpathia had been preparing all night for the rescue work, and for the comfort of the survivors. These were received on board with the most touching care and kindness, every attention being given to all, irrespective of class. Passengers, officers, and crew gladly gave up their state rooms, clothing, and comforts for our benefit; all honour to them.

"The English Board of Trade passengers' certificate on board the Titanic allowed for a total of approximately 3,500. The same certificate called for lifeboat accommodation for approximately 950, in the following boats: Fourteen large lifeboats, two smaller boats, four collapsible boats. Life-preservers were accessible in apparently sufficient number for all on board. The approximate number of passengers carried at the time of the collision was:

First class:	330
Second class:	320
Third class:	750
Total:	1,400
Officers and crew:	940
Total:	2,340

Of the foregoing about the following number were rescued by the Carpathia:

First class:	210
Second class:	125
Third class:	200
Officers:	4
Seamen:	39
Stewards:	96
Firemen:	71
Total of crew:	210
A total of about:	775

"The number saved was about 80 per cent. of the maximum capacity of the lifeboats. We feel it our duty to call the attention of the public to what we consider the inadequate supply of life-saving appliances provided for modern passenger steamships, and recommend that immediate steps be taken to compel passenger steamers to carry sufficient boats to accommodate the maximum number of people carried on board.

"The following facts were observed, and should be considered in this connection:

"In addition to the insufficiency of lifeboats, rafts, &c., there was a lack of trained seamen to man the same (stokers, stewards, &c., are not efficient boat handlers). [19] There were not enough officers to carry out the emergency

---

19. Many of the rescued crew simply didn't know how to row a lifeboat.

orders on the bridge and to superintend the launching and control of the lifeboats, and there was an absence of searchlights. The Board of Trade rules allow for entirely too many people in each boat to permit the same to be properly handled.

"On the Titanic the boat-deck was about 75ft above water, and consequently the passengers were required to embark before the lowering of the boats, thus endangering the operation and preventing the taking on of the maximum number the boats would hold.

"The boats at all times to be properly equipped with provisions, water, lamps, compasses, lights, &c. Life-saving boat-drills should be more frequent and thoroughly carried out, and officers should be armed at boat-drill.

"A greater reduction in speed in fog and ice, as the damage if a collision actually occurs is liable to be less.

"In conclusion we suggest that an international conference should be called, and we recommend the passage of identical laws providing for the safety of all at sea. We urge the United States Government to take the initiative as soon as possible." [20]

The statement is signed by Mr. Samuel Goldenberg, chairman of the passengers committee, and twenty-five others.—*Reuter*.

GRAPHIC STORY
BY THE
WIRELESS OPERATOR

THRILLING NARRATIVE.

BANDSMEN'S HEROISM.

PLAYING AS THE TITANIC
WENT DOWN.

TELEGRAPHISTS' DEVOTION.

SILENCE EXPLAINED.

SPECIAL CABLE
FROM
OUR OWN CORRESPONDENT

NEW YORK, Friday, 5.15 a.m.

The following thrilling statement was dictated to-day by Mr. Bride, the assistant

20. Surely these were American passengers taking a swipe at the British. But whoever sponsored and signed the document made it nearly impossible for the Board of Trade to do anything other than order that all liners carry a full complement of lifeboats.

Marconi operator on board the Titanic, to the *New York Times* representative, in the presence of Mr. Marconi, who is now staying in New York: **21**

THE SILENCE OF THE CARPATHIA.

"In the first place, the public should not blame anybody because more wireless messages about the disaster did not reach the shore from the Carpathia. I positively refused to send Press despatches, because the bulk of the personal messages, with touching words of grief, was so large. The wireless operators aboard the United States cruiser Chester got all they asked for, and they were wretched operators.

"They knew the American Morse code, but not the Continental Morse code sufficiently to be worth while. They taxed our endurance to the limit. I had to cut them out at last, they were so insufferably slow, and go ahead with our messages of grief to relatives. **22**

"When I was dragged aboard the Carpathia I went to the hospital at first, and I stayed there for ten hours. Then somebody brought word that the Carpathia's wireless operator was 'getting queer' from overwork.

"They asked me if I could go up and help. I couldn't walk, as both my feet were broken, or something. **23** I don't know what. I went up on crutches with somebody helping me. I took the key, and I never left the wireless cabin after that. Our meals were brought to us, and we kept wireless working all the time.

"Sometimes the Carpathia's man sent and sometimes I sent. There was a bed in the wireless cabin, and I could

21. According to such sources as the books *The Maiden Voyage* and *The Titanic Disaster Hearings*, the *New York Times* paid either $500 or $1,000 for this exclusive. If Bride received $1,000, it amounted to more than four years' worth of salary.

22. Passenger messages also took precedence because they were being paid for, and Marconi operators were on board ships primarily to take care of Marconi business. Marconi operator Phillips, who perished when the *Titanic* went down, put aside several iceberg warnings, to be taken to the bridge later on, because of the perceived urgency and priority of these passenger messages. Only after U.S. Senate and British hearings into the *Titanic* did priorities for Marconi operators change. Bride's charge that the operators on the *Chester* were incompetent seems unlikely. What seems more likely is that they had nothing to say to the *Chester*. A list of survivors already made it clear that Major Butt, President Taft's aide-de-camp, was dead, and this was what the *Chester* wanted further information on. As for Captain Rostron, he wrote an apology to President Taft saying that he had no idea that the operators had ignored messages from the *Chester* (*Titanic Reports* 170).

23. Badly frostbitten, as it turned out.

sit on it and rest my feet while sending sometimes.

"To begin at the beginning. I joined the Titanic at Belfast. I was born in Nunhead, London, S.E., twenty-two years ago, and joined the Marconi staff last July. I first worked on the Haverford, and then on the Lusitania, and was transferred to the Titanic at Belfast. I didn't have much to do aboard the Titanic, except to relieve Phillips, the senior operator, from midnight until some time in the morning, when he finished sleeping.

MOMENT OF THE DISASTER.

"On the night of the accident I wasn't sending, but was asleep. I was due to be up and relieve Phillips earlier than usual; and that reminds me that if it hadn't been for a lucky thing we never could have sent any call for help. Our wireless installation broke down, and the lucky thing was that this happened early enough for us to fix it up before the collision. We noticed something wrong on Sunday, and Phillips and I worked seven hours to ascertain what was wrong. At last we found a 'secretary' **24** burned out, and repaired it just a few hours before the iceberg was struck. **25**

"Phillips said to me, as he took the night shift, 'You turn in, boy, and get some sleep, and go up as soon as you can and give me a chance. I'm all done for with this work of making repairs.'

"There were three rooms in the wireless cabin. One was a sleeping-room, one a dynamo-room, and one an operating-room. I took off my clothes and went to sleep in the bed. Then I was conscious of waking up and hearing Phillips sending to Cape Race. I read what he was sending. It was only routine matter. I remembered how tired he was, and got out of bed without my clothes on to relieve him. I didn't even feel the shock. I hardly knew it had happened until after the captain had come to us. There was no jolt whatever.

THE HELP SIGNAL, "C.Q.D."

"I was standing by Phillips, telling him to go to bed, when the captain put his head in the cabin, 'We've struck an iceberg.' the captain said, 'and I'm having an inspection made to tell what it has done for us. You had better get ready to send out a call for assistance, but don't send it until I tell you.'

"The captain went away, and in ten minutes, I should estimate, he came back. We could hear terrible confusion outside, but not the least thing to indicate any trouble. The wireless was working perfectly.

"Send a call for assistance," ordered the captain, barely putting his head in the door.

"What call should I send?" Phillips asked.

"The regulation international call for help, just that." Then the captain was gone.

---

24. This perhaps referred to what we would call a transformer.

25. During this time, they no doubt missed pertinent iceberg warnings.

"Phillips began to send 'C.Q.D.' He flashed away at it, and we joked while he did so. All of us made light of the disaster.

"We joked that way while we flashed the signals for about five minutes. Then the captain came back.

"'What are you sending?' he asked.

"'C.Q.D.,' Phillips replied.

JOKING ABOUT THE COLLISION.

"The humor of the situation appealed to me, and I cut in with a little remark that made us all laugh, including the captain. Send 'S.O.S.,' I said, 'it's the new call, and it may be your last chance to send it.'

"Phillips, with a laugh, changed the signal to 'S.O.S.' The captain told us we had been struck amidships, or just aft of amidships. **26** It was ten minutes, Phillips told me, after he noticed the iceberg, but the slight jolt was the only signal to us that a collision had occurred. We thought we were a good distance away.

"We said lots of funny things to each other in the next few minutes. We picked up the first steamship Frankfurt; gave her our position, and said we had struck an iceberg, and needed assistance. The Frankfurt operator went away to tell his captain. He came back, and we told him we were sinking by the head, and that we could observe a distinct list forward.

"The Carpathia answered our signal, and we told her our position, and said we were sinking by the head. The operator went to tell the captain, and in five minutes returned, and told us the Carpathia was putting about and heading for us.

SCENE ON THE DECK.

"Our captain had left us at this time, and Phillips told me to run and tell him what the Carpathia had answered. I did so, and I went through an awful mass of people to his cabin. The decks were full of scrambling men and women. I saw no fighting, but I heard tell of it.

"I came back and heard Phillips giving the Carpathia further directions. Phillips told me to put on my clothes. Until that moment I forgot I wasn't dressed. I went to my cabin and dressed. I brought an overcoat to Phillips, and as it was very cold I slipped the overcoat upon him while he worked.

"Every few minutes Phillips would send me to the captain with little messages. They were merely telling how the Carpathia was coming our way, and giving her speed.

HEROIC TELEGRAPHIST.

"I noticed as I came back from one trip that they were putting off the women and children in lifeboats, and that the list forward was increasing. Phillips told me the wireless was growing weaker. The

---

★ **26.** This would have been a very odd thing for the captain to say since by now Officer Murdoch would have told Smith where the *Titanic* had been struck. It was hardly "amidships."

captain came and told us our engine-rooms were taking water, and that the dynamos might not last much longer. We sent that word to the Carpathia.

"I went out on deck and looked around. The water was pretty close up to the boat-deck. There was a great scramble aft, and how poor Phillips worked through it I don't know. He was a brave man. I learned to love him that night, and I suddenly felt for him a great reverence to see him standing there sticking to his work while everybody else was raging about. I will never live to forget the work Phillips did for the last awful fifteen minutes.

"I thought it about time to look about and see if there was anything detached that would float. I remembered every member of the crew had a special life-belt, and ought to know where it was. I remembered mine was under my bunk. I went and got it. Then I thought how cold the water was.

"I remembered I had some boots, and I put those on, and an extra jacket. As I put that on I saw Phillips standing out there, still sending away, giving the Carpathia details just how we were doing.

"We picked up the Olympic, and told her we were sinking by the head, and were about all done.

"As Phillips was sending this message I strapped his life-belt to his back. I had already put on his overcoat. I wondered if I could get him into his boots. He suggested, with a sort of laugh, that I should look out and see if all the people were off in the boats, or if any boats were left, or how things were. I saw a collapsible boat near a funnel, and went over to it. Twelve men were trying to lower it down to the boat-deck. They were having an awful time.

A COWARD'S ACT.

"It was the last boat left, and I looked at it longingly for a few minutes. Then I gave them a hand, and over she went. They all started to scramble in on the boat-deck, and I walked back to Phillips.

"I said the last raft had gone. Then came the captain's voice:

"Men, you have done your full duty, you can do no more. Abandon your cabin now; it is every man for himself. You look out for yourselves. I release you. That's the way of it at this kind of time; every man for himself.

"I looked out, and saw that the boat-deck was awash.

"Phillips clung on, sending and sending. He clung on for about ten minutes, or maybe fifteen minutes, after the captain released him. The water was then coming into our cabin.

"While he worked something happened I hate to tell about. I was back in my room getting Phillip's money for him, and as I looked out of the door I saw a stoker, or somebody from below decks, leaning over Phillips from behind. Phillips was too busy to notice what the man was doing, but he was slipping the life-belt off Phillips's back. He was a big man too.

"As you can see, I'm very small. I don't know what it was I got hold of, but I remembered in a flash the way Phillips had clung on; how I had to fix that life-belt in place, because he was too busy to do it.

A JUST REPRISAL.

"I knew that man from below decks had his own life-belt, and should have known where to get it. I suddenly felt a passion not to let that man die a decent sailor's death. I wished he might have stretched a rope or walked a plank. I did my duty. I hope I finished him, but I don't know.

"We left him on the cabin-floor of the wireless-room, and he wasn't moving. From aft came the tunes of the ship's band, playing the ragtime tune, 'Autumn.'

"Phillips ran aft, and that was the last I ever saw of him alive.

"I went to the place where I had seen the collapsible boat on the boat-deck, and to my surprise I saw the boat, and the men still trying to push it off. I guess there wasn't a sailor in the crowd. They couldn't do it. I went up to them, and was just lending a hand when a large wave came awash of the deck.

"The big wave carried the boat off. I had hold of an oarlock and I went off with it. The next I knew I was in the boat. But that wasn't all; I was in the boat, and the boat was upside down, and I was under it. I remember realising I was wet through, and that whatever happened I must breathe, for I was under water. I knew I had to fight for it, and I did. How I got out from under the boat I don't know, but I felt a breath of air at last.

"There were men all around me—hundreds of them. The sea was dotted with them, all depending on their life-belts.

her funnels. There must have been an explosion, but we heard none. We only saw a big stream of sparks. The ship was gradually turning on her nose—just like a duck does that goes down for a dive. I had only one thing on my mind—to get away from the suction.

"The band was still playing. I guess all the band went down. They were heroes. They were still playing 'Autumn.'

"Then I swam with all my might. I suppose I was 150ft away when the Titanic, on her nose, with her afterquarter sticking straight up in the air, began to settle slowly. When at last the waves washed over her rudder there wasn't the least bit of suction I could feel. She must have kept going down just as slowly as she had been.

"I forget to mention that besides the Olympic and the Carpathia we spoke some German boat, I don't know which, and told them how we were. We also spoke the Baltic. I remembered those things as I began to figure what ships would be coming toward us.

"I felt after a little while like sinking. I was very cold. I saw a boat of some kind near me, and put all my strength into an effort to swim to it. It was hard work, and I was all done when a hand reached out from the boat and pulled me aboard. It was our same collapsible boat and the same crowd was on it.

LAST GLIMPSE
OF THE TITANIC.

"I felt I simply had to get away from the ship. She was a beautiful sight then. Smoke and sparks were rushing out of

HEARTRENDING
SPECTACLE.

"There was just room for me to roll on the edge. I lay there not caring what happened. Somebody sat on my legs. They were wedged in between the slats, and were being wrenched. I hadn't the heart left to ask the man to move. There was a terrible sight all around; men swimming and sinking everywhere.

"I lay where I was, letting the man wrench my feet out of shape. Others came near, but nobody gave them a hand. The overturned boat already had more men than it would support, and was sinking. At first the larger waves splashed over my clothing; then they began to splash over my head, and I had to breathe when I could.

"As we floated around on our capsized boat and I kept straining my eyes for a ship's lights somebody said, 'Don't the rest of you think we ought to pray?'

"The man who made the suggestion asked what religion the others were. Each man called out his religion. One was a Catholic, one a Methodist, one a Presbyterian, and it was decided the most appropriate prayer for all was the Lord's Prayer. We spoke it over in chorus, with the man who first suggested that we should pray as the leader.

"Some splendid people saved us. They had a boat right side up. It was full to its capacity, yet they came to us and took us all into it.

"I saw some lights off in the distance, and knew a steamship was coming to our aid. I didn't care what happened. I just lay and gasped when I could, and felt the pain in my feet. I feel it still. At last the Carpathia was alongside, and the people were being taken up a rope ladder. Our boat drew near, and one by one the men were taken off of it. One man was dead. I passed him, and went to the ladder, although my feet pained me terribly.

HOW PHILLIPS DIED.

"The dead man was Phillips. He died on the raft from exposure and cold. I guess he had been all in from work before the wreck came. He stood his ground until the crisis passed and then collapsed.

"But I hardly thought that then; I didn't think much about anything. I tried the rope ladder. My feet pained me terribly, but I got to the top, and felt hands reaching out to me. The next I know a woman was leaning over me in a cabin, and I felt her hand waving back my hair and rubbing my face.

"I felt somebody at my feet, and felt the warmth of liquor. Somebody got me under the arms, and then I was carried down below to the hospital. That was early in the day. I guess I lay in hospital until near night, when they told me the Carpathia's wireless man was getting 'queer,' and would I help?

"After that I never was out of the wireless room, so I don't know what happened among the passengers. I saw nothing of Mrs. Astor or any of them.

A TIE WITH FRIENDS AND HOME.

"I first worked the wireless. The splutter never died down. I knew it soothed my hurt, and felt like a tie to the world of friends and home.

"How could I, then, take newspaper queries? Sometimes I let a newspaper ask a question, and got a long string of stuff asking for full particulars about everything. Whenever I started to take such a message I thought of the poor people waiting for their messages to go, hoping for answers to them. I shut off inquiries, and sent my personal messages, and I feel I did the right thing. If the cruiser Chester had had a decent operator I could have worked with him longer, but he got terribly on my nerves with his insufferable incompetence.

"I was still sending my personal messages when Mr. Marconi and the *New York Times* reporter arrived to ask that I should prepare this statement. There were, maybe, 100 left. I would have liked to send them all, because I could rest easier if I knew all those messages had gone to the friends waiting for them.

"Now the ambulance man is waiting with the stretcher, and I guess I've got to go with him. I hope my legs get better soon.

"The way the band kept playing was a noble thing. I heard it first while we were still working the wireless. There was a ragtime tune for us, and the last I saw of the band when I was floating out in the sea with my lifebelt on it was still on deck playing 'Autumn.' How they ever did it I cannot imagine.

"That, and the way Phillips kept sending after the captain told him his life was his own, and to look out for himself, are two things that stand out in my mind over all the rest."

★ Both Harold S. Bride and the *Carpathia*'s Harold Thomas Cottam were sharply criticized in the press for not making a full news report while steaming toward New York (Lord, *A Night* 166). But from Bride's perspective, as an employee of the Marconi Company, his first obligation was to the passengers. They paid for their messages to be sent. Additionally, neither Bride nor Cottam nor Captain Rostron himself could have known of the pent-up demand for news that had developed because earlier wireless messages had been so universally garbled through the interference of incompetent amateur telegraphers relaying only partially understood messages. Rumor had been consistently reported as fact (Davie 149–56).

The fact is, wireless telegraphy was still in its infancy. Most ships did not have the best equipment, and most didn't even have night operators on duty. Bride and Cottam were probably both caught in a situation where if you don't like—or receive—the message, you shoot the messenger.

In any case, by all accounts Cottam's

Wireless operator Harold Bride, due to badly frostbitten feet, is carried off the *Carpathia*.

most serious error was in not sending the following telegram from Captain Rostron on April 15 when he first received it.

> Deeply regret advise you Titanic sank this morning, after collision iceberg, resulting serious loss of life. Further particulars later.

> Bruce Ismay (Kuntz 553)

When finally sent, this message was dated: "Steamship Carpathia, April 17, 1912 (via Halifax). ISLEFRANK, N. Y. C." However, there is nothing sinister here because other ships were able to get the message out that the *Titanic* had been sunk. Most likely, operators Bride and Cottam were swamped with messages from the passengers, and this one was misplaced amidst all the other messages being given to them.

Suspicion of dark commercial plots only ever fell on Bride and Cottam after Marconi official Frederick Sammis telegraphed Cottam on April 18, just before the *Carpathia* docked: "Say old man Marconi Company taking good care of you. Keep your mouth shut and hold your story. It is fixed for you so you will get big money" (Davie 154–55). This was no bribe. Marconi had a secret agreement with the *New York Times* to give them an exclusive from his employees. He was looking after the financial welfare of the two wireless operators.

In the end both Bride and Cottam survived some pretty tough questioning. If they had really wanted to make big money from the *Titanic*'s sinking, they would have gone on the lecture circuit. They might well have earned a small fortune. But both men quickly disappeared from the public eye.

MEMORIAL SERVICE AT ST. PAUL'S.

◆

IMPRESSIVE SCENES.

St. Paul's is the very embodiment of all that is stern and strong in our national character, and it was fitting that the open expression of the nation's sorrow should take place in that grim and massive structure. The sacred edifice boasts a proud list of moving services closely interwoven with some of the most stirring events in our history, yet it is doubtful whether any have rivalled that of yesterday in impressiveness and soul-stirring incident. A vast multitude filled the nave, they thronged the aisles, and they crowded the galleries; yet many more wished to enter, but, finding themselves unable to do so, these stood outside the venerable pile until the service was concluded, associating themselves in that way with the tribute of reverence to the heroic dead which was being so devoutly paid by those within.

It was a remarkable congregation. Row upon row of sombrely-clad men and women, clearly occupying vastly different stations in life, had been drawn together by a common sorrow. No places had been reserved in the body of the Cathedral. The exalted in the land sat side by side with the humble citizen. In the choir, it is true, the Lord Mayor and the civic dignitaries occupied places of honour, grouped around them being members of the Cabinet, distinguished diplomatists, and representatives of many large commercial undertakings, but away and beyond no distinction of any kind was made, for the sentiment which had brought that vast assembly together was the same everywhere.

A SOMBRE SCENE.

An occasional shift of brilliant light filtering softly through the beautiful stained glass lit up the interior from time to time, but the dominant tone was a gloom which reflected the prevailing thoughts of those present. No resplendent ornaments figured on the altar. It had been stripped of everything save the two tall candlesticks, and the Cross between. In front it was draped with folds of black and white, whilst leading up to it the sable-covered steps completed the scheme of outward mourning. One patch of brilliant colour was furnished by the band seated in front of the choir. They had come, 100 strong, from Kneller Hall, to add to the beauty and stately dignity of the service, and their rendering of the music was such as will not be readily forgotten by those privileged to hear.

For some time before noon appropriate pieces had been played, visibly affecting those present, whilst high from the roof came the distant toll of the great bell of the Cathedral to give an added solemnity to the occasion. The Lord Mayor arrived a few moments before the service was timed to begin, being received at the west door by the Dean and members of the Chapter. A short procession was formed, the choir and clergy slowly moved to their places, and the solemn service began. It was simple in character, but well chosen, and calculated to make appeal to the spirit of the hour. The same hymns had been sung before, the same psalms had been chanted again and again, yet they seemed invested with a newer and deeper meaning on this solemn occasion. In the first few moments of that service the hearts of those present were thrown wide open, and tears fell freely and unchecked...

BEREAVED FAMILIES.

PATHETIC SCENES AT SOUTHAMPTON.

"DAILY TELEGRAPH" FUND.

HUNDREDS RELIEVED.

From Our Special Correspondent.

SOUTHAMPTON, Friday Night.

The dreaded proof of widowhood began to be furnished to Southampton wives at breakfast-time to-day. The worst fears of many a wife, mother, and child were realised by noon, and deep gloom settled over the streets wherein the seafaring population have their homes—a gloom unrelieved by any outward display of joy by those who had had good news. Those who had heard their relatives were safe hid their delight lest it should cause pain to women in sorrow and distress.

Knowledge that the pinch of poverty was felt by many families of the Titanic's crew prompted the Mayor, Councillor Henry Bowyer, R.N.R., to begin to distribute the £500 which he has received as the first installment of *The Daily Telegraph* Fund, immediately he procured a list of the survivors. He then could tell from the Board of Trade register who had perished. All the bereaved who were in want were informed that help could be obtained at the Guildhall, and from half-past ten till six o'clock the home of the civic authority was filled with tearful women who required something to tide them over **27** their present desperate position. At one time three large rooms were filled with widows and mothers who had lost the sons supporting them.

When I left at six o'clock, the poor folk were still being brought in, and the Mayor told me he and those assisting him were prepared to wait till midnight to deal with the cases. They will sit again to-morrow, and every day next week, and will cheerfully do anything they can to administer the relief provided by the charitable readers of *The Daily Telegraph*, and so soften the terrible blow which has stunned close upon 2,000 of Southampton's population.

CHIVALRY OF
THE AFFLICTED.

Even in affliction some persons can find time to endeavour to comfort others. This morning I talked to one poor woman, whose two children have been orphaned by the loss of their father, a fireman. She felt acutely the death of her "man," and was beginning to cry when a companion mentioned that a woman in the corner had eight children. "Poor soul," said the widow, "she is worse off than I am. I must do what I can to help her." And off she went to pour sympathy in her ear. When the time came for her case to be investigated by the Mayor she made way for the mother of eight, whose case, she said, was more pressing than her own. Her two children might be hungry, but the problem of providing food for eight empty stomachs was far more urgent. The chivalry of seaman husbands is thus shared by the wives.

Women went into the Mayor's parlour timid and half afraid they were asking for charity. They came out with sufficient money to keep them comfortably for a week, and were told to come again next Friday. All spoke of the tender words of sympathy which the Mayor and his friends had said to them.

At six o'clock the Mayor told me, "We have given away about £150 of *The Daily Telegraph* Fund, and by midnight we anticipate the sum will have reached £200. So far we have relieved from the Fund about 150 widows and mothers, or, with dependents, about 450 persons.

27. This refers to money.

Some of them have received £1. In one case we gave £2, and we told the recipients to come on Friday in each week until such time as a scheme for the final disposition of the funds is settled. The distress is very bad. Prior to the sailing of the Titanic a large number of the sailors and firemen who signed on were out of work for five or six weeks owing to the coal strike. They therefore left their people in very low water, and the wives have been selling furniture and clothing to buy food.

———

"THE WIDOW AND THE FATHERLESS." [28]

———

"We have had widows here to-day who are mothers of eight children, and there were quite a lot with families of six. It was pitiful to see the distress of the poor women. They came in to us crying, shaking, and nervous, but we did the best we could for them, and told them they would not have to worry over money matters for some time. The people are a very good class." [29]

The Mayor was assisted to-day by Alderman Beavis, who superintended the outdoor work, and by Alderman Duniford and Councillor Cheveston, chairman of the Education Committee, inside the Mayor's parlour. Assistance was also given by the whole of the aldermen and councillors in the wards, members of the corporation visiting the homes of the bereaved, and telling them where there was distress that provision for pressing needs could be obtained at the Guildhall. The applicants brought notes bearing on their cases after full investigation. The help which readers of *The Daily Telegraph* have given has been a Godsend to these people, stricken with sorrow.

A person who could have watched without emotion the scene outside the White Star local offices to-day must have had a heart of stone. From the moment when the first name of a sailor survivor was posted till nightfall there was a succession of painful incidents. They were made more harrowing because one could not fail to notice the stern efforts of all the women to be as brave as the heroic men they had lost. Tears—there were floods of them; but the women who could not control their pent-up sorrow bowed their heads, made their way out of the crowd, and allowed their tears to flow unchecked in some out-of-the-way spot far from sympathetic eyes.

28. Deuteronomy 10:18: "He doth execute the judgment of the fatherless and widow, and loveth the stranger, in giving him food and raiment."

29. There are the worthy poor and the unworthy poor, as playwright George Bernard Shaw said through the mouth of Eliza Doolittle's father in *Pygmalion*. The unworthy poor shouldn't expect to receive anything. "The people are a very good class" is meant to reassure readers who have contributed money that their money is being well spent.

Sympathy which was expressed would have made their sorrow harder to bear.

WAITING FOR NEWS.

The progress of these poor widows and mothers through the throng was pathetic enough to move deeply strong men, and many a seafarer held out a helping hand to the relatives of those who had met a cruel fate. Unfortunately, it was not possible to put up the whole list at the same time. The White Star officials very properly posted the information as they received it, holding that it was better to relieve the anxiety of anyone so soon as they were able. But the names came through very slowly, and while there was a prospect of one more survivor being signalled hundreds waited in the belief that the lucky one would be their beloved. When at last the full number was accounted for on the board—the names in some cases had been duplicated and there were nearly 750 names in all posted up—there was a complication owing to the omission of the initials of the stokehold staff. **30**

For instance, a man standing by me said: "Who is Blake? I am anxious about one Blake, but I understand there were four of that name on board the Titanic. It is impossible to know whether one can rejoice or be sad unless more information is given."

This difficulty caused by not forwarding the initials is occasioning a great deal of anxiety. It mainly concerns the firemen, but many people who have relatives of certain names among the seamen are hoping against hope that they have crept in the firemen's list. There are three Allens on the ship's books. One of them only is saved, and his first name is not given. Four Olivers are on the register. Only one is saved. There were two Cunninghams, two Barretts, and three Moores in the ship's company, and one of each survive. Their Christian names have not been given.

The White Star officers here had anticipated this criticism, and as soon as the cablegrams were received they wired to New York, asking for fuller information concerning every member of the firemen's staff saved. At the hour of writing this is not to hand, and the crowd remain, hoping on, but fearing the worst. **31**

While I was in the office lobby a couple of young women made inquiries about a man in the list whose initials did tally with those of the person they sought. One of them insisted that the initials had been copied inaccurately, and asked to see the original cablegram. An officer of the company readily agreed to show it to her, and, when it was produced, it was

---

30. There were 705 actual survivors according to Captain Rostron of the *Carpathia*. Other authorities have stated that either 711 or 712 survived. Seven hundred and twelve may be the most likely figure. That is the figure quoted most often these days (*Encyclopedia*).

31. It took approximately a week for all the correct names and information to reach Southampton.

seen that the words "picked up dead" followed the name.

What struck one most in this sad scene was that the people to whom the blackboard brought tidings joy showed remarkable restraint. "Old Tom's all right," I heard one man mutter as he threaded his way through the press of people to carry the good news to friends. Several people cried, "Thank God!" when they recognised the name they looked for; but there was a deep, reverent note about the exclamations, and no jubilant shout was given, lest it should jar the feelings of men and women watching for the names which never appeared.

SURVIVORS' LIST ANALYSED.

The White Star officials have been at pains to analyse the list of survivors, and to show how many men, women, and children passengers and crew have been saved. They have had a heavy task because the names have in some cases been mutilated in transmission, and especially in regard to foreign third-class passengers it is impossible to identify the sex from the names. The analysis does not pretend to be exact, but it gives figures which may be taken to be approximately correct up to this evening. The names of 729 survivors have been signalled from New York.

Of the passengers, the White Star officials believe 367 to be women and 156 men. Of the 205 crew saved 190 are men and 15 women, two of them cashiers in the restaurant, the remainder stewardesses. If these figures prove accurate, 392 women and 346 men have been saved.

Mr. Lawrence Beesley, whose thrilling narrative of the sinking of the Titanic appears elsewhere, is a son of Mr. H. Beesley, of Wirksworth, Derbyshire, formerly manager of the local branch of the Capital and Counties Bank. Yesterday morning his parents received a cable from Mr. Beesley stating that he was saved. **32**

ACCOUNT
BY A
LONDON PASSENGER.

A RUDE AWAKENING.

NEW YORK, Thursday (11.45 p.m.).

The following account of the disaster is given by Mr. Beesley, of London: **33**

"The voyage from Queenstown was quiet and successful. We had met with very fine weather. The sea was calm, and

---

32. The paper had earlier reported Mr. Beesley lost.

33. Lawrence Beesley's great book, written shortly after the sinking, is *The Loss of the S. S. Titanic: Its Story and Its Lessons*. The *Daily Telegraph*'s account is quite faithful to what Beesley says in his book.

the wind was westerly to south-westerly the whole way. The temperature was very cold, particularly on the last day. In fact, after dinner on Sunday evening it was almost too cold to be on the deck at all. I had been in my berth about ten minutes, when, at about a quarter past ten, I felt a slight jar. Then, soon afterwards, there was a second shock, but it was not sufficiently large to cause any anxiety to anyone, however nervous they may have been. The engines, however, stopped immediately afterwards.

"At first I thought that the ship had lost a propeller. I went up on deck in my dressing-gown, and I found only a few people there, who had come up in the same way to inquire why we had stopped, but there was no sort of anxiety in the mind of anyone. We saw through the smoking-room window that a game of cards was going on, and I went in to ask if they knew anything. They had noticed the jar a little more, and, looking through the window, had seen a huge iceberg go by close to the side of the boat. They thought that we had just grazed it with a glancing blow, and they had been to see if any damage had been done.

"None of us, of course, had any conception that she had been pierced below by part of a submerged iceberg.

A GAME OF CARDS.

"The game of cards was resumed and, without any thought of disaster, I retired to my cabin to read until we started again. I never saw any of the players or the onlookers again.

"A little later, hearing people going upstairs, I went out again, and found

that everybody wanted to know why the engines had stopped. No doubt many of them had been awakened from their sleep by the sudden stopping of the vibration to which they had become accustomed during the four days we had been on board. Going up on the deck again, I saw that there was an unmistakable list downwards from the stern to the bows; but, knowing nothing of what had happened, I concluded that some of the front apartments had filled and had weighed her down.

"Again I went down to my cabin, where I put on some warmer clothing. As I dressed, I heard the order shouted, 'All the passengers on deck with lifebelts on.'

"We all walked up slowly, with the lifebelts tied on over our clothing, but even then we presumed that this was merely a wise precaution the captain was taking, and that we should return in a short time to go to bed. There was a total absence of any panic or expression of alarm. I suppose this must be accounted for by the exceeding calmness of the night and the absence of any signs of an accident. The ship was absolutely still, and, except for the gentle tilt downwards, which I don't think one person in ten would have noticed at the time, there were no visible signs of the aproaching disaster. She lay just as if waiting for the order to go on again when some trifling matter had been adjusted. But, in a few moments, we saw the covers being lifted from the boats, and the crews allotted to them standing by and uncoiling the ropes which were to lower them. We then began to realise that it was a more serious matter than we had at first supposed.

"My first thought was to go down to

get more clothing and some money, but, seeing people pouring up the stairs, I decided that it was better to cause no confusion to people coming up by attempting to get to my cabin.

OFFICERS' ORDERS.

"Presently we heard the order, 'All men stand back away from the boats. All ladies retire to the next deck below,' which was the smoking-room or B deck. The men all stood away, and waited in absolute silence, some leaning against the end railings of the deck, others pacing slowly up and down. The boats were then swung out and lowered from A deck. When they were level with B deck, where all the women were collected, the women got in quietly, with the exception of some, who refused to leave their husbands.

"In some cases they were torn from their husbands and pushed into the boats, but in many instances they were allowed to remain, since there was no one to insist that they should go.

"Looking over the side, one saw the boats from aft already in the water, slipping quietly away into the darkness.

"Presently the boats near me were lowered, with much creaking as the new ropes slipped through the pulleys and blocks down the 90ft which separated them from the water. **34**

"An officer in uniform came up as one boat went down, and shouted, 'When you're afloat row round to the companion-ladder, and stand by with other boats for orders.'

"'Aye, aye, sir,' came up the reply, but I don't think any boat was able to obey the order, for when they were afloat and had their oars at work, the condition of the rapidly settling liner was much more apparent. In common prudence the sailors saw that they could do nothing but row from the sinking ship and so save, at any rate, some lives. They, no doubt, anticipated that the suction from such an enormous vessel would be more than usually dangerous to the crowded boat, which was mostly filled with women.

NO TRACE OF DISORDER.

"All this time there was no trace of any disorder. There was no panic, or rush to the boats, and there were no scenes of women sobbing hysterically, such as one generally pictures happening at such times. Everyone seemed to realise so slowly that there was imminent danger that when it was realised that we might all be presently in the sea, with nothing but our lifebelts to support us until we were picked up by passing steamers, it was extraordinary how calm everyone was, how completely self-controlled we were as one by one the boats, filled with women and children, were lowered and rowed away into the night.

"Presently word went round among us that men were to be put in boats on the starboard side. I was on the port side. Most of the men walked across the deck

34. It was much less than 70 feet to the water by this time.

to see if this was true. I remained where I was, and shortly afterwards I heard the call, 'Any more ladies?' Looking over the side of the ship, I saw boat No. 13 swinging level with B deck. It was half full of women. Again the call was repeated, 'Any more ladies?' I saw none coming. Then one of the crew looked up and said, 'Any ladies on your deck, sir?' 'No,' I replied.

"'Then you'd better jump,' said he. I dropped and fell into the bottom of the boat as they cried, 'Lower away'…"

A CREW OF COOKS.

"The crew seemed to me to be mostly cooks. They sat in their white jackets two to an oar, with a stoker at the tiller. There was a certain amount of shouting from one end of the boat to the other, and the discussion as to which way we should go was finally decided by our electing as captain the stoker who was steering, and by all agreeing to obey his orders. He set to work at once to get into touch with the other boats, calling upon them, and getting as close to them as seemed wise, so that when search boats came in the morning to look for us, there would be more chance that all would be rescued.

"It was now one o'clock in the morning. The starlit night was beautiful, but as there was no moon it was not very light. The sea was as calm as a pond. There was just a gentle heave as the boat dipped up and down in the swell. It was an ideal night, except for the bitter cold.

"In the distance the Titanic looked enormous. Her length and her great bulk were outlined in black against the starry sky. Every porthole and saloon was blazing with light. It was impossible to think that anything could be wrong with such a leviathan, were it not for that ominous tilt downward in the bows, where the water was by now up to the lowest row of portholes.

LAST HOPELESS CRIES FOR HELP.

"At about two o'clock we observed her settling very rapidly, with the bows and the bridge completely under water. She slowly tilted straight on end, with the stern vertically upwards. As she did so the lights in the cabins and the saloons, which had not flickered for a moment since we left, died out, flashed once more, and then went out altogether. At the same time the machinery roared down through the vessel with a groaning rattle that could have been heard for miles.

"It was the weirdest sound, surely, that could have been heard in the middle of the ocean. It was not yet quite the end. To our amazement, she remained in that upright position for a time which I estimate at five minutes. It was certainly for some minutes that we watched at least 150ft of the Titanic towering up above the level of the sea, looming black against the sky. Then with a quiet, slanting dive she disappeared beneath the waters. Our eyes had looked for the last time on the gigantic vessel in which we set out from Southampton.

"Then there fell on our ears the most appalling noise that human being ever heard—the cries of hundreds of our fellow-beings struggling in the icy water, crying for help with a cry that we knew could not be answered. We longed to return to pick up some of those who were swimming, but this would have meant the swamping of our boat and the loss of all of us." —*Reuter's Special Service.*

MR. ISMAY'S STATEMENT.

LAST WORD IN SHIPBUILDING.

INQUIRY WELCOMED.

NEW YORK, Friday (1.30 a.m.).

Mr. Bruce Ismay, of the White Star line, gave out the following prepared statement on the pier:

"In the presence and under the shadow of this catastrophe of the sea, which overwhelms my feelings too deeply for expression in words, I can only say that the White Star officers and employés will do everything humanly possible to alleviate the sufferings and sorrow of relations and friends of those who perished. **35**

"The Titanic was the last word in shipbuilding. Every regulation prescribed by the British Board of Trade had been strictly complied with. The master, officers, and crew were the most experienced and skilful in the British service. **36** I am informed that a committee of the United States Senate has been appointed to investigate the circumstances of the accident.

"I heartily welcome a most complete and exhaustive inquiry, and any aid which I and my associates and our builders and navigators can render is at the service of the public and the Government both in the United States and Great Britain. Under these circumstances, I must defer making any further statement at this hour."

Mr. Ismay said informally before giving out his statement that he left the ship in the last boat, one of the collapsible boats on the starboard side. **37** "I do not know the speed at which the Titanic was going," said Mr. Ismay, in reply to a question; "she hit the iceberg a glancing blow." Mr. Ismay went to his rooms at Ritz Carlton Hotel.—*Reuter.*

---

35. The *Compact Edition of the Oxford English Dictionary* states that "employé" stands for a male worker and the word "employee" means a female worker.

36. This fact will turn out to be of little practical use since it only makes the sinking of the *Titanic* seem more implausible.

37. Collapsible boat C (Butler 126).

PERSONAL STORIES OF THE WRECK.

HEARTRENDING EXPERIENCE

LADY'S LEGS BROKEN.

NEW YORK, Friday.

Mrs. Churchill Candee, of Washington, was taken from the Carpathia with both her legs broken, and hurried off in an ambulance to the hospital. She received her injuries while getting into the lifeboat. Most of the men saved, she declared, were picked up from the water, having plunged overboard after the lifeboats had been launched. **38**

"Major Archibald Butt and Colonel Astor died like heroes," she continued.

But before she could relate details she was hurried away. **39**

Mrs. Edgar J. Meyer, of New York, highly praised the officers and men of the Titanic. Her husband was among those who went down with the ship. She said that after the first shock she and Mr. Meyer ran to the lifeboats. She pleaded with her husband to be allowed to remain with him. He finally threw her into the lifeboat, reminding her of their nine-year-old child at home. Mrs. Meyer, with an English girl, rowed in her boat for four and a half hours. "We were well away from the steamer when it sank," she said, "but we heard the screams of the people left on board. There were about seventy of us widows on board the Carpathia. The captain and the passengers of the Carpathia did all they could for us."

A HONEYMOON TRIP.

Mrs. W. D. Marvin, of New York, who was on her honeymoon trip, was almost prostrated when she learned, on reaching the dock, that her husband had not

38. It would be sniping at this story to report all the inaccuracies that are in it, starting with the report that Mrs. Candee broke her legs in getting off the ship. Six men had been looking after the attractive woman's welfare, and she was one of the few passengers who was most assured of being put into a lifeboat. One suspects that, as so often happens in journalism, very earnest reporters were still trying to make the actual story of the *Titanic*'s sinking fit their preconceived notions as to what should have happened. This problem plagues this particular narrative, but in fairness to the reporter, survivors may have been inclined to embellish their accounts out of simple relief that they were now well and back on solid ground.

39. Mrs. Candee's own account of how she was rescued can be found in the May 4, 1912, cover story of *Collier's Weekly*. It is titled "Sealed Orders."

been picked up by some other boat. "As I was put into the boat he cried to me," she said, "It's all right, little girl; you go; I will stay." As our boat shoved off he threw me a kiss, and that was the last I saw of him."

Mr. Edward Beane, of Glasgow, who, with his wife, occupied a second-class state-room, declares that fifteen minutes after the Titanic hit the iceberg there was an explosion in the engine-room, which was followed a few minutes afterwards by a second explosion.

Mr. A. H. Barkworth, of Tranby House, East Yorkshire, said he was sitting in the smoking-room when the boat struck the iceberg. He saw Mr. W. T. Stead on deck. He described how the forecastle was full of powdered ice. He noted the foremast was listing heavily to starboard. As Captain Smith was telling the women to put on their lifebelts he went down to his cabin and changed his clothes. All the boats had left his deck. He put on his lifebelt and fur coat and jumped overboard. While he was swimming hard to get away he was struck by wreckage, and a huge wave passed over his head. Swimming about, he found a boat, which was rather crowded. He clutched at it and was helped on board. After that they helped another man in. Two men died after being helped into the small boat.

George Rheims of New York, who was on the Titanic with his brother-in-law, Mr. Joseph Holland, a London resident, said that none seemed to know for

twenty minutes after the boat struck that anything had happened. Many of the passengers stood round for hours with their lifebelts on. He saw the people getting into the boats. When all the boats had gone he shook hands with his brother-in-law, who would not jump, and leaped over the side of the boat. He swam for a quarter of an hour and reached a lifeboat. It had eighteen occupants, and was half under water. The people were in the water up to their knees. Seven of them died during the night. Only those who stood all the time remained alive.—*Reuter's Special Service.* **40**

The following further stories are related by survivors:

Mr. Robert E. Daniel, a young cotton broker of Philadelphia, said:

"I was in my cabin dictating to the stenographer when the ship struck the berg. The shock was not violent. The officers who survived told me afterwards the Titanic slipped up on the iceberg and tore her bottom out. No one seemed alarmed at first. I went on dictating until somebody knocked at my door and cried out that the ship was sinking. I grabbed a life preserver and went to the deck. The sixteen boats were filled with passengers, most of them women. Twelve of the boats pulled away from the port side and four from the starboard. There was no panic. Had there been sufficient lifeboats it is my opinion that practically all the passengers would have been saved." **41**

40. This may well have been the overturned collapsible that Second Officer Lightoller took charge of (Lord, *A Night* 153).

41. Except there might not have been enough time to get the remaining 1,500 people into the boats.

Mr. Daniel leaped overboard when he discovered that the ship was sinking and was picked up by one of the boats.

NOVELIST'S DEATH.

Mr. Jacques Futrelle was one of those who parted from his wife and steadfastly refused to accept a chance to enter a lifeboat when he knew that the Titanic was sinking under him. How he went to his death is told by Mrs. Futrelle, who said:

"When the Titanic hit the iceberg there was the most appalling excitement, and who after passing through such experiences could blame those poor people for the panic which overwhelmed them. Jacques is dead, but he died like a hero, that I know. Three or four times after the crash I rushed up to him and clasped him in my arms, begging him to get into one of the lifeboats. 'For God's sake, go!' he fairly screamed, and tried to push me towards the lifeboat. I could see how he suffered. 'It's your last chance, go,' he pleaded. Then one of the ship's officers forced me into a lifeboat, and I gave up all hope that he could be saved…"

A REMARKABLE FEAT.

Mr. August Wemmerstrom [Wennerstrom], of Sweden, spied a collapsible boat behind one of the smoke stacks as the vessel was sinking. With three other men he managed to tear it from its lashings, and the four jumped overboard with it. The boat turned over four times, but each time they managed to right it. While drifting about Mr. Wemmerstrom said he saw at least 200 men in the water who were drowned. Finally he and his three companions were all picked up by the Carpathia.

Mr. George Brayton, of California, related how he was standing beside Mr. Henry B. Harris when the latter bade his wife good-bye. Both started towards the side where the lifeboat was being lowered. Mr. Harris was told of the rule that the women should leave first. "Yes, I know," he replied; "I will stay." Shortly after the lifeboat left a man jumped overboard, and the other men followed. It was like sheep following their leader. Captain Smith was washed from the bridge into the ocean. Shortly before the ship sank there was an explosion which made the ship tremble from stem to stern. Mr. Brayton also said that he saw one of the stewards shoot a foreigner who tried to press past a number of women in order to gain a place in the lifeboats. **42**

Mr. Taylor, another survivor, jumped into the sea just three minutes before the boat sank. He told a graphic story when he landed from the Carpathia.

"I was eating when the boat struck the iceberg. I did not realise for some time what had happened, and no one seemed to know the extent of the accident.

---

42. "Foreigners" or "Italians" were thought to be highly excitable and even irrational as compared to calm, stoic Anglo-Saxons. A good deal of racial profiling does come through in survivors' reports. The Irish weren't thought too well of either, but at least they spoke English.

We were told that an iceberg had been struck by the ship, and we felt the boat rise. It seemed as though she was riding over ice. I ran on deck, and then I could see the ice. There was a veritable sea of it. I should say that parts from the iceberg were 80ft high, but it had been broken into sections, probably by our ship. I jumped into the ocean, and was picked up by one of the boats. I never expected to see land again. I waited on board the ship until the lights went out. It seemed to me the discipline maintained was wonderful."

DOCTOR'S EXPERIENCE.

Dr. J. F. Kemp, the Carpathia's physician, says that their wireless operator happened by chance to have delayed turning in on Sunday night for ten minutes. Thus it was that he was at his post and got the Titanic's call for help. Had he gone to rest as usual, there would have been no survivors. Dr. Kemp describes the iceberg which sank the Titanic as being 400ft long and 90ft. high. **43** The Carpathia cruised twice through the icefield in the vicinity of the fatal spot, and picked up the bodies of three men and a baby. These corpses were committed to the deep on Monday evening. Among the congregation at the funeral service were thirty widows, twenty of whom were under 23 years of age, most of them being brides of only a few weeks or months. Pitiful tales were related by some of the steerage passengers who came off the Carpathia. A few of them were met by relatives or friends, but the majority of them were taken care of by charitable organisations.

A thrilling story was told by Ellen Shine, a 20-year-old girl from county Cork, who crossed to America to visit her brother. "Those who were able to get out of bed," said Miss Shine, "rushed to the upper deck, where they were met by members of the crew, who endeavoured to keep them in the steerage quarters. The women, however, rushed past these men, and finally reached the upper deck. When they were informed that the boat was sinking most of them fell on their knees and began to pray. I saw one of the lifeboats and made for it. In it there were already four men from the steerage, who refused to obey an officer who ordered them out. They were, however, finally turned out."

RACQUETS CHAMPION.

Mr. Charles Williams, the racquet player of Harrow, who was on his way to New York to defend his title of world's champion, said he left the squash court on the Titanic at 10.30. He was in the smoking-room when he first felt the shock. He rushed out and saw an iceberg, which seemed to loom over 100ft above the deck. It broke up admidships and floated away. Eventually he jumped from the

---

43. The *Carpathia* arrived four and a half hours after the *Titanic*'s sinking. The iceberg would have been long gone from the scene. Another case of creative remembering at work.

boat-deck on the starboard side into the sea, getting as far away from the steamer as possible. He was nine hours in a small boat, standing with the water up to his knees, before he was picked up. Mr. Williams said that the sailors conducted themselves admirably.

One of the many tragedies was the loss of the parents of four girls and three boys who were placed together in one of the lifeboats. Two of these children, whose names could not be ascertained, were removed to hospital on their arrival here. One of them is suffering from scarlet fever, and the other from meningitis.—*Reuter's Special Services.*

WHITE STAR STATEMENTS.

The following statement was issued yesterday by the White Star Line:

> The managers of the White Star Line state that they will be quite prepared to reply to any charge which might be properly brought against them when the time comes for doing so, and they gladly welcome the information which has come from New York that an inquiry is going to be held there. **45**

The following cable has been received by the White Star, Liverpool, from their New York office:

> Press here to-day comment most favourably on the behaviour of the officers and crew of Titanic under extraordinary and trying circumstances, and are satisfied the discipline was everything they could desire.

With reference to the statements as to lack of provisions and covering in the Titanic's boats, inquiries in Liverpool show that there is a regular system on liners for providing water and biscuits in boats in cases of disaster. Water beakers and biscuit tanks are part of the boats' equipment, and this equipment was on White Star boats.

LAST MAN SAVED.

SUCKED DOWN WITH THE SHIP.

NEW YORK, Friday.

Of all the recitals of personal adventure in the Titanic disaster, that of Colonel Gracie, of the United States Army, who jumped from the topmost deck of the

---

44. Impossible; almost all survivors tended to exaggerate how long they waited for rescue (Lord, *A Night* 176).

45. Remarkably, all court proceedings were settled in a matter of only four years (Lord, *The Night* 172–77).

Titanic when she sank, and was sucked down with her, is the most extraordinary. **46** Colonel Gracie, on reaching the surface again, swam until he found a cork raft, and then helped to rescue others. He gives the exact time of the sinking of the Titanic as 2.22 a.m., which was the hour at which his watch was stopped by his leap into the sea.

"After sinking with the ship," he said, "it appeared to me as if I was propelled by some great force through the water. This might have been occasioned by explosions under the water, and I remembered fearful stories of people being boiled to death. The second officer has told me that he has had a similar experience.

"Innumerable thoughts of a personal nature having relation to mental telepathy flashed through my brain. I thought of those at home, as if my spirit might go to them to say 'Good-bye' for ever. Again and again I prayed for deliverance, although I felt sure that the end had come. I had the greatest difficulty in holding my breath until I came to the surface. I knew that once I inhaled the water would suffocate me. When I got under water I struck out with all my strength for the surface. I got to the air again after a time which seemed to me to be unending. There was nothing in sight save the ocean, dotted with ice[.]

"The second officer and Mr. J. B. Thayer, jun., who were swimming near me, told me that just before my head appeared above the water one of the Titanic's funnels separated and fell apart near me, scattering the bodies in the water. I saw wreckage everywhere, and all that came within reach I clung to."

A CROWDED RAFT.

Colonel Gracie relates how at last by moving from one piece of wreckage to another he reached the raft.

"Soon," he continued, "the raft became so full that it seemed as if she would sink if more came on board her. The crew, for self-preservation, had, therefore, to refuse to permit any others to climb on board. This was the most pathetic and horrible scene of all. The piteous cries of those around us ring in my ears, and I will remember them to my dying day.

"Hold on to what you have, old boy," we shouted to each man who tried to get on board. 'One more of you would sink us all.' Many of those whom we refused answered as they went to their death, 'Good luck! God bless you!' All the time we were buoyed up and sustained by the hope of rescue. We saw lights in all directions. Particularly frequent were some green lights, which, as we learned later, were rockets fired in the air by one of the Titanic's boats. So we passed the night with the waves washing over and burying the raft deep in water.

"We prayed through all the weary night, and there never was a moment

---

46. He was indeed on the topmost deck, but he only had a few feet to jump to reach the ocean. The ship was about to disappear beneath the waves, the water conveniently rising to meet him (Lord, *A Night* 95).

when our prayers did not rise above the waves. Men who seemed long ago to have forgotten how to address their creator recalled the prayers of their childhood, and murmured them over and over again. Together we said the Lord's Prayer again and again."—*Reuter's Special Service.* **47**

GETTING NEWS.

---◆---

REPORTER'S DARING.

CAPTAIN AND PRESSMAN.

INTERESTING DIALOGUE.

From Our Own Correspondent.

NEW YORK, Friday (11.58 a.m.).

As regards Press messages, the Carpathia, until she arrived alongside the pier last night, remained silent and unapproachable from first to last. The newspaper correspondents, who had chartered tugs to meet the Cunarder at sea, spent hours lurking around in fog and rain, only to find permission to board the Carpathia and interview the survivors was refused, and they were compelled to return to port suffering from exposure and mortification. Incidentally, they found the Carpathia able to outpace them and land her passengers, while the smaller vessels, with the disappointed interviewers aboard, were still groping their way towards New York Harbour.

All sorts of schemes to board the Carpathia in the harbour without permission were devised, and just as promptly frustrated. One tug swung close to the Carpathia when it was within an hour of the landing-stage, and a daredevil reporter of the *New York American* jumped aboard.

AN ADVENTUROUS
REPORTER. **48**

A number of the crew were at hand to impede his way, but the reporter finally reached the bridge of the Carpathia, where he met Captain Rostron.

---

47. Gracie's account here stands out as being very consistent with what he records in his book, *Titanic: A Survivor's Story.* Within a year, the colonel was dead, perhaps from heart strain brought about by his night on the ocean (Butler 232).

48. The direct quotes here are a total mystery. One can only assume that the man who got on board later told his story to other reporters. One of these reporters who heard the story must have been a reporter for the *Telegraph*, but all of this is wild surmise. To the reporters, Captain Rostron was simply wrong in not giving them the access they demanded.

"What do you mean by being on this ship?" the captain asked. "You are under arrest, and will be put in irons."

"Why haven't you given the public the truth about this affair?" the reporter asked him. "My hands were tied," the captain replied. "I could not do so. There were a thousand reasons why I couldn't answer."

"Why didn't you answer the President's message regarding Major Butt?"

The captain refused any answer to this question.

"Can I see some of the passengers?" Captain Rostron was next asked. "I am a friend of Mrs. Jacques Futrelle. Can I see her?"

"No, you cannot see any passengers," replied Captain Rostron, "and when the ship reaches the pier, I intend to turn you over to Captain Roberts, who has charge of the pier. I won't permit you to talk to anybody."

"I want to see Mr. Ismay," said the irrepressible newspaper representative. "I want to see him for the American people."

"You cannot do so," declared the captain. "You are under arrest."

"That's all right," said the reporter, "but you have not given out the news, and we have waited almost a week; will you let me get it now?["]

"You stay on the bridge with me, or I'll put you in irons," said Captain Rostron, grimly.

MEMORIAL SERVICE AT SEA.

"Did you hold a memorial service before the iceberg that sent the Titanic to her doom?"

"We did," replied the captain. "I stopped the ship and held a service on Monday morning."

"Did you save the bodies the Carpathia either did pick up or might have picked up?"

"What do you mean?" asked Captain Rostron.

"I mean of thirty-five persons in one lifeboat at 2.20 o'clock in the morning, only sixteen were found alive when it was picked up, and at that time three dead bodies were in the boat?" **49**

"I won't talk to you. I want you to stay here where I can watch you," was all the reply vouchsafed by the captain.

"Captain Rostron," urged the Pressman, "do you realise this is the most gigantic tragedy in the history of the sea, and the world won't accept your whims about giving it the information it wants?"

"I realise, sir, that you came aboard this boat in spite of orders, and I won't be catechised or criticised by you."

"Captain, I want to see Mr. Bruce Ismay. The American people would like to hear from him?"

"You be quiet. You can't see anybody, I tell you."

---

49. It is a wonder Captain Rostron didn't chuck the reporter overboard. There was no such lifeboat, as the best observers—Beesley and Gracie—make clear.

"Is either John Jacob Astor, Major Archibald Butt, William T. Stead, Artist Millet, Isador Strauss, Mrs. Isador Strauss, or Benjamin Guggenheim aboard?"

"I think not," replied the captain.

"Do you still refuse to let me see Mr. Ismay?" was the next question.

"I'll let you see no one," replied Captain Rostron.

"After this," says the New York reporter, in describing the episode, "the Carpathia's master paced the bridge like a man suffering under a great load of anxiety, and in spite of the general opinion that he was master of his ship he seemed conscious of the fact that he had subordinated his position, advisedly or otherwise, to more powerful influences, and appeared to realise the error of having remained mute up to this time." **50**

CHINESE STOWAWAYS.

REMARKABLE RESCUE.

From Our Own Correspondent.

NEW YORK, Friday.

Among those rescued from the sinking Titanic were six Chinese, who stowed themselves away in one of the vessel's boats before she left England. **51** When the crash came the Chinese did not become excited. They knew the lifeboat would be lowered if there was any danger of the Titanic going down. All had shawls, and when they heard the shouts of those on board, "Women to be saved first," they covered themselves with the shawls, leading the crew to believe that they were women.

50. More than likely Captain Rostron was still considering whether he might chuck this reporter overboard.

51. There was one Japanese stowaway on Fifth Officer Lowe's boat. Other accounts, including one by Bruce Ismay, state there were stowaway Filipinos on board who might have been mistaken for Chinese emigrants (*Encyclopedia* "Chinese sailors on the Titanic").

★ ★

Whoever the stowaways were—whether Japanese, Chinese, or Filipino—they would have been illegally in the United States. It is likely, though no records seem to exist on this issue, that even European emigrants would have been sent back to their home countries. However, no one can really be sure if there were stowaways on the ship. Recordkeeping was extremely imprecise. A search reveals that there were Chinese passengers on board, but they had *paid* to be there.

In the darkness they escaped detection. It was not known that they were Chinese until they were taken on board the Carpathia. Then some of the Carpathia's crew wanted to toss them into the sea, it was said, but the officers of the Cunard vessel put them in irons instead. How the Chinese escaped being discovered by the crew of the Titanic or some of her passengers puzzled those on board the Carpathia.

To-day the Federal officials took the imprisoned Chinese while the necessary arrangements preparatory to sending them back to their native country are being made.

APPALLING
DISASTER
TO
TITANIC

FEA

1,68

UNK IN

AN IC

REPO

,358 O

NEW YO

c sank at

NEW YO

ing statemer
officials:
Haddock, of t
at the Titanic
passengers
s and transfe
amer Carpat
from the Tit
—Reuter.
a.m. we rec
age from Nev
y:
e Star offic
een lost.—R

YORK, Mo

ng despatch
Race:
her Olympic reports that the steamer
ached the Titanic's position at   day-
ound boats and wreckage only.
ted that the Titanic foundered about
at. 41 deg 16 min, long. 50deg 14min.
age adds:
anic's boats are accounted for. About
re been saved of the crew and passen-
er are nearly all women and children.
nd Liner California is remaining and
vicinity of the disaster.

NEW YORK, Monday (9.10 p.m.).
The Titanic's survivors on board the Carpathia are
stated at the White Star offices to include all the
first-class passengers.
    She is expected to reach New York on Friday
morning.—Reuter.

NEW YORK, Monday (9.50

tude rarely, if ever, equalled in the long history of
disasters at sea.
    It was at 6.7 a.m. yesterday that the first news
was received that the Titanic had struck an iceberg
while on her maiden voyage from Southampton to
New York.
    Both in shipping circles and among the general
public the utmost excitement and consternation
were caused.
    As has happened on several previous occa-
sions the first

the collision Captain Smi
Titanic, sent out the reco
help, consisting of the lett
frequent intervals.
    The etheric waves were
late on Sunday night, and
mitted to London, New
or assistance
ng the Cuna
erranean, the
and the Balti
to the White
s at once hea
far as can be
nts of the disa
the Carpathia

al circumstan
hentic is yet
captains hav
of ice in that
Liners which
at they enco
large fields
four days ou
into this da
half-past ten
time, which
day morning
eberg.
e effect of th
ons striking
extensive inj
ture.
the latest te
in the direct
e went down
t is not yet kn
e difficulties
have been w

N HOU

MAYOR'S

The Daily Te

by your cou
opened a fu
mmediate ai
ows, orphan
—whether th
e lost their
y, and to in
erous assistance of the benevo
tempting to relieve, in some d
which has been occasioned in
of families by a disaster fort
leled in the history of ocean
taking this step, I feel sure the
responding to the wishes of the
the keen sympathy universally
entertained for those who ha
been plunged into misery and

SUNDAY,
APRIL 21, 1912

DAY SIX

Remember the Sabbath Day, to Keep It Holy

(There was no Sunday newspaper.)

THE DAILY TELEGRAPH,

APPALLING
DISASTER
TO
TITANIC

FEAR

1,68

NK IN

AN IC

REPO

,358 O

NEW YO

sank at 2

NEW YO

ng statemer
officials:
addock, of t
t the Titanic
passengers
s and transfe
ner Carpat
rom the Tit
—Reuter.
m. we rec
ge from Nev

Star offici
en lost.—R

ORK, Mo

g despatch
ce:
er Olympic reports that the steamer
ched the Titanic's position at   day-
and boats and wreckage only.
ed that the Titanic foundered about
t. 41 deg 16 min, long. 50deg 14min.
e adds:
nic's boats are accounted for. About
been saved of the crew and passen-
r are nearly all women and children.
d Liner California is remaining and
vicinity of the disaster

NEW YORK, Monday (9.10 p.m.).

The Titanic's survivors on board the Carpathia are
stated at the White Star offices to include all the
first-class passengers.

She is expected to reach New York on Friday
morning.—Reuter.

NEW YORK, Monday (9.50

tude rarely, if ever, equalled in the long history of
disasters at sea.

It was at 6.7 a.m. yesterday that the first news
was received that the Titanic had struck an iceberg
while on her maiden voyage from Southampton to
New York.

Both in shipping circles and among the general
public the utmost excitement and consternation
were caused.

As has happened on several previous occa-

the collision Captain Smit
Titanic, sent out the reco
help, consisting of the lett
frequent intervals.

The etheric waves were
late on Sunday night, and
mitted to London, New
or assistance
ng the Cunar
erranean, the
and the Baltic
to the White S
at once head
far as can be
nts of the disas
the Carpathia

al circumstanc
hentic is yet k
captains have
of ice in that
Liners which
at they enco
large fields o
four days out
into this dan
half-past ten
time, which c
day morning
eberg.
e effect of the
ons striking
xtensive inju
ture.
the latest tel
in the directi
e went down,
t is not yet kn
e difficulties i
have been we

N HOUS

MAYOR'S A

The Daily Te

by your cour
opened a fun
nmediate aid
ws, orphans
—whether the
e lost their li
y, and to inv
erous assistance of the benevol
tempting to relieve, in some de
which has been occasioned in
of families by a disaster fortu
leled in the history of ocean
taking this step, I feel sure tha
responding to the wishes of tho
the keen sympathy universally
entertained for those who have
been plunged into misery and

INTRODUCTION

———◆———

First, the joy of recovered survivors, then the grief for the priceless lost: The deaths of 1,500 souls could not be a mere accident; such a number demands a reckoning. There are questions now, and there will be more questions. Captain Smith, though, is already a sainted hero.

Head of the U.S. Senate Inquiry William Alden Smith (no relation to the captain) can only say of the *Titanic*'s commander:

"Those of us who knew him well, not in anger but in sorrow, file one specific charge against him: *overconfidence* and neglect to heed the oft-repeated warnings of his friends" (Wade 288).

Yet, who to blame? Who will be the luckless person?

Fortunately, an obvious target lies close by—the executive director of the White Star Line has survived the disaster. Why didn't he have the good grace to go down with his ship like the captain? Joseph Bruce Ismay will see himself pilloried in the press and savaged by the investigation (Eaton and Haas, *Titanic: Destination* 126).

Ismay's ordeal begins with the *Daily Telegraph*'s account of the first day of Senate proceedings. It will end only after he has been driven into retirement by the directors of the White Star Line themselves, eager to get rid of any reminder of their greatest failure.

Though others will also testify, this is a day J. "Brute" Ismay will never forget (Lord, *The Night* 180).

CLEARING A MYSTERY.

IMPORTANT STATEMENT BY THE CAPTAIN OF THE OLYMPIC.

FALSE REPORTS
OF
SAFETY.

TAPPING WIRELESS MESSAGES.

From Our Special Correspondent.

SOUTHAMPTON, Sunday Night.

When the White Star leviathan Olympic had landed her passengers here to-day, Captain H. J. Haddock, her commander, in an interview sought by me, made a very important statement concerning the telegram published throughout the world on Monday that all the Titanic's passengers were safe, and that the liner was proceeding to Halifax under her own steam. The interview is of extreme importance considering the criticism which has been made to the effect that the publication of the telegram resulted in reducing the rate for reinsurance on the Titanic from 60 guineas to 20 guineas per cent. **1**

I give Captain Haddock's statement in his own words, and anything I may introduce to make it absolutely clear to the public I put in parentheses:

"On the passage from Cherbourg to Southampton I received a letter from two newspaper correspondents on board requesting me to explain a telegram sent from America to England on Monday that 'All Titanic passengers safe. Titanic proceeding slowly to Halifax under her own steam,' and which caused a drop from 60 to 20 guineas in reinsurance at Lloyd's on Monday afternoon. It was stated in the letter handed to me that the telegram was supposed to emanate from the Olympic, because it came through Reuter. The correspondents asked whether that message was sent from the Olympic, and if so how it came to be sent if it was not true.

"A wireless message was received on the Olympic on Monday from one of our old passengers, a lady living in New York, who has crossed many times by White Star liners. On it were the words, 'Are all Titanic passengers safe?' (or saved, I am not sure which). I thought the lady had friends on the Titanic. That message was received on board at 10.20 or 10.27 New York mean time, which is equal to 3.20 or 3.27 Greenwich time. At another period of

1. A false report had circulated that the *Titanic* was saved and under tow to Halifax, but this report cannot be traced to anyone trying to influence the market. See the rest of the article.

the day—I think it was earlier—we were in communication with the ship Asian, from which I tried to get information about the Titanic. The Asian could give us very little, but amongst the words used to us was the statement that she (the Asian) was towing an oil tank steamer to Halifax."

HOW THE ERROR OCCURRED.

Captain Haddock showed me the letter-book copy of his letter sent to the owners of the Olympic at Liverpool, giving his answer to the request for information. This letter, after stating the application of the correspondents, proceeds:

I, in the presence of our Marconi operator, have denied that such a message was received by or sent from this ship. The only solution that I can offer for the Reuter message is the enclosed Marconigram ("Are all Titanic passengers safe?"), which may have been tapped in transmission and the "are" missed. The remaining words, "Titanic making Halifax," being suggested by the Asian message, a copy of which is already in your possession.

The message is probably from a constant White Star traveller—(Captain Haddock mentions the name in his letter, but I am not at liberty to give it, and it is of no public interest to do so)—and I on receipt of the message made the same mistake and left out "are," and telephoned the inquiry office (the Olympic's inquiry office) to put up a notice reading, "All Titanic's passengers safe."

Nothing more was added. We have been most carefully through every message from the ship. No copy of my error, plain or code, or the remainder of the sentence, was sent from this ship.

H. J. Haddock.

This statement, on a subject which has been agitating the public mind on both sides of the Atlantic, will be read with great interest. I asked Captain Haddock what the Olympic did on receiving the distress signal from the Titanic in the early hours of Monday morning. The Olympic's commander replied, "When we picked up the Titanic's message we were 505 miles away. We steamed hard towards her for fourteen hours."—(from another source I ascertained the Olympic steamed twenty-three knots an hour during this period)—"and then we picked up the Carpathia's signals. The Carpathia is a Cunard passenger boat, and when we heard she had done everything possible to rescue the Titanic's passengers and crew, there was nothing more we could do. We resumed our course."

I also asked Captain Haddock if he saw any ice, and he answered in the negative. "A week before the disaster," he said, "the Olympic passed over the spot where the Titanic sank, or a few miles to the north of it. It was broad daylight, and we never saw a particle of ice of any description, and from the bridge of the Olympic we could see about twenty miles on either side. The observations in the locality were perfect, and there was no sign of ice whatever. That is the tragedy of the whole thing. The field of ice which caused the disaster was travelling south at a more rapid pace than I had ever known."

————

BOATS ENOUGH
FOR ALL.

————

While I was on board the Olympic I noticed that the White Star Company are not waiting for any revised Board of Trade regulations before increasing the supply of boats for the huge ship. The Olympic on her last voyage carried sixteen large lifeboats and four big rafts. When she sails again she will treble that number, and will have enough boats to accommodate every person on board. I watched the process of hauling extra boats to the hurricane deck. The new boats are of the collapsible type—long, beamy craft, fully stored with water casks and biscuits, and fully equipped. I saw one boat on deck, and nine others in a barge alongside, while in the dock were others. As far as could be ascertained, the Olympic will carry forty collapsible boats, in addition to her lifeboats and rafts.

———◆———

From an
Unsigned Editorial

————

A week has passed since the Titanic sank after collision with a detached iceberg off the Newfoundland Banks. So long as human records last, the memory of the discipline, heroism, and self-sacrifice displayed by passengers and crew—by the men in their strength, who calmly met death, and by the women, in their weakness, who as calmly faced life anew, lonely and grief-stricken—will be cherished as among the proudest, if saddest, chapters in the history of the two English-speaking peoples. As we have been wont to tell the story of the wreck of the Birkenhead, so our children's children will dwell on the terrible, and yet beautiful epic of the sea which was recounted in the special cablegrams published in *The Daily Telegraph* on Saturday. **2** As a page from life's day-book, the story is now complete. There will, of course, be searching inquiries both here and in America as to the causes of the collision and the circumstances which account for so heavy a toll of life. But in its essential details the narrative is ended, and the public have already begun to wonder what steps can be taken to render such a disaster not, perhaps, impossible, but at least less likely, in future, and, if it should happen, less appalling in its results. One confession has been exacted by Nature from man, which ocean travellers without expert knowledge never thought to see set down in black and white as an incontrovertible fact. We must recognise that, as there is no building which is absolutely fireproof, no train which can be guaranteed against accident, no

★ **2.** The HMS *Birkenhead*, a troop-ship, went down in 1852. Troopers stood at attention on deck so that women and children could be evacuated first. More than six hundred soldiers lost their lives (Wikipedia "HMS *Birkenhead*").

reservoir dam which may not burst, so there is no ship which is unsinkable. While that is so, there are ships which do not readily sink, and of these the Titanic was a notable example. Not until she practically faced her doom was the iceberg seen. Then the helm was starboarded, and she received a slanting blow from the razorlike edges of her treacherous foe. In an instant, the great vessel's side was laid open to the sea— iron plates were cut with the precision with which a sardine tin is opened, or were so bent and punctured that the rivets sprang. Thus some of her compartments filled instantly, and others soon gave way under the strain. In order to remain afloat, with a fraction of an inch above sea-water level, it was necessary that the water should give the Titanic an upward support of about 60,000 tons. After the collision this essential force was withdrawn. If she had charged the iceberg end-on, it is probable that her bow would have been merely driven in, and she would have maintained sufficient reserve of buoyancy to enable her to reach an American port for repairs. But her navigating officer, in seeking safety, sealed her doom. In endeavouring to avoid all damage he laid the ship's side against the steel-like shears of the iceberg, with the result that she was cut open in a manner unique in maritime records. Had she been of smaller dimensions, of less stout build, and with fewer watertight compartments, she

would probably have sunk with hardly a minute's delay, and the proportionate loss of life would have been far greater. Under conditions which the mind of man never conceived as possible, the vast mass of steel remained afloat for no less than two and three-quarter hours. From what is known of ship construction, it may be doubted if a foreign-built vessel of similar size would have emerged from this deadly duel as well as she did. Though the Titanic has sunk, though the Titanic has been proved to be not unsinkable, British shipbuilders are not disgraced, but may claim the 705 survivors as living witnesses to the character of British design and workmanship. In all the elements of construction making for safety, this vessel excelled; she did not merely comply with the requirements of the Board of Trade and Lloyd's Register—the highest standards in this respect in the world—but she exceeded them in a manner and to an extent that foreign ships do not exceed them. **3**

But while we may draw this consolation from the story of the loss of the Titanic, the question may be asked— and will be asked—whether there are not measures which could be taken to render such ships—for the day of big ships is assuredly not ended—even less liable to disaster. It is clear, beyond all question, that higher standards are urgently necessary. A community always gets for its use the vessels it deserves— the ships it wants. An American Senator,

---

★ **3.** British pride was taking a beating in many American newspapers because editorialists felt the English could have built and should have built, for all the expense of the *Titanic,* a much safer ship (Marcus 204–05).

indeed, confessed that the American people are more to blame for the catastrophe than any others, because they have been the most exigent. From both sides of the Atlantic has come the demand for high speed. High speed means danger. Yet speed has been developed. It has been urged that ocean travel shall approximate in comfort, and even luxury, to the conditions of a first-class hotel. The shipbuilders of all the great maritime nations have responded. The Titanic was a palace—the apotheosis of luxury at sea. If those who voyage to and fro across the Atlantic are prepared to accept less comfort and less speed, then the question will arise whether the weight which may be saved can be employed so as to insure a larger margin of safety in case of accident. It may be that this can be done, but one thing is certain—the peril of the sea never can and never will be eliminated. Precautions may be taken—every possible precaution should be taken suggested by human ingenuity—but when all has been done it is always the unexpected that happens. Steps are adopted to guard against this or that danger, and it is some new and unthought-of danger that proves our undoing, for Nature in her manifestations is always surprising us and undermining our confidence. In the history of navigation no vessel has had an experience resembling that of the Titanic—collision on a starlight night with an iceberg, seen by the lookout man in the high-perched crow's nest too late to avoid violent concussion; a smooth sea, in which even collapsible boats could live; passengers with a high sense of discipline and courage, officers and men of the crew realising to the full their responsibility. We may legislate for the iceberg's deadly blow—the rare phenomenon of Atlantic travel—and it may be that the next rude awakening will come from some other cause. But while that is true, a wide field for investigation in ship construction is opened up by this catastrophe, because the precautions taken against ice may conceivably prove valuable in the next emergency, due to some other peril. We cannot sit down in complacency under the heartrending blow; we must strive for improvement, even though we know that the perfect ship, the ship which cannot be sunk, will never ride the waves…

While there was no great revolution in ship construction as a result of the *Titanic*'s sinking, supposed watertight bulkheads were vastly improved. For one thing, they were made to go higher in ships so that there was less likelihood of water filling a compartment and spilling over the top and into another compartment. Even longitudinal bulkheads were considered in an effort to protect ships from iceberg puncture wounds, but the liner *Lusitania* had longitudinal bulkheads and sank anyway when struck by a German torpedo during World War I. There is a limit to what technology can do.

———◆———

MR. ISMAY
AT THE
SENATE
INQUIRY.

———

TITANIC'S SPEED.

———

ABOUT 21 KNOTS.

———

IMPORTANT EVIDENCE.

———

SPECIAL CABLE
FROM OUR OWN
CORRESPONDENT.

NEW YORK, Sunday.

Mr. Bruce Ismay was the first witness called on Friday before the Investigating Committee. **4**

He said, under oath: "I am the managing director of the White Star Line, but I travelled on the Titanic as a voluntary passenger. The accident took place on Sunday night. The exact time I do not know. I was in bed asleep when it happened. The ship sank, I am told, at 2.20 a.m. That is all I think I can tell you at this moment.

"The ship had never been at full speed. This would have been seventy-eight revolutions, working up to eighty. She had not all her boilers on. It was intended, if we had fair weather on Monday afternoon or Tuesday, to drive the steamship at full speed. Unfortunately, the catastrophe prevented this.

"I came off on the last starboard boat."

"Can you describe what you did after the impact or collision?"

———

WHEN THE SHIP STRUCK.

———

"I presume the impact awakened me. I lay for a minute or two, and then I got up and went into the passageway, where I met a steward and asked him what was the matter. He replied, 'I don't know, sir.' Then I went back to my stateroom, put on my overcoat, and went up to the bridge, where I saw the captain. 'What has happened?' I asked. 'We struck ice,' he replied. 'Is the injury serious?' I asked. He replied, 'I think so.' Then I came down, and in the entry-way I saw the chief engineer. I asked him if he thought there was any serious injury. He said he believed there was. Walking along the deck I met an officer on the starboard side and assisted him as best I could in getting out women and children. I stayed on deck until the starboard collapsible boat was lowered."

★ **4.** The investigating committee was really a subcommittee of the Senate Committee on Commerce. William Alden Smith had himself appointed chairman and did the bulk of the interrogations. None of the subcommittee members had any nautical expertise, but they were chosen to be bipartisan with regard to political affiliation. There were seven members total (Butler 179–81).

"Was she the last boat?"

"The last, so far as I know. Certainly the last on that side."

"Was the captain then on the bridge?"

"That I do not know."

"Did the captain remain on the bridge?"

"I don't know."

"Then the statement of the captain that the ship was seriously in danger, and that of the chief engineer, were to the same effect, with hope?"

"Yes."

"The pumps could be kept going?"

"Practically that."

"Did you have any talk with any officers other than the captain, the chief engineer, and the steward you met?"

"No."

"Did the officers seem to know the serious character of this collision?"

"That I couldn't tell. I had no conversation with them."

"Did any officer say it was not serious?["]

"No, sir."

THE CAPTAIN ON THE BRIDGE.

"You went to the bridge immediately after you left your room?"

"Yes, after I put on my coat I went straight to the bridge. The captain was there."

"In what part of the ship were your quarters?"

"On B deck, just aft the main companionway."

"Do you know how many passengers were on this deck?"

"I had no idea how many passengers."

"You say your trip was voluntary?"

"Absolutely, and for the purpose of seeing the ship in action. I had no business in New York at all. It was simply a case of wishing to see how the vessel behaved and of getting ideas for improvements in the new ship which we are building." **5**

"Was there any official or representative of the builders on board?"

5. This would have been the planned next ship in the White Star Line's constellation of big luxury ships: the *Gigantic*. It was renamed *Britannic* to give it a less ostentatious identity (Eaton and Haas, *Titanic: Destination* 55).

J. Bruce Ismay being questioned by the Senate Investigating Committee.

"Yes, the representative of the builders was Mr. Thomas Andrews."

"What was the occasion of his voyage?"

"To see whether everything was satisfactory, and also how he could improve on the Titanic."

"Was he among the survivors?"

"Unfortunately, no."

"How old a man was he?"

"I should say 42 or 43. He may have been less."

"Then you were the only executive officer, outside the ship's customary officers, aboard?"

"Yes, sir."

NO CONSULTATION
WITH THE CAPTAIN.

"Did you have occasion to consult the captain about the movements of the ship?"

"Never."

"Did he consult you?"

"Never. Perhaps I am wrong in that. What we talked about was not to attempt to arrive at New York Lightship before five o'clock on Wednesday morning. That was arranged before we left Queenstown."

"Was it supposed you could reach New York by that time without putting the steamship to full capacity?"

"Oh, yes. Nothing was to be gained by arriving sooner."

Senator Smith: "You spoke of the revolutions being increased as the voyage proceeded?"

Mr. Ismay: "They were gradually increased. With a new steamship you always begin with a low speed."

"Did you exceed seventy revolutions?"

"Yes."

"You were going seventy-five on the Saturday, the day before the accident?"

"Yes; but that, of course, was nothing to full speed."

"During the voyage did you know at any time you were in close proximity to icebergs?"

"I knew ice had been reported."

"Did you personally see any icebergs, or any large bodies of ice?"

"Not until after the collision. I had never seen an iceberg."

"Had you ever been on the northern route before?"

"We were on the southern route…"

THE ORDER TO
LOWER THE BOATS.

"Were you on deck when the order was given to lower the lifeboats?"

"I heard the captain give the order when I was on the bridge."

"Will you tell us what he said?"

"It is difficult to remember exactly. As I recall it he said, 'Lower the boats.' As soon as I heard him give this order I left the bridge."

"Did you see any boats lowered?"

"Yes."

"How many?"

"Certainly three."

"Will you tell us how they were lowered?"

"They were swung out, people were put in from the deck, and then the boats were lowered to the water."

"On which decks were the boats?"

"They were all on one deck, the sun deck?"

"Were any orders given, or supervision

exercised, by the officers of the ship in lowering the lifeboats?"

"I can only describe what I saw myself. The boats were filled, and the crew put in and sent away."

"How many?"

"That I couldn't tell."

"How many men were in the boat in which you left the steamship?"

"Four."

"Does that mean of the crew?"

"Four of the crew."

"What positions did they occupy?"

"I believe one was a quartermaster."

"You saw three boats lowered?"

"Yes…"

and seven o'clock next morning?" **6**

"Of that I know nothing. I couldn't say 'yes' or 'no.' I didn't see such a thing."

"Were you, when you first went on deck, only partly clothed, and did you make inquiries of the officers, or started and then returned?"

"That's right."

["]How long were you on the ship after the collision?"

"That is difficult to answer. Practically until she sank."

"How long was that?"

"It is difficult to judge the time. I could not answer that. I should say an hour and a quarter, perhaps longer."

NO SELECTION
OF WOMEN.

"Were the women passengers designated as to which should go in the boats?"

"They simply picked out the first women they could find, and put them into the boats. I myself put a great many women into the boats."

"Did you see any lifeboat without a complement of oarsmen?"

"No."

"Did you see the first lifeboat lowered?"

"That I cannot answer. I saw the first lowered on the starboard side."

"It has been intimated that some of the lifeboats did not contain men enough, and that a number of women were obliged to row from 11.30 at night until between six

HOW MR. ISMAY
LEFT THE SHIP.

"Did you during this time see any passenger you knew?"

"I saw a good many passengers, but I don't remember recognising any of them."

"What were the circumstances of your departure from the ship; in what way did you leave?"

"I was immediately opposite the lifeboat. A certain number of people were in it. An officer called to know if there were any more women. No women were in sight on the deck then. There were no other passengers about, and I got in."

"How did she collide? Was there a side blow?"

6. Women had to row in some cases because the lifeboats were short of crew who were familiar with rowing. Every launched boat was taken from the water by the rescue ship *Carpathia* (Marcus 171–94).

"I have been told she hit the ice somewhere between the breakwater and the bridge on the starboard side."

"Did you see the passengers or any men on the boats with life-preservers on?"

"Nearly all the passengers I saw had life-preservers on."

"When you entered the lifeboat yourself you say there were no passengers on that part of the ship?"

"None."

"Did you at any time see any struggle among the men to get in?"

"None."

"Any attempt as the boats were lowered between decks to get on?"

"None; there were no passengers there to take on." **7**

"Before you boarded the lifeboat did you see any passengers jump into the sea?"

"I did not."

"After you were taken off did you see any of the passengers or any of the crew with life-saving apparatus on in the sea?"

"No."

"What course did your boat take?"

"We saw a light in the distance and attempted to pull the boat toward it."

"How long were you in the lifeboat?"

"About four hours."

"Were any others in the vicinity?"

"Yes."

"How many?"

"I can't say; one we hailed, but got no answer."

"Did you see any rafts in the open sea?"

"None..."

WOULD NOT SEE
THE SHIP GO DOWN.

"What can you say about the sinking and disappearance of the ship?"

"Nothing. I did not see her go down."

"How was that?"

"I was sitting with my back to the ship. I did not wish to see her go. I was pushing with an oar. I am glad I didn't see her go."

"When you last saw her had she broken in two?"

"No."

"When did you last see her?"

"I could not say. It might have been ten minutes after I left her. It was impossible to judge the time. I gave only one glance over my shoulder."

"Was there much apparent confusion?"

"My back was turned. When I glanced around I saw the ship's green light."

"Did you get a message from the captain?"

"No..."

★ **7.** Ismay is painting a picture of the situation that Senator Smith is finding hard to believe. Others have also had their doubts. Jack Thayer Jr. is reported to have said: "A large crowd was pressing to get into them [the boats]. No women were around as far as I could see. I saw Ismay, who had been assisting in the loading of the last boat, push his way into it. It was really every man for himself" (Marcus 309).

THE TITANIC'S SPEED.

"What speed were you making?"

"Seventy-five revolutions. I should think that would mean twenty-one knots."

The committee put their heads together, and wanted to know about how much that would mean in land miles.

A member of the committee suggested it was about twenty-six miles an hour.

Mr. Ismay: "I should say somewhere about that." (It is twenty-four.)

"Did you have anything to do with the selection of the men who accompanied you in the lifeboat?"

"No."

"How were they designated? I presume by the officer in charge of the boat?"

"By Wilde, the chief officer. I believe the men of the crew were allotted to certain boats on a station list."

"Can you describe the rafts?"

"There were none on board the ship."

"Did you see any rafts?"

"None." **8**

"Is it customary to carry rafts?"

"Not in recent years."

"Why?"

"I believe they are not considered suitable for modern ships. This ship was especially constructed so as to float with any two compartments—any two of biggest compartments full of water, and I think I am right in saying there are very few ships—perhaps I had better not say it."

Mr. Ismay was urged by Mr. Franklin and Mr. Parvin to say what he intended.

Mr Ismay: "Well, I believe I had better continue in order to avoid misapprehension. I was going to say I believe there are very few ships to-day of which the same can be said. When we built the ship we had this in mind. If the ship had hit ice head on, in all human probability the ship would have been afloat to-day." **9**

---

8. It was futile questions such as this that earned Senator Smith a good deal of criticism in the British press. To them, he should have already known that rafts were not a good idea as a safety device, as they would provide no protection from the cold water of the sea. The folly of having absolutely no naval expertise on the committee itself tainted everything it did (Marcus 215–17).

9. Apparently this statement is true. On the other hand, an estimated 200 people lodged in the front of the ship would have died in such a head-on collision. First Officer Murdoch had only a matter of a few seconds to make his steering decision. It is also true that if the *Titanic* had only been punctured in a couple of places along the side, she would have remained afloat in that situation as well. Thus, many religious commentators of the day came to the conclusion that the loss of the *Titanic* was ordained of God to punish the pride of Modern Man in his overconfidence in technology and the Mighty Machine. A less prominent ship's sinking might not have required religious comment at all (Cox 74–5).

HOW THE SHIIP STRUCK.

Senator Newlands: "How did the ship strike the iceberg?"

Mr. Ismay: "The information I received was that she struck a glancing blow between the end of the forecastle and the captain's bridge."

Senator Newlands: "If any two compartments had been filled with water she would still have floated?"

Mr. Ismay: "Any two of the largest."

Senator Smith: "What time did you dine on Sunday evening?"

Mr. Ismay, "7.30, with the ship's doctor."

"And the Captain?"

"No, he did not dine with us."

"Was there any ice about when you went to bed?"

"I saw no ice until daylight next morning."

"Do you know if any people were killed by the ice coming on deck?"

"I do not. That would only be a matter of hearsay."

"Were all the women and children saved?"

"I am afraid not."

"What proportion would you say?"

"I don't know. Since the accident I made very few inquiries."

"Did any of the collapsible boats sink?"

"I don't know."

Senator Newlands: "What was the full equipment of the ship?"

Mr. Ismay: "I couldn't answer that. The Board of Trade regulations were complied with—regulations which I understand are accepted by the United States."

MR. ISMAY'S PLANS.

"Did you attempt to interfere with the wireless communication between the Carpathia and other stations?"

"The captain of the Carpathia could tell you I hadn't moved out of my room until the night we arrived in New York."

"What were you wearing when you left the Titanic?"

"A suit of pyjamas, a pair of slippers, a suit of clothes, and an overcoat."

"How many officers were on the ship?"

"I think, seven."

"How many of a crew?"

"I don't know the full number. There are always three officers on watch."

"How many men were in the lifeboat with you?"

"I couldn't tell. I suppose nine or ten."

"Was there anybody you knew?"

"I knew Mr. Carter. As far as I could see, all the rest of the men were third-class passengers."

"You indicated your willingness to supply the Committee with any data that may be necessary regarding the construction and equipment of the vessel?"

"It is absolutely at your disposal. Any one of the surviving officers or crew you may wish to see is at your disposal."

"What are your plans?"

"I understand that depends on you."

"I want to thank you for responding so promptly to our request, and I am going to ask you to hold yourself subject to our call."

Mr. Ismay: "I am entirely at your disposal, gentlemen."

HEROIC CONDUCT
OF
WOMEN
SURVIVORS.

THRILLING
NARRATIVES.

LADIES PULLING OARS.

SUFFRAGISTS' CLAIM.

"WOMEN BRAVER
THAN MEN."

SPECIAL CABLE
FROM OUR OWN
CORRESPONDENT.

NEW YORK, Sunday.

Instances accumulate here that womanhood will never find anything for which it need blush in the Titanic disaster.

Every virtue shown by the men had its duplicate many times in the women, and the manifestations are numerous. I collected to-day from the survivors enough evidence to prove that if bravery is essential to suffrage, many women who landed from the Carpathia on Thursday should have not one vote, but a dozen.

The world now knows of the devotion of Mrs. Isador Strauss, who would not forsake her husband, and, likewise of Mrs. Allison, of Montreal, who was joined by her daughter.

"I won't go without you," said Mrs. Strauss to her husband, and she resolutely fought off the efforts of the crew to put her into a boat. "No," said Mrs. Allison bravely, and she eluded those who would have saved her and her daughter. **10**

Physical force got Mrs. Astor into the boat, as it did Mrs. Walter Clark, of Los Angeles; Mrs. George Widener, of Philadelphia; Mrs. Jacques Futrelle, Mrs. John Thayer, Mrs. Turrell Cavendish, and many others, English and American alike.

GAVE HER LIFE
FOR ANOTHER.

The heroism of Edith Evans, who gave up her own life that another might be saved, stands out conspicuously.

★ **10.** There is a strange story to the Allisons. The nurse they chose for their children, Helen, age 2, and Hudson, age 11 months, was a convicted child murderer, fleeing from notoriety. Nurse Cleaver, at some point during the *Titanic*'s sinking, simply took the boy, Hudson, and got on a lifeboat, without telling either of his parents. The parents went down with the ship as they searched for their "lost" son, who was eventually found and rescued by relatives in New York (Geller 15–18).

Miss Evans was nearly 30 years old, and, independently well-to-do, she spent much of her time in travel. She was a passenger on the Titanic, travelling with her aunts, Mrs. Cornell, Mrs. Appleton, and Mrs. Brown. **11** The signal came for the women and children to go, and Mrs. Cornell and Mrs. Appleton secured seats in one of the lifeboats. Mrs. Morgan **12** and Miss Evans sought another. It was one of the last boats to go. They found places, but as the boat was about to be lowered it was seen to be overcrowded. One person would have to get out. Miss Evans arose, although her aunt put out a restraining hand, announcing she would go. "I must be the one to go," declared the young woman. "You stay; you have children at home; I have nobody." She jumped out and the lifeboat was lowered. That was the last seen of her.

Mrs. Brown thereafter showed a spirit which made her volunteer to leave the boat. There were only three men in the boat, and but one of them could row. Mrs. Brown, who was reared on the water, immediately picked up one of the heavy sweeps, and began to pull. In the boat, which carried Mrs. Cornell and Mrs. Appleton, there were places for seventeen more than were carried. This boat, too, was undermanned, and two of the ladies at once took their places at the oars.

COUNTESS OF ROTHES' BRAVERY.

The Countess of Rothes is now at the Ritz-Carlton Hotel, New York, under the care of a physician. I learn it is not so much exposure and shock which have made her ill, as the effects of her hard labour in pulling at the oars. Her boat was likewise undermanned, because the crew preferred to stay behind.

One able-bodied seaman, who shipped aboard the Titanic when she left Southampton, is tired and a little listless and subdued from the things he lived through last Monday. But his eyes light up and his speech becomes animated when you ask him what part the women played in the trying hours after the Titanic sank.

"There was a woman in my boat as was a woman," he told *The Daily Telegraph* representative yesterday. "She was the Countess of Rothes. I was one of those who was ordered to man the boats, and my place was in No. 8 boat. There were thirty-five of us in that boat, mostly women, but some men along with them. I was in command, but I had to row, and I wanted someone at the tiller. When I saw the way she was carrying herself, and heard the quiet, determined way she spoke to the others, I knew she was more of a man than any we had on board, and I put her in command. I put

11. Mrs. John Murray Brown, not the "unsinkable" Molly Brown (Butler 129). Molly Tobin Brown was traveling among the extremely well-to-do but was reluctant to leave the ship until she was bodily thrown into a lifeboat.

12. Brown

her at the tiller, and she was at the tiller when the Carpathia came along five hours later."

"And there was another woman on board who was strong in the work we had to do. She was at the oar with me, and though I never learned her name she was helping every minute. It was she who suggested we should sing. 'Sing?' you say! I should think we did! It kept up our spirits. We sang as we rowed, all of us, starting out with 'Pull for the shore,' and we were still singing when we saw the lights of the Carpathia. Then we stopped singing, and prayed."

Mrs. Allen Becker, a missionary of the Lutheran Church, was aboard the Titanic with her three children, Ruth, Marion, and Richard. Fearing confusion, she kept her three children in the stateroom until the stewards came with their cries of "Last call for the boats!"

WOMAN SAVES SAILOR.

Of Miss Bentham it is related that she was sleeping soundly when the stewards came for her. She arose, dressed herself warmly, and was handed into a boat. This was very crowded; so much so that one sailor had to sit with his feet dangling in the icy-cold water. As time went on, the sufferings of the man from cold became apparent. Miss Bentham arose from her place and had the man turned round while she took his place with her feet in the water.

Miss Mary Young showed her spirit by compelling those in command of one boat to take on more passengers. When her boat got away it was found there was room for many more. There were twenty-six aboard when Miss Young thought forty could be carried safely. "Twenty-six is the limit," said one sailor. The young woman declared more should be taken, and she was so emphatic that they picked up several who were swimming in the water.

PERIL OF OVERCROWDING.

The lives in many of the boats were imperilled because they took from the water more people than the craft could safely hold. **13** Mrs. Joel Swift was another woman who took her turn at the oars. There were twenty-four persons in her boat, four of them men, all members of the crew. "Let me help," she said; and she did. She induced other women to turn in, saying it would warm them up.

Miss Marie Young, **14** who taught music to the children of President Roosevelt, was another oarswoman. She was in a boat which she said was marked to have a capacity of eighty persons,

---

13. A lovely sentiment, but official testimony at both U.S. and British inquiries disproves this. Most boats were underloaded, not overloaded.

14. In a preceding paragraph there is a mention of a "Mary Young." There is no record of such a woman surviving, but Marie Young did survive (Lord, *A Night* 194).

although there were only twenty-eight in it. Miss Young, finding only four men to do the rowing, took her seat at the rowlock and went to work. She was very cool, and even reproved a sailor for puffing strong tobacco.

Mrs. Marvin could not row, but she helped by taking care of a little brown-eyed French girl who was handed into the boat as it was being lowered. There was no one to claim the youngster, and she still carried the child in her arms nearly five hours later, when the Carpathia had come to the rescue. The youngster is now in the care of the Women's Relief Committee.

Miss Jessie Leitch, of London, a second-class passenger, came ashore with the six-months-old infant of her cousin, the Rev. John Harper, of London, who was drowned. Mr. Harper handed the child to her, kissed the little one good-bye, and remained to perish. Miss Leitch wrapped the child in her own clothing, and stoically endured the cold until help came. **15**

Six or seven little babies, all orphans, are now nestling in cots provided by the relief committee. All are doing well. **16**

Mrs. Fred Kenyon got into a boat in which three men; not members of the crew, were at the oars. Mrs. Kenyon discovered that none of these men could handle an oar. She and several of her sisters in the boat contemptuously ordered the men out of their places, and picked up the sweeps. They and one sailor handled the boat until help came.

A SUFFRAGIST'S CLAIM.

And so one could enlarge the list by the score. Apropos of the women's heroism, as developed in the tragic story of the Titanic, several of our most notable women suffragists are declaring that "women are naturally braver than men," and should refuse to go first into the lifeboats.

This novel view was expressed yesterday by Miss Lida Stokes-Adams, a prominent Suffragist, of Philadelphia, who declares that women lost one of the greatest chances ever presented in the cause of female suffrage, when they did not assert themselves even more, and prove they were on a superior plane to men from the point of view of personal courage.

"Of course," she conceded, "it is hard to answer whether the women and children should have had the preference in such a disaster, but I don't think they should have had. I think the women should have insisted that the boats be filled with an equal number of men and women, or that the men should have had an equal chance of saving themselves, even though in brute strength they are the stronger. It would have been a wonderful thing for the suffrage cause if this had been done. Years from now there

---

15. Oddly, John Harper's wife does not seem to be listed among the passengers (Tibballs 487).

16. None of the children rescued off the *Titanic* needed to be sent to an orphanage as they all had either parents or relatives living (Wikipedia, "Michel Marcel Navratil").

will be similar accidents, and I venture to say men and women will share the disaster alike, and women will endeavour to save the men."

After making this prediction Miss Adams praised the men of the Titanic for their heroic conduct.

———◆———

CHILDREN'S
PATHETIC STORIES OF
THE WRECK.

———

SPECIAL CABLE
FROM OUR OWN
CORRESPONDENT.

NEW YORK, Sunday.

Several of the children who were saved from the Titanic have told pathetic stories of how they were rescued before the big ship down. Jack Thayer, aged 14, and William Carter, aged 10, two small survivors of the Titanic, are the spokesmen for the members of their family who were saved. Little Jack was thrown overboard by his father just prior to the Titanic's final plunge, and was picked up by one of the drifting lifeboats. His account of the last farewell with his mother and father is graphic and touching.

"Mother and I were about to go to bed when we were thrown headlong to the floor of our state room," said Jack. "In a few minutes father came hurrying to our aid, and it didn't take us long to reach the main deck. Men and women were running in every direction. Everyone was excited, and women fainted, and the cry soon went up that the Titanic had struck an iceberg.

———

QUIETING THE
PASSENGERS.

———

"Officers and sailors soon began shouting 'No danger,' and quieted many. Father and I did our utmost to quiet mother, but the collision had unnerved her.

"Soon the crew began lowering the lifeboats. Officers shouted orders for the women to be taken off first, and that the men must stay aboard. I could see women all around me refusing to leave their husbands. Mother was one of them. She took me by the arm and endeavoured to drag father to the man in charge of the boats. Father told her to get in, but she clung to me. I didn't want to leave father, and I kissed mother good-bye. I told her not to worry; that we would join her later. For the next hour nothing could be heard on the deck but cries and curses. **18**

"Father and I stood together. There

★ **17.** This account is quite different from his account recorded in *The Sinking of the Titanic: 1912 Survivor Accounts,* abridged and edited by Bruce M. Caplan from the Logan Marshall original. See Chapter XV.

18. According to Thayer's later account, he actually became separated from his mother and father and was not with them as the ship took its plunge. Mrs. Thayer also survived (Lord, *A Night* 194).

was nothing more to do. Most of the women had been taken off. At last father saw the boat was about to sink. He put a life preserver about my neck and told me to jump, and said he would follow. Next thing I knew I was flying down the side of the boat. Whether I jumped or father threw me overboard I do not know. I struck the water and floated around until I was almost frozen.

"I THOUGHT OF FATHER."

"A big stick of wood came within my reach and I grabbed it. I became numb, and I thought of father. I believed mother was saved. I felt no pain, but I lost consciousness. I think I floated around for hours. I don't remember being picked up. I don't remember being carried aboard the Carpathia, but when I awakened I was there, and mother was leaning over me. Nobody knew anything about father."

Young Carter, whose father, mother, and sister were saved, said he saw several men shot for disobeying orders.

"Mamma awakened me just after the accident," said the little boy. "She told me there had been an accident, and I was to be a brave boy and dress myself quickly. While she and my sister were dressing I dressed myself, and we all went out on deck, where we had been ordered to go. We found the women crowded in one part of the deck and the men in another.

BOYS AND GIRLS WITH THE WOMEN.

"All the boys and girls were with the women, and once in a while a man would try to break through. It came our time to get into the boat. It was hard on that boat, and we found there very little to eat. Everybody began to worry and wonder if we would be picked up. Some were brave, but a lot cried. I cried too. We rowed away from the big ship, and mamma helped to row. Her hands were all blistered in the daylight.

"We saw another steamer, and we were picked up. I was awfully glad my mamma and my sister were saved, and I feel awfully sorry for the other people. It is awful sad."

Arthur Olsen, a little eight-year-old Norwegian, who lost his father, but was saved himself, was one of the children left unclaimed when the Carpathia arrived at New York. [19] Through an interpreter he said:

"In our boat everybody was crying and sighing. I kept very quiet. One man got very crazy, and then cried just like a little baby. Another man jumped right into the sea and was gone. It was awful cold in the boat, but I was dressed warm like we dress in Norway. I had to put on my clothes when my papa told me to. On the big ship I couldn't talk to anybody because I don't understand the language."

Henry Christiana, another lad, told the following story. [20]

19. Listed as a third-class survivor (Tibballs 494).

20. No Henry Christiana is listed on passenger lists, but a Marshall Drew is listed as surviving from second class (Tibballs 487).

LIKE BAD DREAMS.

["]It all seems like the bad dreams I used to have," he said. "I never want to go to England again. I went over there with my uncle and aunt, Mr. and Mrs. James Drew, to visit my grandpa. We had a good time in England, and started back on the Titanic. The night of the wreck my aunt woke me, and said she was going to dress me and take me out on deck. I was sleepy, and didn't want to get up. I could hear funny noises all over the ship, and sometimes a woman talking loud in the corridor. My aunt didn't pay any attention to what I said, but hurried me into my clothes and rushed me with her up to the deck. There everyone was running about, and some men were laughing, and saying that there was no danger. They were taking all the women and hurrying them into the boats, along with the children. We couldn't see what for. I thought at first we had got home.

"Aunt Lulu put me into the boat, and then stood back with Uncle James, but in a moment someone hurried her into the boat, too, and we went down the side. Uncle James was waving his hand at us, and Aunt Lulu was standing up and looking at him. Then our boat pulled away from the ship, and there was a lot of talking and screaming. We were a long time on the water, and finally got something to eat on the Carpathia."

AMERICAN MARKETS.

REUTER'S AGENCY.

NEW YORK, April 20—Events in the financial world this week have been almost completely overshadowed by the great marine tragedy, which acted as a depressing influence. Political and other events having a bearing on Wall Street were almost ignored in the gloom that prevailed. There were indications in yesterday's late trading, however, that the market is breaking loose from these conditions...

BOATS FOR ALL.

PROBLEM OF SAFETY.

A flood of suggestions, challenging accepted practice at innumerable points, has followed upon the loss of the Titanic. Apart from the questions of speed, lookout and course to be followed during the ice season, these suggestions chiefly relate to three principal matters. They are:

1. Number, character, and launching position of boats and kindred life-saving appliances.

★ Keep in mind what deadline pressure these journalists reporting to England must have been under. It would be difficult to get names of all children correct under any circumstance.

2. Provision of an adequate number of trained men for the launching, handling, and navigation of boats.

3. Structural arrangements to secure the added safety of the ship.

To set out these three heads of discussion is to indicate that the practice of the shipowner, the sufficiency and efficiency of the seamen, and the complete success of the naval architect are all called in question.

It is well, in commenting upon this subject, to accept the view that the big ship has come to stay. During the past twenty years the tonnage of Atlantic liners has gone on steadily increasing, with valuable consequences to the public from the standpoint of safety. The big ship, so far as ability to fight the elements is concerned, has proved the safe ship. What we have now to deal with are problems arising out of the unsuspected vulnerability of the big ship embodying the latest ideas in structural strength and sub-division. In other words, it is demonstrated for the first time that the life-saving appliances of the big ship must equal in proportion those of the small ship, to the extent of offering a chance to everybody on board. That is the minimum which the public demands, and the shipping companies will no doubt accept the formula, whatever it costs.

DETACHABLE DECKS.

This will mean in the case of some Atlantic liners not merely the doubling, but the trebling, of the boat accommodation, unless some adequate substitute can be provided. A proposal has been made that ships should be provided with detachable decks, which would float when the vessel herself sinks. This idea has the support of some seamen, who argue that a detachable portion of the deck might be so carried as to remain an integral part of the ship, until released by a tap of the carpenter's hammer... **21**

The boat deck of the Titanic was at least 75ft above the water-line, and expert opinion was rather disposed to think that this had its disadvantages. It appeared to be generally agreed by both British and German builders that if ships ever got any higher the boats would have to come down. It is worth noting, however, that the Titanic's boats were successfully launched from this great height, and with gear that was quite new. Only one boat was swamped, it is said. It might have been very different, of course, had there been a heavy swell, and if the vessel had been rolling considerably. But in such circumstances boat-launching might be difficult and dangerous work in the case of any ship. That, and the risk to the boats after launching, only shows that the safe ship is the primary desideratum.

QUESTION OF STABILITY.

There is good reason to believe that the early boat-deck plan of the Titanic

---

21. This idea was never tried. We are talking about a section of ship weighing several tons being released by the "tap of the carpenter's hammer." Unlikely.

contemplated the carriage of thirty-two big boats on the boat-deck, instead of sixteen. The double-acting type of davit was fitted throughout, according to Mr. Welin, so that it would be possible to double or treble the number of boats without structural alterations, if official regulations required it. Hence there was apparently never any idea that a largely-increased provision of boats on the boat-deck would in any way interfere with the stability of the vessel. **22**

But if there is any scruple on that point, or if, on balance, expert opinion holds that there are advantages in carrying boats at a lower level, and in the hull of the vessel, then, at all costs, space will have to be found for the purpose. The problem of giving every passenger a chance is not insoluble, even in the case of a huge vessel like the Titanic.

Mechanical power is already furnished in the case of ships' launches. There seems to be no reason why a proportion of ships' lifeboats should not have a motor installation... **23**

We have dealt, so far, with the question of life-saving appliances. Their service-ability obviously depends upon the use that can be made of them. Here, always subject to the overwhelming forces of Nature, comes in the human element. The disaster to the Titanic suggests:

1. Need of an adequate number of executive officers to direct the launching of boats, and to assume navigational control of them after launching.

2. Need of a sufficient number for each boat of trained seamen, used to boat handling.

3. Correlation of passengers and crew with a boat-launching programme, the initial stages of which shall be rehearsed soon after the ship leaves port.

In other words, what is wanted is system. A doubt may be expressed whether half a dozen officers, in addition to the commander, are sufficient for the modern mammoth. If we cannot hope for the formula, "One officer for one boat"—and clearly we cannot—the next best thing will be that the responsibility for the control of an individual boat shall be definitely placed upon an officer, quartermaster, boatswain, or other competent person. Then we come to the question of manning.

UNSKILLED SEAMEN.

Here it is as well to be frank. We are paying for the change from sail to steam. We are paying for the current and excusable

---

22. No, the ship would not have been unstable, but it would have looked cluttered with an additional sixteen boats, making a safe launch of them even more problematic in a mere two hours and forty minutes. I personally suspect that little could have been done to save any more lives, given the inexperienced nature of the crew in handling lifeboats.

23. Lifeboats with motors never made it to production either, possibly because of the difficulty in maintaining the motors and in keeping the fuel safe.

notion that what is wanted as the deck hand of to-day is a sort of ocean warehouseman. He must have had sea experience, of course, but it does not follow that he can handle a boat to which many precious lives may have to be committed. The "crowd" on the Titanic was necessarily new to a new ship, and that was not in favour of the best use in an emergency of the best available material. But any system stands condemned under which with a total crew of 900 to choose from, it is found that some at least of the sixteen or twenty boats depended for their handling on stokers and cooks. In a given condition of sea, the very best lifeboats available would have had no chance unless most capably managed.

The remedy is obvious. The complement of more lifeboats is the provision of a sufficient number of skilled seamen to man them and handle them. This is essentially a shipowner's question. Owners are at great pains in these days to train young men on sailing ships in order that they may become executive officers. It is now clear that they must take steps to provide trained sailors for the work of life-saving, for which the trained sailor is indispensable. Moreover, the general effect of this casualty will be to focus much needed attention upon the general question of personnel. The drilling of the passenger—if possible without unduly alarming him—is, of course, a desirable feature of any new régime. **24**

Naval architects, meanwhile, must be called upon to do their part in grappling with unexpected problems. Double bottoms, divided into watertight compartments, and running the full length of the ship, transverse watertight bulkheads, extending from bottom to upper deck— these are shown to be inadequate in the event of serious bilge damage. One suggestion is that ships should have watertight decks, instead of vertical bulkheads, the idea being that if the lower part of the ship were injured the upper part would still keep afloat... **25**

OWNERS AND THE PUBLIC.

In his own interests, if from no other motive, the shipowner is going to put himself right with the public. But it seems impossible that he can escape serious additional expense. More lifeboats, more trained seamen, structural changes, loss of space—these are all possible heads of outlay. Then there is the question of wireless telegraphy. This has been so widely installed that the Board of Trade, unlike the authorities of some other countries, has never had to make wireless equipment compulsory. But it may deem it desirable to do so now in the case of every ship carrying a certain number of passengers. This would affect a good many boats not at present equipped. If the Board of Trade does not act, the installation will be made by owners in the case of all fairly

24. Of course, this is now standard practice.

25. An improbable design alteration that never got off the ground.

large ships, because if the intending passenger's first inquiry is, "Has she plenty of boats?" his second is sure to be, "Has she got wireless?"

Thus the outlook for the shipowner is one of expense and of reorganisation, leading gradually to the restoration of public confidence. And the cost of it all? Some of it may possibly be attained by the cutting down of luxury. We may get ships that will be both simpler and safer, and perhaps there will be no real regret.

HASTY PURCHASES.

In the past few days an exceptionally large number of orders have been placed for lifeboats for ships' use. The steamship companies are evidently not going to wait for the Board of Trade to decide what the future regulations in the matter of boat accommodation shall be. They are bowing immediately to public opinion, clearly recognising that the liners which can show that they are adequately equipped with life-saving appliances will in future be assured of patronage. This is shown by the effort which is being made to get further boats supplied immediately. Not only are builders being pressed to furnish new boats without delay from their stocks, but the inquiry extends to secondhand boats in good condition.

The essential requirement is that they shall be delivered quickly.

One of the easiest ways of adding to the life-saving equipment is by taking on board collapsible boats. **26** These have the advantage of being stowed without difficulty, since they occupy but little space. It is obviously not a simple thing at a moment's notice to alter the entire boat installation of a ship. New boats might be dumped down on the boat deck and safely lashed, but unless the davit installation is taken into account, the thing is only half done. It may be supposed, therefore, that some of the purchases of collapsible boats represent a tentative measure, designed to carry the ship along until additional boats of the usual type, whether built of wood or of steel, are forthcoming, and the davit arrangements have been altered.

BUILDERS' HEAVY ORDERS.

Builders of ships' boats report a great influx of orders, sufficient to keep them busy for many months to come. This is not surprising, when it is remembered that if public opinion is to be satisfied there are Atlantic lines which, in some form or other, must treble their boat accommodation. How this is to be done may, in the case of each steamer, present a more or less serious problem that cannot be finally dealt with at the moment.

26. These were probably Engelhardt boats, which were collapsible only in the sense that their sides could be raised and lowered, being made of canvas. The boats' bottoms were firmly made of wood.

But the essential thing is to make sure of the necessary boats, as far as the stocks of both new and secondhand will admit. In this, as in other instances, it is a case of "first come, first served." **27**

In the case of steamers now in North American ports, or on the way thither, somewhat peremptory cables with respect to the provision of additional boats have been despatched in certain cases. The fact that stocks on the other side can be drawn upon will to a considerable extent alleviate the position. Their more favourable situation as regards current boat equipment makes the problem one of less urgency for various lines trading to the Southern Hemisphere, but, generally speaking, it may be stated that the question of boat accommodation is receiving the close consideration of the steamship companies.

SOUTHAMPTON'S MOURNING.

ACUTE DISTRESS.

IMPRESSIVE MEMORIAL SERVICE.

From Our Special Correspondent.

SOUTHAMPTON, Sunday.

Wherever you move about this growing seaport town, you are confronted with plain evidence of stricken families, bowed down with grief, at the loss of breadwinners. It is doubtful whether you could walk 100 yards without meeting someone who is mourning a husband, father, or brother, and on every side you hear a tale of woe. You hear it, that is, if you inquire; sorely-tried people do not parade their sorrow or their distress, but only a blind man could fail to notice it. **28**

27. Engelhardt boats served their purpose but eventually proved unreliable in rough waters. Canvas is not a good substitute for wood in stormy seas.

28. According to Daniel Allen Butler in his book *"Unsinkable": The Full Story*, Southampton was the port city most heavily hit by the loss of the *Titanic*: "Four out of every five crewmen aboard her had come from this proud old seafaring town, whose ties to ships and the sea dated back to Roman times." Because of a coal strike affecting not only Southampton but other ports, men had been especially fortunate to have been able to sign up for the *Titanic* voyage, which was considered a godsend by the city's out-of-work seamen. The effect of the sinking was so great that entire streets were "hung with black crepe, whole rows of houses bereaved" (172). Over a third of the dead, some 540 people, came from this vital seaport town.

In 2012, the city is set to open a permanent *Titanic* museum on the 100th anniversary of the sinking. The museum is long overdue. The city has over 4,000 artifacts for display, and, currently, only has a statue in a park honoring the ship's lost engineers (Bates).

The scenes in the Audit Hall, where the Mayor and his committee are dispensing relief, were as depressing yesterday as on Friday. They were much the same in character, and could not very well be different; but as you watched the people in the waiting-rooms and corridor you realised that the deeper gloom had settled upon the widows and bereaved mothers. Some of the cases were extremely pathetic. One young woman, scarcely out of her teens, came in carrying two tiny children. She broke down completely when one tried to comfort her, and a mother, who had lost her sole support, cared for her little ones till the flood of tears ended. Then the poor girl, on receiving back the younger baby, smothered it with kisses, and cried, "How shall we live?" A sympathetic soul near by said the fund would provide for her; but the poor creature replied that there were so many people to look after that she could not believe she would get help, and her children would want. She was told that her babies would also be looked after, but she said that was too much to believe, and refused to be comforted. The Mayor was able to allay her fears, but the prospect of the future was terrible for her, and she went away full of doubt.

This young widow, with heavy cares upon her, felt her position more, possibly, than anyone else in that melancholy heartbroken throng, but her case was typical of the rest. All are deeply thankful for the temporary assistance which is in the first instance being provided out of *The Daily Telegraph* Fund, but they see a desperate future unless the response of the philanthropic is adequate. A feeling of doubt and uncertainty is extending to those whose friends and relatives among the crew have been notified as survivors. The correction of the lists of first and second class passengers has caused a very uneasy feeling. Those who should be jubilant at the news that their friends are living are saying if mistakes could be made in regard to passengers they could also be made in the names of the crew. The lists have been removed from the front of the White Star offices, and it is to be hoped that the alarm of relatives is groundless. I am assured the names of the crew surviving have been received twice, and there is every reason to believe the published lists are accurate. There will be dreadful tragedies in homes which to-day are happy if this confidence is misplaced...

The Mayor's fund last night reached £10,000, and it will be considerably added to to-day. The passengers and crew of the Olympic have subscribed £1,500, and other incoming vessels are making collections.

SUMMARY.

As a direct outcome of the disaster to the Titanic, big shipping companies are ordering more lifeboats without waiting for Board of Trade regulations.

In the American Senate a resolution was carried suggesting that international treaties should be adopted regulating the course and speed of Atlantic liners, and various provisions for the safety of passengers.

Passengers and crew who have been rescued alike declare emphatically that Captain Smith died a sailor's death.

As the last boat was launched he was standing on the bridge, over which the sea was already breaking.

"Well, boys," he shouted, "you've done your duty, and done it well. I release you. It's every man for himself now. God bless you."

A little child had climbed on to the bridge. Seizing her, he jumped overboard, hoping to give her to the occupants of one of the boats.

The fireman who gives this account did not see the captain again.

Exciting details of the sinking of the Titanic were told to the Senate Investigating Committee.

Subpœnas were served on Mr. Bruce Ismay and many others as soon as the Carpathia was berthed last Thursday night.

Mr. Bride, assistant wireless operator on the Titanic, stated that the Frankfurt, of the North German Lloyd Line, was the first to acknowledge the cry for help.

"We gave the Frankfurt our position, and we never heard from her again," declared Mr. Bride.

Further inquiries are being made into these allegations.

Pathetic stories of the wreck are told by some of the children who were rescued by the Carpathia.

A little boy of ten describes how his mother helped to row the boat in which they left the Titanic.

Jack Thayer tells how his father, just as the great liner was going down, threw him overboard. **29**

During the week-end no less than £3,871 was received for our Fund for the dependants of the crew, making a grand total of £9,649...

★ **29.** Thayer was the son of John B. Thayer, president of the Pennsylvania Railroad. According to his later recounting in *The Sinking of the Titanic: 1912 Survivor Accounts* (Caplan 185–91), young Thayer jumped into the ocean and surfaced near collapsible B, where Lightoller was directing operations. Some of the men on B helped him aboard, and later he was reunited with his mother. Tragically, his father perished.

HEROES
OF THE
TITANIC.

◆

PUBLIC APPEAL.

THE DAILY TELEGRAPH FUND
FOR THE WIDOWS & ORPHANS.

A WONDERFUL LIST.

NEARLY £10,000

IN FOUR DAYS.

...At the request of many subscribers, *The Daily Telegraph* is taking steps to offer to the family of the heroic Marconi operator, Phillips, a substantial gift from the Fund in recognition of the splendid services of the man who died for others, continuing to send out the signals for help after the captain had told him to save himself. It is also felt that Bride, his assistant, who left hospital in the Carpathia to help the exhausted operator on that vessel, has a strong claim upon the generosity of our readers, and we do not doubt that we have their sanction for including him in our scheme. **30** There is also an earnest and general desire that something should be done at once for the families of the bandsmen, who to the last had no thought of saving themselves, and were heard playing "Nearer, my God, to Thee," before the vessel sank. It is well within our province to undertake to provide for the immediate wants of the musicians' widows, orphans, and other dependents. Some of these men, moreover, were Londoners, and, therefore, outside the operation of the scheme of immediate relief organised in Southampton. The support extended by the musical profession to *The Daily Telegraph* matinée at Covent Garden demands from the Fund in return the readiest recognition of the gallantry of the musician-heroes of the Titanic...

★ **30.** It is doubtful that Harold Bride received any money when it came to light that he had earned nearly four years' worth of salary by selling his story as an exclusive to the *New York Times*.

★ ★

Because the bandsmen were not considered passengers, nor part of the crew, for a brief time aid to their widows fell between the cracks of public generosity; but the public at large and other musicians in particular were not about to forget these heroic men. Eventually, a substantial fund was raised for widows and orphans of band members. One fundraising effort in particular included the London Symphony, the New Symphony, the Beecham Orchestra, and "those of two opera houses." Sir Edward Elgar, Sir Henry J. Wood, Landon Ronald, and Thomas Beecham conducted (Bryceson 237).

TRAGEDY
OF THE
TITANIC

---◆---

SEVERE INQUIRY BY THE AMERICAN SENATE

MR. ISMAY EXAMINED
FORBIDDEN TO LEAVE THE COUNTRY.

MR. BRIDE'S STATEMENT.

STRANGE ALLEGATIONS.

GERMAN SHIP MYSTERY.

SPECIAL CABLE
FROM OUR OWN
CORRESPONDENT.

NEW YORK, Sunday.

After listening to the sensational details given in connection with the catastrophe, the Senate Investigating Committee, which has been hearing witnesses here, decided yesterday afternoon to adjourn, and resume the inquiry in Washington.

This Committee subpœnaed Mr. Bruce Ismay and other officials of the White Star Line on Thursday night, and also many of the officers and survivors, and by means of searching questions succeeded in securing a flood of valuable information bearing upon the tragedy.

HURRIED CONGRESSIONAL ACTION.

Americans are greatly exasperated because they had to wait so long for detailed and authentic news of the loss of the Titanic, and pressure was at once brought to bear by influential newspapers at Washington, with the result that a subcommittee of the Senate's Committee of Commerce was hastily assembled to subpœna witnesses and secure sworn statements before Mr. Ismay and the others returned to England. The subpœnas were served immediately the Carpathia arrived on Thursday night, and, as a result, Americans are now seeing the chief participants in the Atlantic horror, and hearing at first hand their sworn statements, which yesterday and the day before were of absorbing interest.

Senator William Smith, of Michigan, a leading member of the Congressional Committee, was asked, before the first session began, whether it was true, to his knowledge, that Mr. Ismay sent three wireless messages ashore from the Carpathia directing the steamship Cedric, at New York, to be held, so that the surviving members of the Titanic's crew could be sent back to England.

SENATOR SMITH'S EXPLANATION.

Mr. Smith replied:

"Why, yes, of course. That is one

reason why this hearing began so soon. A Government boat picked up messages stating that Mr. Ismay desired to sail on the Cedric, and they were forwarded to Washington. That made me take an early train to New York, and it was that which made me go to the pier on Thursday night when the Carpathia docked. Mr. Ismay was anxious to go back, and to have the crew of the Titanic go back immediately. He wanted to go back on the Lapland on Saturday, and I had to tell him rather emphatically he couldn't go." **31**

Many survivors of the Titanic will be called. Mrs. John Jacob Astor, Colonel Archibald Gracie, and relatives of all the prominent men who lost their loved ones will probably be placed in the witness-box. The members of the committee expressed their determination to call "every man, woman, or child" who can tell anything about the disaster. **32**

GERMAN SHIP'S STRANGE CONDUCT.

Something in the nature of a sensation was created yesterday afternoon when Mr. Harold Bride, the assistant to Mr. Phillips, the dead wireless operator on the Titanic, swore that the steamship Frankfurt had been the first to acknowledge the cry for help from the stricken ship. **33**

The inquiry, which is being held in the ballroom of the Waldorf-Astoria Hotel, immediately attracted a vast interest, and when word of Mr. Bride's remarkable and unexpected declaration was circulated the people in the hotel corridors flocked in to such an extent that the room became uncomfortably crowded. Mr. Ismay, looking very worried and pale, was present, with a bodyguard of detectives, and also Mr. Franklin, the White Star Line's New York manager,

---

31. Ismay claimed he was only trying to be a humanitarian by rushing crew and himself back to England. *Titanic* workers lost their jobs when the ship went down. They needed to get back to Southampton quickly (Butler 181–82).

32. To his everlasting credit, Senator William Alden Smith listened to at least one, if not more, third-class passenger's testimony, but in general the very important witnesses were first- and second-class passengers. Most third classers would have been emigrants taking their chances on any boat that would carry them. Considered the safest ship of its day, the *Titanic* would have been an excellent choice for them.

33. For all of the sensation caused by Bride's testimony, the *Titanic* telegrapher, Phillips, had made a good choice in ignoring the *Frankfurt* operator. The *Frankfurt* turned out to be 150 miles away and unable to participate in the rescue (Lord, *A Night* 51–2).

and vice-president of the International Mercantile Marine Company.

Mr. Marconi, and many plain, bronzed men of the sea were also present...

SECOND OFFICER'S STORY.

SAILOR-LIKE TESTIMONY.

A MIRACULOUS ESCAPE.

From Our Own Correspondent.

NEW YORK, Sunday.

In previous cablegrams published in Saturday's *Daily Telegraph*, short summaries were given of the evidence by participants in the shipwreck. Several of these statements are so important, and the stories so dramatic, that I now send the text of this testimony. There was such an extraordinary pressure of matter relating to the disaster on Friday that many people here ignored the witnesses before the Committee on the same day, and probably that was also the case on your side of the Atlantic. One gives first place to the dramatic story of Mr. Charles Lightoller, second officer of the Titanic, and senior surviving officer of the ship, who in plain sailor fashion told the Committee what happened while the women were being taken away in the boats, as the good men stood by, and when the Titanic took her last dip. **34**

Mr. Lightoller, after having sent off boatloads of women, stuck to the ship until the water came up to his ankles. There had been no lamentations and no demonstration either from the men or the passengers as they saw the last lifeboat go, and there was no wailing or

---

★ The role of the earliest telegrapher is a modern-day enigma. Paid like a serf, he had at his fingertips the power to call other ships with iceberg warnings or to alert the world to collisions in which rescuing ships could be called to aid. He was hindered in his job by unclear work rules that made him the employee of the Marconi company, or some other firm, rather than an employee of the ship. His first duty, then, was to Marconi, and Marconi wanted his men to serve passengers. Passengers paid for their messages, and the telegraphic service was like the modern cell phone. Passenger chitchat occupied most of a telegrapher's time. After the disaster of the *Titanic*, the telegrapher's safety role became of first importance, and clearly established procedures were set for delivering important messages to the captain.

★ ★

34. C. H. Lightoller did indeed become a "first place" witness at both the American and British hearings. He was the *Titanic*'s senior surviving officer and, though still young, "had experienced fire at sea, been a castaway, stood as second officer on a three-sky sail clipper...and later had been involved in the Yukon Gold Rush." His testimony here is consistent with what he always maintained throughout his life as to what happened the night the *Titanic* sank (Butler 46).

It must be kept in mind that Lightoller is called a "second" officer because he was second in the ranking system of White Star Line officers. For some unknown reason, Captain Smith brought his own chief officer with him to the *Titanic*, perhaps because they had a comfortable working relationship. This decision bumped Lightoller back a step. But such an event would have only been temporary. Before the *Titanic* went down, Lightoller had every expectation of becoming a commander of a White Star liner. After the *Titanic* went down, because of his association with the great disaster, his hopes of advancing within the White Star Line ended.

crying, no outburst from the men who lined the ship's rail as she disappeared from sight. The men, he said "stood as quietly as if they were in church." Only one man other than about two seamen to each boat, of the seven sent off by Mr. Lightoller, was taken from the ship in his presence. That man was Colonel Pouchen, of Montreal, a brave man, Mr. Lightoller said, who had been put in the boat by him in place of a seaman, because there was not a seaman handy.

"What happened next?" he was asked after he told about his last boat.

"The ship took a dive," he said, without emotion. "I looked forward, and I took a dive."

Mr. Lightoller was sucked to the side of the ship against the grating over the blower for the exhaust. There was an explosion, at least he believed it was an explosion, though he was not certain of it. It blew him to the surface of the water again, only to be sucked back once more by the water rushing into the ship. This time he landed against the grating over the pipes which furnish the draught for the funnels and stuck there. There was another explosion, and again he came to

the surface not many feet from the ship, and on the other side of her. The ship had turned round while he was under the water. He came up near a capsized collapsible lifeboat and clung to it. Many men were in the water near it. A funnel fell within four inches of him and killed many swimmers. Thirty clung to the capsized boat, and a lifeboat with forty survivors in it already finally took them off.

RULE OF
HUMAN NATURE.

Only once did Mr. Lightoller raise his voice perceptibly, and that was when he denied that there was any favouritism for the crew that militated against the chances of escape for the passengers. Asked if he had been ordered by Captain Smith to send the women first or had done so because it was the rule of the sea, he sid: "It is the rule of human nature."

Mr. Lightoller is a trim man, with blue eyes, brown hair, and a smooth-shaven, clean-cut face. He said that he had been in the service of the White Star Line for thirteen years, and an officer in various grades for seven years. He was on the Titanic when she made her turning tests and her trial trip. The turning tests lasted five hours, and the trial trip about four. These tests were made in smooth water, and, in fact, the Titanic had not met any rough weather in her brief career up to the time she hit the iceberg. Mr. Lightoller did not know what the maximum speed of the Titanic was. Talking with officers and others, he had heard that her maximum was between 22½ and 23 knots, but he did not know the Titanic had been put to her maximum speed. The builders, he said, expected to get 21 knots out of her. **35**

As to the life-saving apparatus on board Mr. Lightoller said that the Titanic was perfectly complete. She had fourteen lifeboats, two emergency boats, which were really lifeboats of a lighter type, and four collapsible canvas boats. They were new, and in their proper places, with the necessary lowering apparatus, when the Titanic hit the iceberg. All the apparatus had been tested, and Mr. Lightoller described the method prescribed by the British Board of Trade as to lowering boats, equipping them, and testing the gear. The boats were on the top of the sun deck, about 70ft above the water. It was Captain Clark, of the British Board of Trade, Mr. Lightoller said, who made the examination of the Titanic before she was approved by the British authorities.

Senator Smith, of Michigan, who conducted the examination of Mr. Lightoller, asked him how Captain Clark was regarded by the officers of ships.

"Speaking of Captain Clark," said Mr. Lightoller, with the suggestion of a smile, "he was considered a nuisance. He is so strict. He insists upon every bit of life-saving apparatus being exhibited and taken out on the decks—lifebelts and such, lowering of boats and manning them, and he will have it done until he is satisfied that everything is all right."

"Was the steerage equipped with the same apparatus for the preservation of life in emergency?" Senator Smith asked.

"Identically the same," said the witness.

Senator Smith took another tack. He asked Mr. Lightoller if he had ever been in the sea with a life-belt on. Mr. Lightoller said he had.

"When?" asked the Senator.

"After the Titanic sank," said the witness.

"How long?"

"From half an hour to an hour."

"Did you leave the ship?"

"No, sir."

"Did it leave you?"

"Yes, sir."

"Did you stay until the ship sank?"

"Yes, sir..."

ABSENCE OF CONFUSION.

"Did all the passengers have the right to go on that deck [the boat deck]?"

"Yes, sir."

"Did the steerage passengers?"

---

35. A knot is 1.15 mph. The *Titanic* was going at about 24 to 25 mph into ice.

"No, sir."

"At such a time?"

"Oh, yes, sir," answered Mr. Lightoller, indicating that it was a time when the ordinary routine was not observed. **36**

"There must have been a good deal of confusion, was there not?"

"Not at all, sir."

It appeared that the lifeboat which stuck was about 15ft from the deck, and Mr. Lightoller said there was no opportunity to get to it. The boat never was lowered. It went with the ship. **37**

"Referring to the collision, when did you see Mr. Ismay, after it?"

"Only once. It was about twenty minutes after the collision."

"And he was alone on that boat deck?"

"He was the only one I noticed. I would notice him quicker than I would some passengers, as I knew him."

At that moment, Mr. Lightoller said, he did not know where Captain Smith was, but he had seen him on the bridge shortly before.

"Did you believe the Titanic was in danger?" Senator Smith asked.

"No, sir."

"Did you believe that there had been a serious accident?"

"No, sir," was the answer, with a slight emphasis on each word.

"What was the force of the impact when the Titanic struck the berg?"

"There was a slight grinding, then a shock."

"Any noise?"

"Very little."

Mr. Lightoller said he had not seen Mr. Ismay that night before the collision. He himself was in his berth, but was not asleep. He was not fully dressed, when he walked forward and saw the captain and the first officer on the bridge.

TAKING THE
TEMPERATURE.

"What time elapsed between the impact and your appearance on deck?"

"Two minutes."

"Who else was on deck?"

"No one but the third officer."

"Did you confer with him?"

"Yes, sir."

"Well, did you think there had been a collision?"

"Not necessarily a collision."

"Well, what did you think you struck?"

"Ice."

"Well, why?"

"I naturally jumped at that conclusion. There was ice around the Banks." **38**

---

36. Normally, third-class passengers were not allowed into areas of the ship reserved for first- and second-class passengers. But during a disaster, of course, this rule did not apply, though there may well have been some confusion on the part of ship's stewards, who were not fully alerted to the fact that the *Titanic* was actually sinking.

37. Actually, all lifeboats were successfully launched.

38. Outer Banks of Newfoundland.

Mr. Lightoller said that tests of the water had been made for ice. Water was taken from the side of the ship in canvas buckets, and the temperature learned by putting a thermometer in it. As second officer, Mr. Lightoller said, he had been in charge of it on Sunday from six o'clock p.m. until ten, or until less than two hours before the collision. He would not admit that the water tests were being made solely for the purpose of looking out for ice. **39** It was part of the routine of the ship. Tests were made for routing and other purposes.

"What does the temperature indicate?" the Senator asked.

"Nothing more than the temperature of the air."

"Does it indicate proximity to icebergs?"

"Well, it indicates cold water."

"How cold?"

"I was in it. It wasn't much over freezing."

Witness said he did not know what the earlier tests of the water that day showed. No reports had been made to him. He did not think it necessary that night, when he was on the bridge in charge of the ship, to make tests for the purpose of finding out if the Titanic were in the vicinity of icebergs.

ICEBERGS REPORTED.

"Did you know that the steamer Amerika reported to the Titanic the location of icebergs in that neighbourhood?"

"I can't say I saw the message. I heard of a message, and that it came from some ship; but I did not know it was the Amerika. The message gave the longitude, but not the latitude. The icebergs were reported between 49deg and 51deg."

"Did you get from the captain that night any information about icebergs?"

"Not that night. I think it was in the afternoon, about one o'clock. I was on the bridge, having relieved First Officer Murdock, who had gone to lunch."

Mr. Lightoller said Captain Smith had told him of the wireless messages about icebergs. He could not recall just what position the ship was in then, but he could work it out on a chart. Chief Officer Murdock returned to the bridge, and Mr. Lightoller told him exactly what the captain had communicated to him.

"What did Murdock say?"

"All right."

"So the chief officer of the ship was fully advised by you of the proximity of icebergs?"

"Yes, sir."

"How fast was the boat going at that time?"

"Between 21½ and 22 knots."

"Was that her maximum speed?"

"I don't know, sir."

"Do you know if she made her maximum speed at the time of her trip?"

"So far as we know, she could go faster than that if pushed. We understood that that was not her maximum speed."

"Then you understood there was a reserve of power?"

"Yes, sir."

★ **39.** There was no water test for detecting icebergs.

THE SPEED QUESTION.

"Had you received any instructions to exhaust that reserve power to make the ship go faster?"

"No, sir."

"Well, did you want her to go faster?"

"Yes, sir, some time or other."

It was true, witness said, that he and other officers had talked about the maximum speed, and what this new craft of the sea could do in the way of rapid progress for a ship of her size. Mr. Lightoller did not hesitate in making this statement, but answered as if he could not understand why an officer of a ship should not be interested in how fast she could go. When Chief Officer Murdock relieved him, Mr. Lightoller went to his room. He did not tell the other officers about the icebergs. The look-out had not been increased when he went on the bridge again at six o'clock. On the deck there were two junior officers. Captain Smith was not on the bridge at that time, and he did not see Captain Smith until 8.55 o'clock. There were two men in the crow's nest, one man at the wheel, and one man standing by.

"How was the weather that night?" Senator Smith asked.

"Clear and calm."

"Were you apprehensive because of the proximity of icebergs?"

"No, sir."

"For that reason you did not consider it necessary to increase the look-out?"

"No, sir."

"Did you see the captain between six o'clock and 8.55, when he came on the bridge?"

"I did not."

"What did the captain say to you, or what did you say to him when he came on the bridge?"

"Probably one of us said, 'Good evening.'"

"Didn't you say anything else?"

"Yes, sir. We spoke of the weather, the calmness of the sea, the clearness of the night, and about the time we should be getting to the vicinity of the ice. I was impressed, and I had on my mind the proximity of the ice. The captain and I talked for about twenty-five minutes."

"Was there any reference to the wireless message from the Amerika?"

"No, I think not; but there may have been. Captain Smith observed that there was a slight haze, which might mean the nearness of icebergs.["] So far as Mr. Lightoller knew, the Titanic did not reduce speed. Speed might have been reduced without his knowing it.

"How so?"

"The captain did not tell me to slow up. I don't know that he sent word to the engine-room. He might have done so by word of mouth, and I would not have known. The commander might have sent word to slow the ship by reducing the number of revolutions, say, from seventy-six to seventy-two. I don't know he did that."

"How long did the captain remain on the bridge?"

"Until 9.20..."

CAPTAIN'S LAST ORDERS.

"What were the last orders you heard the Captain give?"

"When I asked him, 'Shall I put the women and children in the boats?' he answered, 'Yes, lower away.' I don't know how long the vessel was afloat. I was told it sank at 2.20 o'clock. We came to that conclusion afterwards, but no officer told me the exact time."

Mr. Lightoller then described the operation of loading the boats, and what happened to him. There was a collapsible boat on the top of the officers' quarters. The boat was cut away. As it went over the side a number of men jumped on it. This was the boat which he found overturned later on, with no one on it.

"I was standing on the top of the officers' quarters. There was nothing more to be done. The last boat had been sent away. The ship took a dive. I faced forward and I also took a dive. As I went under water I was pulled to the grating over the exhaust pipes. I don't know how long I was there. I do know my head was under water. Then this explosion or whatever it was blew me clear out of the water. I did not see débris then. I was not thrown far from the ship. I was barely away from her. As the ship went down and the water rushed over her I was drawn in and against the grating over the funnel. I don't know how I was released. I think the boilers must have exploded again."

"Where did you find yourself next; on the raft or near it?"

"I was in the same position, but the Titanic had come around. There were a lot of us in the water around it. I got to the collapsible boat which was overturned. There was no one on it then. I think Colonel Gracie had somewhat the same experience as I had in being sucked under the water. When I got to the overturned boat one of the funnels of the Titanic fell within four inches of the boat. It fell on all the people who were there."

"Was anybody saved of those struck?"

"I could not say, sir."

DEATHS FROM THE COLD.

About thirty men eventually got to the capsized boat. Among them were John Thayer, of Philadelphia, **40** Colonel Gracie, Phillips (the senior Marconi operator on the Titanic), and Bride, his assistant. Mr. Lightoller said he thought that all the rest of the thirty were firemen of the Titanic. Three or four men slipped off the boat and were lost. One of them was Phillips, the wireless operator.

"Did these men die of cold?"

"Presumably."

Witness said that no effort was made to keep any of those in the water from getting to the capsized boat. He took command of the boat as far as was necessary. He remembers that they were about half a mile away from the Titanic.

"When you left the ship, did you see any women and children on her?"

"None whatever."

Everybody he saw in the water had a life-preserver. He believed the men on the capsized boat were firemen, because they were used to discipline, and obeyed the few orders he gave. Soon a lifeboat with passengers from the Titanic picked up the capsized boat.

"I counted sixty-five heads, not

40. Actually John Thayer's son.

including my own, when we got aboard the lifeboat. This did not include those in the bottom of the boat; approximately, there were seventy-five in the boat altogether after we got in."

"How were the passengers selected for the lifeboats?"

"By their sex."

No women were turned back except, perhaps, a stewardess. He saw women refuse to go into the lifeboats. He did not know why they refused to go. He thought one or two families asked to be taken together, but only women went in the first lifeboat. He put off about twenty-five women and only two sailors. The same rule was followed until the third lifeboat was lowered, when it was evident that the ship was going down, and then the women were crowded to the boats as fast as possible; the small number in the first boats being due to the fact that Mr. Lightoller did not believe the ship would sink. **41**

"By the time I had got to the third boat I was aware that the situation was serious. Therefore I took chances, and after that I took greater risks in crowding the women into the boats."

It took a long time to get enough women to fill the last boat that was put off, because the men were searching the ship to find them. For the benefit of the Committee, Mr. Lightoller estimated that of those picked out of the water alive, five out of every six were members of the crew.

RETURN OF THE CREW.

DEPARTURE
FOR
ENGLAND.

From Our Own Correspondent.

NEW YORK, Sunday.

The Titanic's rescued crew sailed home by the Red Star's liner Lapland yesterday, apparently in a rather surly mood. Escorted aboard the Lapland almost before the Carpathia had warped into her berth, they were ordered not to go ashore, except with special permission, it was stated, and no one was allowed to visit them in their quarters. A number of them found their way to seamen's paradises along the waterfront, or to the home of the Seamen's Society, where a service was conducted for them yesterday morning, and clothing and tobacco were distributed for the voyage home.

Away from the supervision of their superiors, the sailors told their stories freely. One could not help feeling that the line for which many of their comrades had laid down their lives, and whom they themselves served to the point of death, received but few

41. Lightoller was also unaware that the lifeboats had been tested at full capacity hanging from the davits. Thus, he feared the boats might not hold sixty-five to seventy people while being lowered (Cox 53).

kind words. Had it not been for the Seamen's Institute, one man declared, many of them would have gone home without shoes. **42** They were told that no money would be forthcoming from the company on this side of the water, and that when they reached the other side they would be paid only up to the time the Titanic sank. The line's indebtedness to them ended at that moment, they were told.

"Half sorry I didn't go down with the steamer," one man declared. "Then my wife and children would have been cared for by the company, but now they get nothing. I come home to them without a job, and only a few shillings in my pocket. Like many of my mates, I gave my coat and jacket to the women in the boat with me, but I have to buy a new one with the little coming to me on the other side. As far as I can see, the line is not worrying whether I and my family have anything to wear." **43**

The courage of Captain Smith was a favourite topic with all the men he once commanded. According to them, he would be the last man that ever trod a bridge to anticipate what the sea had in store for him by the use of a revolver. That story they denounced as a "damnable lie." Each and every one of them who mentioned him declared that he went down with the ship.

———

RESCUE SHIP.

———◆———

CARPATHIA RESUMES HER INTERRUPTED VOYAGE.

———

SPECIAL CABLE
FROM OUR OWN
CORRESPONDENT.

NEW YORK, Sunday.

The Carpathia, which rescued the survivors of the Titanic, started again yesterday on her interrupted trip to the Mediterranean. Her flag, like every flag in sight, and there are many on shipping and tall buildings which can be seen from the water front, was at half-mast in honour of the Titanic's gallant dead.

Captain Rostron had another crowded hour, and between the times when he was not busy looking after the preparations for departure he attended the Congressional Committee investigation into the loss of the White Star liner. He reported to officials of the line here, and wrote his report for the home office at Liverpool. This report, just before sailing, he made public, and he declared it was the only statement he had given out since the rescue.

He and his crew had very little rest since the Sunday night when the

---

42. The Institute was most likely a charity for seamen and not a union.

43. The White Star Line was not required to regard surviving crew members as employees. Their employment ended when the *Titanic* sank. No ship, no job (Lord, *A Night* 127).

Carpathia picked up the Titanic's distress signal. Even though many did not realise the plight of the Titanic, the crew turned out to prepare the boats, to make sandwiches, and get ready accommodation for the survivors, and turn the vessel into an emergency hospital in case of need. A steward paid this tribute to Captain Rostron yesterday:

FULL SPEED AHEAD.

"Captain Rostron is a soldier as well as a sailor. He ordered the hot water to be shut off all over the ship, and turned every bit of heat into steam. It was speed we needed to get there, and we got there. The captain did everything that could be done, and he did not content himself with sticking to brainwork alone. He got down and did the hardest kind of work.

"One of the first things done was to muster the stewards in the saloon, and Chief Steward Hughes told us a wireless had been received that the Titanic had struck an iceberg and would probably be wanting help."

When the wireless word was received here that the Carpathia had decided to turn back to New York, instead of making Halifax with the survivors, the real work of getting ready for her departure within a day of her arrival fell upon Captain Roberts, superintendent of the Cunard Line. Captain Rostron ordered the supplies he needed to fill his larder by wireless and in code. In the anxiety to get some news every wireless flash from the Carpathia was picked up.

This particular code message was caught by the wireless station at Brooklyn, and an hour later a reporter appeared at the Cunard Line office, and, producing the code, asked one of the officials to translate it. He had suspicions when he was told it meant herrings, beef, and other articles of everyday necessity. It was explained that a code was used to shorten the message, but the reporter was sure it was another suppressed message about which the New Yorkers were hearing so much. **44**

PRESENTATION TO CAPTAIN ROSTRON.

When the Carpathia departed yesterday there was a small army of sightseers at the pier all the morning and until sailing time. These were kept in check by the police. No one was allowed on the pier except on business. As sailing time approached this order was modified, and those who were able to give the names of the friends they wished to see were allowed to go on the pier and the vessel.

Quite a number of persons obtained admission, and long before the vessel cast off they overran the decks, anxious for

44. This last sentence is puzzling, but not all that mysterious. The *Carpathia* would have had to resupply after docking so that it could head back for its original points of destination in the Mediterranean. Perhaps a code was used. New York's reporters simply couldn't believe the *Carpathia*'s telegrapher didn't have the time to send out news stories for public consumption. Hence a conspiracy theory was born.

glimpses of the rooms occupied by the survivors, to listen to stories of the rescue, and especially to climb to the wireless operator's room. The stewards and sailors were busy cutting up life preservers stripped from the survivors for souvenirs.

The committee of survivors met at noon aboard the Carpathia and presented a loving-cup to Captain Rostron.

As the Carpathia sailed late in the afternoon people cheered heartily for Captain Rostron, a fine, clean-cut type of the British officer, who made a splendid impression on the Senate Committee when he gave evidence. Standing on the bridge, he doffed his cap and smiled gravely as the Cunarder steamed from the pier towards the fairway.

CONGRESS DEBATE.

SENATOR'S ATTACK ON THE WHITE STAR LINE.

MR. ISMAY'S ANGER

EMPHATIC PROTEST.

"UNFAIR AND UNJUST."

SPECIAL CABLE
FROM OUR OWN
CORRESPONDENT.

NEW YORK, Sunday.

Speaking in the Senate at Washington, Senator Rayner, of Maryland, bitterly attacked Mr. Bruce Ismay. The reports in the papers here on Friday were brief and inaccurate, and in view of the importance of the occasion I did not cable them to *The Daily Telegraph*. Yesterday, however, the speech was reported more or less fully by the leading papers, and I take the following from the *New York Times*.

Senator Rayner declared that Mr. Ismay, as well as the directorate of the White Star Company, was criminally responsible for the loss of 1,500 lives, and he predicted the justice of England would speedily "bring to bay this criminal directorate. If the Titanic had been an American ship, subject to our criminal procedure," he said, "they would be convicted of manslaughter, if not of murder."

Senator Rayner's denunciation of Mr. Ismay came up in a discussion on the power of the Senate to bring him and any other witnesses to Washington to testify about the wreck. Of that power, said Mr. Rayner, there could be no doubt. Congress had given power in a statute to Congressional Committees, and provided a penalty, varying from £20 to £100, or imprisonment, not exceeding one year, for the disobedience of witnesses to appear, and the Courts, at least once, had inflicted the maximum penalty.

"The sinking of the Titanic was a crime, and in the investigation of that crime the Committee has full powers. There is no other jurisdiction in America," he asserted, "that has power to reach the case."

SENATORIAL DIGNITY.

"Mr. Ismay," said Senator Rayner, "should be brought here, and be made to explain. He should not be requested to come. It is not a question of his good will, and the hearings should be here in Washington, and not in New York, as this accident has developed into a national disaster. He should be asked particularly to explain how he, the directing manager of the company, the superior of the captain, and not under the captain's orders, directed the northern route, which ended so fatally, and then left hundreds of passengers to die, while he took a boat to safety." **45**

Senator Simmons, of North Carolina, a member of the sub-committee appointed to investigate the wreck, interrupted to say that the Committee had already decided that the hearings should be held in Washington, as they considered it beneath the dignity of a Committee of the Senate to proceed to New York for the convenience of steamship officials. The trip of the chairman, Senator Smith, to New York last night, he said, had not been to prepare for the hearings in that city, but simply to get certain information for use later on in the Washington sittings.

"Mr. Ismay claims, according to the reports, that he took the last lifeboat," cried Senator Rayner. "I don't believe it. And if he did it is cowardly to take any lifeboat for the managing director of the line, who, with his board, is criminally responsible for this appalling tragedy.

ATLANTIC ROUTES.

"I haven't the slightest doubt the northern route was taken in obedience to Mr. Ismay's direct orders, and he risked the life of the entire ship to make a speedy passage. I care not what the rules of the English Admiralty are. Here you have the spectacle of the head of a line failing to see that his ship is properly equipped with life-saving apparatus, heedless of the warnings that he was sailing in dangerous seas, forsaking his vessel, and permitting 1,500 of her passengers and crew to be swallowed by the sea. The martyrdom of agonies of separation that took place on board the sinking ship are too fearful for the mind to dwell upon and contemplate; but Mr. Ismay, the officer primarily responsible for the whole disaster, has reached his destination in safety, and unharmed.

"No legislation can bring back to earth a single life lost upon that fatal night. What we can do is to help to fix the responsibility, if possible, and to rely upon British justice to bring to bay the guilty directorate of this company. All civilised nations will applaud the prosecution of the management of this line. If they can be made to suffer, no sympathy will go out to them, and if it does it will be submerged in the overwhelming lamentation that to-day re-echoes throughout the civilised world for the victims of their culpable carelessness; a recklessness that has sent hundreds of their

45. Senator Rayner is wrong. The ship was on a more southern course, directed so by Captain Smith himself in a late move to avoid the ice (Marcus 117).

fellow-beings into eternity, has desolated homes and firesides, and turned this land into a house of mourning.

"In this hour of our calamity we appeal to the majesty of the law to deal out retributory justice to this guilty company to the last degree."

VIRULENT PRESS ATTACKS.

Senator Rayner's speech is a type of others equally virulent, all clamouring against the unfortunate chairman of the White Star Line, and they are only equalled by the editorials in the leading "yellow" papers, which are beside themselves with impotent rage.

It is usual in the case of a big calamity to find a victim, and the fact that Mr. Ismay forgot to go down with the ship and is the head of a big corporation makes him, in the view of inflammable politicians and equally choleric "yellow" journals, a peculiarly fine target. It should not be forgotten, also, on your side, that the American Government is now prosecuting the Atlantic "Shipping Trust," and the White Star Company is one of the alleged monopolistic corporations "co-operating to crush out competition and secure a monopoly."

The newspapers yesterday published what purports to be "practically the first personal statement" Mr Ismay has made since the wreck, apart from the statement given before the Senate Committee on Friday.

In answer to the *New York World's* representative, Mr. Ismay is reported as saying,

"What do you think I am? Do you believe I am the sort that would have left that ship as long as there were any women or children aboard her? That is the thing that hurts; and it hurts all the more because it is so false and baseless. It is so utterly false," he exclaimed, his naturally low voice rasping under his nervous strain.

"UNFAIR; HORRIBLY UNFAIR."

"This whole thing seems unfair; horribly unfair. I cannot understand it. I mean the Senatorial Inquiry. They are going at it in a manner that seems unjust, and the injustice lies heaviest upon me. Why, I cannot even protect myself by having my counsel ask questions."

"Don't misunderstand me by thinking I mean questions calculated to twist witnesses up. On the contrary, I mean questions intended to simplify involved meanings. A glaring example of this was when I was asked about rowing in the boat, and I said I had been at one of the oars and had not seen the ship go down. At once I was asked how I could have failed to see her, since, if rowing, I must have been facing her. It would have been easy for my counsel to show that, as I was pushing at an oar, which was being handled by two or three of us, there was not room for me to sit in the proper oarsman's position. So I helped as best I could by shoving on the handle."

Mr. Ismay strode up and down the corridor outside the room in the Waldorf-Astoria Hotel where Senator Smith's Committee was assembled. He had been under examination the greater part of the morning, and when the afternoon session began he could contain himself in a chair no longer, so the next two hours he spent pacing up and down.

The *New York World's* correspondent says:

"Mr. Ismay was dressed with scrupulous care, and wore a dark suit, with a black scarf running through a high turned-down collar. His tones were those of a cultivated Englishman, but at present they are not at their best; his inner distress is making itself felt."

AMERICAN REPROACHES.

Some of the newspapers here have openly reproached Mr. Ismay, as the chairman of the White Star Line, for not going down with the ship, like the captain.

"I tell you," Mr. Ismay is reported as saying to the *New York World's* interviewer, "my conscience is clear; and I have not been a lenient judge of my acts. I took the chance when it came to me. I did not seek it. I repeat, every woman and child had been cared for before I left the boat. **46** And more, all the men within reach had been taken care of before I took my turn. And why shouldn't I take my turn?

"There are only two classes on a ship—crew and passengers. I was a passenger. It is true I am president of the company, but where would you draw the line? Would you stop a shareholder from taking his place in the lifeboats because he has a financial interest in the corporation? I didn't consider myself any different from the rest of the passengers. With me, as with them, it was a case of women and children first, and then the men had their chance. I took no other man's place."

"When I entered my boat, the last to leave, I was practically the last waiting. There may have been others waiting for other boats to be lowered away, but I had no reason to suppose they would not get away all right. I was sure absolutely of one thing; every woman, except those who would not quit their husbands, or, perhaps, a few who never came up from their cabins, had left the Titanic before I set foot in the boat.

AN APPEAL FOR FAIR PLAY.

"All I want is a fair chance from the Press and public. I am sure things will be seen in their proper light, and the rather free disposition to criticise will disappear."

As an illustration of the manner in which Mr. Ismay believes the inquiry is doing him severe injustice, he mentioned one feature of the second officer's, Mr. Lightoller's, testimony, in which Mr. Lightoller said two minutes after the collision, when he ran out of his room, he saw Mr. Ismay on the boat deck alone.

"I am quite sure," said Mr. Ismay,

46. What Ismay probably meant was that every *first-class* woman and child had been cared for.

"the officer did not mean that. Either he was misunderstood, or he made a mistake. He meant that when he came out of his room the second time and went on the boat deck to clear away the lifeboats he found me there. This was at least twenty minutes later. I had gone there to help in boat work and to load in women and children. I am sure he must have meant that, because I am certain I was not on the boat deck until a long time after she struck." **47**

"Oh, yes, that is what Lightoller meant. There could be no other meaning," chimed in Mr. Burlingham, counsel for the White Star Line, who had come up at that moment, and the other with him solemnly nodded assent.

ANXIOUS
TO RETURN

Mr. Ismay said he was anxious to get back to England as soon as possible. "I would like to leave on the Lapland," he said, "but the Committee have asked me to await their pleasure. My wife and family are naturally much disturbed. I have received cables imploring me to return forthwith, if it could be arranged. I should much like to get away and hold myself ready to return upon notice from the Committee."

Mr. Ismay is further reported as saying: "I had no hand whatever in any

suppression of news. I had nothing to do with the way in which the wireless was handled on the Carpathia. I want to emphasise one thing—that the White Star Line has nothing to fear from investigation. Everything humanly possible was done, but the forces of nature are stronger than our most elaborate defences.

"I have the utmost respect for the Senate of the United States, but the inquiry, as it is proceeding now, may wreak injustice rather than clear up the points in question. In England such a hearing would be attended by counsel for me, and their questions would help in getting at the bottom of things."

Some papers here are most vindictive in assailing Mr. Bruce Ismay and the White Star Company in connection with the disaster, and are printing most maliciously cruel cartoons, alleging that a few minutes before the accident Mr. Ismay and the captain were in evening dress, and had just been dining with a few other men in a private room. It is admitted now that the captain was actually on the bridge, and not the first officer, when the vessel was on the verge of the fatal plunge, and that Captain Smith wore the regulation uniform…

WASHINGTON, SATURDAY.

During the debate in the Senate today on the resolution concerning

---

★ **47.** Information on Ismay's exact whereabouts is hard to piece together, but he was certainly among the first on the bridge to consult with Captain Smith about what had happened. He was not likely to be concerned about his personal safety until he had heard the worst (Lord, *A Night* 22).

the regulation of ocean traffic, Mr. McCumber [48] took occasion to register a protest against "the trial, conviction, sentencing, and execution of one who is connected with the Titanic on the floor of the Senate yesterday without fair, honest, and full consideration."

Mr. McCumber was evidently referring to the speech of Mr. Raynor [Rayner], in which he made a violent attack on Mr. Bruce Ismay.—*Reuter.*

★ **48.** Porter James McCumber, Republican Senator from North Dakota

★ ★

Bruce Ismay, English director of the White Star Line and president of the International Mercantile Marine, had the misfortune of being the senior executive survivor of the worst maritime disaster in history—at least up to that time. He also had the misfortune of coming before U.S. senators inflamed by corporate acts of greed so outrageous they had earned for that era the name "the Gilded Age." It was an era that had allowed men like J. P. Morgan, a principal stockholder in the International Mercantile Marine, to amass large sums of wealth at the expense of workers and small businesses he had driven out of existence. Fellow capitalists like Rockefeller, Andrew Carnegie, and Jay Gould had led a drive for business consolidation that had made them the most wealthy and powerful men in America. Therefore, they and those associated with them, like Bruce Ismay, were natural targets of senators envious of their success and power and elected by a populace eager to see such power curbed. Although Ismay was treated better by his British interrogators than by his U.S. ones, his career was at an end. British historian Geoffrey Marcus comments:

"Never again would he stride confidently down James Street with his friend and colleague, Harold A. Sanderson, on his way to the head office of the Line at No. 30. Never again would he dominate the Board in his old high-handed style. His continued presence at the head of affairs was felt to be a handicap and embarrassment; opposition to Ismay gathered head; and the Line presently hove its Jonah overboard. As one of the principal shipping magnates of Europe, Ismay was finished. He eventually relinquished most of his business interests and withdrew to a remote corner of western Ireland" (207–08).

AFTERMATH

———◆———

So—UNBELIEVABLY, INEXORABLY—THE *TITANIC* WAS LOST IN the greatest maritime disaster of its age. A ship driven at some twenty-four miles per hour could not survive the glancing blow of an iceberg, no matter how modern and "unsinkable" she was.

The iceberg had a "right" to be there, a clergyman sermonized; the *Titanic* not necessarily so. Due precautions had not been taken.

Yet Captain E. J. Smith was exonerated of any wrongdoing: he had gone down with his ship in a blaze of Anglo-Saxon glory so important to the spirit of the age. Nor could he have anticipated the *Titanic*'s loss, there having been no similar disaster in the short history of coal-fired liners built of steel. No, his ship kept the usual complement of two lookouts in the crow's nest. That should have been enough.

Still, Lord Mersey, at the conclusion of British Wreck Commission hearings, admonished that while Captain Smith was not at fault for what happened, any subsequent captain operating in a similarly complacent manner would not find himself so innocent. New knowledge brings responsibility—and liability.

Bruce Ismay survived his American inquiry ordeal, but just barely. Within a year, he would lose the chairmanship of the White Star Line and step down from the board of the International Mercantile Marine. His presence was an embarrassment to the organization. After a long retirement to the west coast of Ireland, Ismay died in 1937, a lonely and socially ruined man.

The *Titanic*'s passengers in general proved remarkably resilient. Although some could never get over that terrible night when they lost a precious loved one, many survivors did go on to pick up the individual threads of their lives.

The emigrants who could stay in America tended to prosper over time, but even those who had to return to their homelands were able to rely on the comfort and support of old friends, family, and charity. We do know of at least two survivors who, very much later, did commit suicide. But Jack Thayer took his life after the death of a son, and lookout Frederick Fleet took his life after the death of his spouse. Their *Titanic* experiences do not appear to be the proximate cause of their respective actions.

One thing is certain. Never again would ships be allowed to run at high speed into ice-choked waters. Nor would passenger liners and other steamships be allowed to shut down their telegraphs at night. Investigators on both sides of the Atlantic castigated Captain Stanley Lord of the *Californian* and his crew for not waking the ship's sleeping telegrapher after seeing the *Titanic* fire rockets into the night sky. Variously, the *Californian* was estimated as being only seven to a maximum of twenty miles away from the sinking liner. In any case, Captain Lord was sleepy, the telegrapher was asleep. Why bother about the peculiar actions of an unknown ship when nothing could be the matter anyway? The *Californian* lay quietly unaware of an appointment with destiny.

Although Captain Lord spent much of his life seeking exoneration for his actions that night, the Mercantile Marine Association, to whom he applied for assistance, never succeeded in getting Lord's case before an official inquiry. In 1992 the Marine Office Investigation Branch finally issued a report that pleased nobody who either approved or disapproved of Captain Lord.

Two veteran seamen came to utterly different conclusions on the actual location of the *Californian* on the night of the *Titanic*'s sinking, but both seamen agreed that whether the *Californian* was only seven miles away or some twenty miles away, as Captain Lord always maintained, he and his crew still knew about rockets being fired and should have gone to the distressed liner's aid. To view the Marine Office Investigation Branch report, visit the organization's website—a must-read for *Titanic* inquirers.

★ ★ ★

Two other websites also deserve mention. *Encyclopedia-Titanica.org* is an exhaustive source of information about all things *Titanic*. Its numerous message boards contain insightful discussions on the miscellaneous and not so miscellaneous esoterica of the *Titanic*'s history. Warning: This site is addictive.

Also addictive is the site *BBC-Archive-Survivors of the Titanic: Survivors of the Titanic Tell Their Stories*. *Titanic* researchers can hear recorded accounts of what happened the night the *Titanic* went down. Of particular interest is the information provided by Second Officer C. H. Lightoller.

Officer Lightoller became something of a legend: Having survived a previous shipwreck, he became the White Star Line's most important witness, and his skillful, not to say brilliant, handling of American and British investigators probably saved his company from a finding of negligence. Later, at the beginning of World War II, Lightoller would take his own boat to the beaches of Dunkirk and aid in the rescue of the collapsing British army. His own small craft carried more than a hundred soldiers to safety.

Good As Gold author Lady Louise Patten has suggested that her grandfather, the self-same Lightoller, and three other officers had time to meet, just before the *Titanic* sank, and agree to conceal the fact that a steering error had caused the ship to hit the iceberg. This seems highly unlikely. Charles Herbert Lightoller's whereabouts are known for nearly the entire time the *Titanic* was sinking: He was getting passengers into lifeboats. He had no more time for a cover-up than did the other officers, who were also similarly occupied.

In addition, Quartermaster Robert Hitchens, at the wheel of the *Titanic*, had many years' experience at sea and would have known how to turn the *Titanic* to the right or to the left. It's what he did for a living.

The doomed *Titanic*.

No, you simply do not drive a ship at twenty-five miles per hour into an ice field. Beyond this fact nothing else really matters.

True, it was discovered at the British hearings that the *Titanic* had had a coal fire in one of its bunkers the entire time it had been at sea. A few researchers have tried to make much of this coal fire, but it still remains just a coal fire, in a steel bunker on a steel-plated ship. No, the fire had been fought, the bunker emptied, and the sides of the bunker cleaned—before the ship ever encountered the iceberg. Therefore, there was never any conspiracy to keep the fact of this coal fire a secret, as some theorists have claimed. The fire was mentioned early in the British proceedings before a crowded room of some 200 people.

However, it is true that many in the lifeboats thought they saw the light of a nearby ship and rowed for hours toward that light without ever getting any nearer to it. This does remain an unexplained mystery for naval men to mull over. You can find much of this speculation online.

It is also true that Robert Ballard proved the *Titanic* went down some thirteen miles from its last telegraphed position, a serious error in plotting location on the part of one of the ship's officers, but that doesn't really matter either because the rescue ship *Carpathia* had no trouble finding *Titanic*'s lifeboats anyway.

What really matters in the aftermath of the sinking is that so many others have been saved by lessons learned from the *Titanic*'s destruction. New regulations require ships to carry enough lifeboats for every passenger, to have regular lifeboat drills, to pay more attention to the location of ice fields, and to keep their wireless radios manned at all times.

The tragedy is that it took the death of so many innocents to achieve these needed results.

BIBLIOGRAPHY

———◆———

Aldridge, Rebecca. *The Sinking of the Titanic*. New York: Chelsea House, 2008. Print.

Ballard, Robert D. *The Discovery of the Titanic*. New York: Time Warner, 1987. Print.

Bartlett, John. *Familiar Quotations*. 16th ed. Boston: Little, Brown, and Co., 1992. Print.

Bates, Stephen. "Titanic Museum to Open in Southampton." *The Guardian* [London] 31 Mar. 2009, Main sec.: 15. *Guardian.co.uk*. Guardian News and Media Limited, 31 Mar. 2009. Web. 1 Apr. 2011.

Beesley, Lawrence. *The Loss of the S. S. Titanic: Its Story and Its Lessons*. Boston: Houghton Mifflin Company, 2000. Print.

———. "The *Titanic*: Lessons of the Disaster, A Survivor's Telegram." *The Times* [London] 20 Apr. 1912: 8. *Times Archive*. Times Newspapers Ltd, 2010. Web. 7 Apr. 2011.

British Parliamentary Papers. *Shipping Casualties. (Loss of the Steamship "Titanic")*, Cd 6352. "Report of a Formal Investigation into the circumstances attending the foundering on 15th April, 1912, of the British Steamship 'Titanic,' of Liverpool, after striking ice in or near Latitude 41° 46' N., Longitude 50° 14' W., North Atlantic Ocean, whereby loss of life ensued." London: His Majesty's Stationary Office, 1912. Print.

"British Wreck Commissioner's Inquiry." *Titanic Inquiry Project: Electronic Copies of the Inquiries into the Disaster.* Ed. Rob Ottmers. Titanic Inquiry Project, 2009. Web. 30 July 2010.

Bryceson, Dave. *The Titanic Disaster: As Reported in the British National Press April–July 1912.* New York: Norton, 1997. Print.

Burns, John F. "Millvina Dean, *Titanic*'s Last Survivor, Dies at 97." *The New York Times.* The New York Times Company, 1 June 2009. Web. 22 Apr. 2010.

Butler, Daniel Allen. *"Unsinkable": The Full Story.* Mechanicsburg: Stackpole Books, 1998. Print.

Caplan, Bruce M., ed. *The Sinking of the Titanic: 1912 Survivor Accounts.* Seattle: Seattle Miracle Press, 1997. Print.

Chambers Biographical Dictionary. Rev. ed. 1984. Print.

Cox, Stephen. *The Titanic Story: Hard Choices, Dangerous Decisions.* Chicago: Open Court, 1999. Print.

Davie, Michael. *Titanic: The Death and Life of a Legend.* New York: Alfred A. Knopf, 1986. Print.

Eaton, J. P., and Charles A. Haas. *Titanic: Triumph and Tragedy.* 2nd ed. New York: Norton, 1998. Print.

Eaton, John P., and Charles A. Haas. *Titanic: A Journey through Time.* New York: Norton, 1999. Print.

_____. *Titanic: Destination Disaster: The Legends and the Reality.* New York: Norton, 1987. Print.

"Eleanor Robson Belmont." *The Internet Movie Database.* IMDB.com, Inc., 2010. Web. 10 Dec. 2010.

Encyclopedia Titanica: Titanic Facts, Survivors Stories, Passenger and Crew Biography and Titanic History. Encyclopedia Titanica, 2010. Web. 1 Sept. 2010.

Foster, John Wilson, ed. *The Titanic Reader.* New York: Penguin, 1999. Print.

Geller, Judith B. *Titanic: Women and Children First.* New York: Norton, 1998. Print.

Gracie, Archibald, and John B. Thayer. *Titanic: A Survivor's Story* and *The Sinking of the S. S. Titanic*. Chicago: Academy Chicago Publishers, 1998. Print.

Heyer, Paul. *Titanic Legacy: Disaster as Media Event and Myth*. Westport: Praeger, 1995. Print.

Howells, Richard. *The Myth of the Titanic*. New York: St. Martin's Press, 1999. Print.

Hyslop, Donald, Alastair Forsyth, and Sheila Jemima. *Titanic Voices: Memories from the Fateful Voyage*. New York: St Martin's Press, 1994. Print.

Kuntz, Tom. *The Titanic Disaster Hearings: The Official Transcript of the 1912 Senate Investigation*. New York: Pocket Books, 1998. Print.

Lightoller, Charles H. *Titanic*. Ludlow: 7C's Press, 1975. Print.

Lord, Walter. *A Night to Remember*. New York: Bantam Books, 1997. Print.

———. *The Night Lives On*. New York: William Morrow, 1986. Print.

Lynch, Don. *Titanic: An Illustrated History*. New York: Hyperion, 1992. Print.

Marcus, Geoffrey. *The Maiden Voyage*. New York: Viking Press, 1969. Print.

Marriott, Leo. *Titanic*. New York: Smithmark Publishers Inc., 1997. Print.

Matsen, Brad. *Titanic's Last Secrets*. New York: Hachette, 2008. Print.

Mccarty, Jennifer Hooper, and Tim Foecke. *What Really Sank the Titanic: New Forensic Discoveries*. New York: Citadel Press, 2008. Print.

McDonnell, Vincent. *Titanic Tragedy*. Cork, Ireland: The Collins Press, 2007. Print.

Nichol, Mark M. "The Mystery of the SS *Naronic*." *Titanic and Other White Star Line Ships*. Nov. 2006. Web. 10 Sept. 2010.

O'Donnell, E. E. *The Last Days of the Titanic: Photographs and Mementos of the Tragic Maiden Voyage*. New York: Roberts Rinehart, 1997. Print.

Officer, Lawrence H., and Samuel H. Williamson. "Measuring Worth—Purchasing Power of US Dollar." *Measuring Worth—Home*. Measuring Worth, 2010. Web. 26 July 2010.

Priestly, J. B. *The Edwardians*. New York: Harper & Row, 1970. Print.

Quinn, Paul J. *Titanic at Two A.M.* Saco: Fantail, 1997. Print.

Richman, Joe, and Teal Krech, prods. "'Ship Ablaze': Remembering the *General Slocum*: NPR." *All Things Considered: Radio Diaries*. NPR. 15 June 2004. *NPR: National Public Radio: News & Analysis, World, US, Music & Arts: NPR*. NPR, 2010. Web. 12 Sept. 2010.

Sadur, Jim. "*Titanic*: Facts & Figures." *Jim's Titanic Website*. 11 Mar. 2010. Web. 2 Aug. 2010.

Sinclair, David. *Dynasty: The Astors and Their Times*. New York: Beaufort Books, 1984. Print.

Steinbrunner, Chris, and Otto Penzler, eds. *Encyclopedia of Mystery and Detection*. New York: McGraw-Hill Book Company, 1976. Print.

"Survivors of the *Titanic*: Survivors from the Famous Shipwreck Tell Their Stories." *BBC Archive*. BBC, 2010. Web. 1 Dec. 2010.

Tibballs, Geoff, ed. *The Mammoth Book of the Titanic*. New York: Carroll & Graf, 2002. Print.

"Titanic Claimants to Accept $664,000." *The New York Times* 18 Dec. 1915. *The New York Times*. The New York Times Company, 2010. Web. 15 Aug. 2010.

"*Titanic* Letter Sells for a Record £55,000." *BBC News*. BBC, 18 Apr. 2010. Web. 6 Aug. 2010.

The Titanic Reports: The 1912 Inquiries by the US Senate and the British Wreck Commission. St. Petersburg: Red and Black Publishers, originally published 1912. Print.

"Treasure of the R.M.S. *Republic*." *The Official RMS Republic Website*. MVSHQ, Inc., 7 Mar. 2009. Web. 03 Aug. 2010.

United Kingdom. Marine Accident Investigation Branch. Her Majesty's Stationery Office. *RMS "Titanic": Reappraisal of Evidence Relating to SS "Californian."* London: Crown, 1992. *MAIB: Marine Office Investigation Branch*. MAIB, 2010. Web. 5 Sept. 2010.

"United States Senate Inquiry." *Titanic Inquiry Project: Electronic Copies of the Inquiries into the Disaster*. Ed. Rob Ottmers. Titanic Inquiry Project, 2009. Web. 30 July 2010.

Wade, Wyn Craig. *The Titanic: End of a Dream*. New York: Penguin Books, 1986.

Wels, Susan. *Titanic: Legacy of the World's Greatest Ocean Liner*. Alexandria: Time-Life Books, 1997. Print.

Wikipedia contributors. "HMS *Birkenhead* (1845)." *Wikipedia, The Free Encyclopedia*. Wikipedia, The Free Encyclopedia, 30 Nov. 2010. Web. 11 Dec. 2010.

Wikipedia contributors. "Michel Marcel Navratil." *Wikipedia, The Free Encyclopedia*. Wikipedia, The Free Encyclopedia, 1 Apr. 2011. Web. 8 Apr. 2011.

Wikipedia contributors. "Question Time." *Wikipedia, The Free Encyclopedia*. Wikipedia, The Free Encyclopedia, 27 Oct. 2010. Web. 28 Oct. 2010.

ACKNOWLEDGMENTS

———◆———

Thanks to all who helped with this book. I extend my appreciation to the *Daily Telegraph* of London for permission to quote from their articles of 1912 on the sinking of RMS *Titanic*.

The Library of Congress provided the microfilm of these articles, and I acknowledge this help as well as the help of the interlibrary loan services of the Nashville Public Library. Special thanks go to the library staff who helped me numerous times to get the ancient microfilm readers to work once again after they had jammed or had otherwise broken down in some way.

My thanks also to the Brentwood Public Library for the use of their excellent facilities.

And many thanks to Ron Pitkin and others who encouraged me in the making of this book. These include Sara Kase, my initial contact at Sourcebooks, and Kelly Bale, who edited and supervised the proofreading of it.

Kevin and Deniece Clarke gave me a copy of Logan Marshall's *The Sinking of the Titanic*, which was published in 1912 and which proved useful.

Thanks also go to Denise Brewer, who provided photos from a long-forgotten 1912 book belonging to her grandfather that have enriched the pages of this volume.

Last, special thanks to my wife Gwen and daughter Megan for their countless hours of editing and corrective commentary—and blessings on my daughters Laura and Amy who phoned in their encouragement from time to time from afar.

INDEX

———◆———

ABOUT THE AUTHOR

Stephen W. Hines is the owner of the literary prospecting enterprise known as Seer Green Press. He presents the findings of his research to the public through general trade book publishers such as Sourcebooks, Inc., Penguin Putnam Inc., Bantam Doubleday Dell, and the University of Missouri Press.

Titanic: One Newspaper, Seven Days, and the Truth That Shocked the World is his eighteenth book and joins such bestsellers as *Little House in the Ozarks*—a *Publishers Weekly* list-maker—and *The Quiet Little Woman*—a *USA Today* bestseller.

Hines holds an MA in journalism from Ball State University and lives with his wife near Nashville, Tennessee.